MEDIA AND THE POLITICS OF FAILURE

PALGRAVE MACMILLAN SERIES IN INTERNATIONAL
POLITICAL COMMUNICATION

Series editor: Philip Seib, Marquette University (USA)

From democratization to terrorism, economic development to conflict
resolution, global political dynamics are affected by the increasing
pervasiveness and influence of communication media. This series examines
the participants and their tools, their strategies and their impact. It offers a
mix of comparative and tightly focused analyses that bridge the various
elements of communication and political science included in the field of
international studies. Particular emphasis is placed on topics related to the
rapidly changing communication environment that is being shaped by new
technologies and new political realities. This is the evolving world of
international political communication.

Editorial Board Members:

Hussein Amin, American University in Cairo (Egypt)
Robin Brown, University of Leeds (UK)
Eytan Gilboa, Bar-Ilan University (Israel)
Steven Livingston, George Washington University (USA)
Robin Mansell, London School of Economics and Political Science (UK)
Holli Semetko, Emory University (USA)
Ingrid Volkmer, University of Otago (New Zealand)

Books Appearing in this Series

*Media and the Politics of Failure: Great Powers, Communication Strategies,
and Military Defeats*
    By Laura Roselle

MEDIA AND THE POLITICS OF FAILURE

Great Powers, Communication Strategies, and Military Defeats

Laura Roselle

MEDIA AND THE POLITICS OF FAILURE
© Laura Roselle, 2006.

First published in 2006 by
PALGRAVE MACMILLAN™
175 Fifth Avenue, New York, N.Y. 10010 and
Houndmills, Basingstoke, Hampshire, England RG21 6XS
Companies and representatives throughout the world.

PALGRAVE MACMILLAN is the global academic imprint of the Palgrave Macmillan division of St. Martin's Press, LLC and of Palgrave Macmillan Ltd. Macmillan® is a registered trademark in the United States, United Kingdom and other countries. Palgrave is a registered trademark in the European Union and other countries.

ISBN-13: 978–1–4039–7525–6

Library of Congress Cataloging-in-Publication Data

Roselle, Laura.
    Media and the politics of failure : great powers, communication strategies, and military defeats / Laura Roselle.
       p. cm.—(Palgrave series in international political communication)
    Includes bibliographical references and index.
    ISBN 1–4039–7525–6
       1. Vietnamese Conflict, 1961–1975—Mass media and the conflict.
    2. Mass media—United States. 3. Communication in politics—United States. 4. Afghanistan—History—Soviet occupation, 1979–1989—Mass media and the war. 5. Mass media —Soviet Union. 6. Communication in politics—Soviet Union. 7. War in mass media. I. Title. II. Series.

DS559.46.R68 2006
070.4′333—dc22   2006041590

A catalogue record for this book is available from the British Library.

Design by Newgen Imaging Systems (P) Ltd., Chennai, India.

First edition: September 2006

10 9 8 7 6 5 4 3 2 1

Printed in the United States of America.
Transferred to Digital Printing in 2007.

CONTENTS

ACKNOWLEDGMENTS

I have been fortunate to have the support of many people while conducting my research and writing this work. Dick Brody and David Holloway were supportive at the very beginning. I also benefited enormously from the late Gabriel Almond's generosity, time, and intellectual encouragement. Alexander George's comments on case selection were also very important early on. Readers of more recent versions to whom I owe thanks include Ken Rogerson, Robin Brown, Steve Livingston, Sarah Oates, Clyde Ellis, and anonymous readers at *International Studies Quarterly*. Colleagues in the International Communications section of the International Studies Association have been consistently supportive of my work. Phil Seib took interest in the manuscript and was wonderful to work with.

At various times I have received funding to support this project from Stanford University, the Berkeley-Stanford Program in Soviet and Post-Soviet Studies, and the Stanford Center on Conflict and Negotiation. In addition, the Carter Center supported me through a Hewlett Fellowship, and a year and a half-long stint as Assistant Director of the Soviet Media and International Communications Program.

I cannot thank Ellen Mickiewicz adequately for all her gifts to me. She has been a mentor and friend for many years, and I simply cannot imagine having completed this without her. She offered advice, counsel, and opportunities for experiences and travel.

Finally, I thank my family for their support. My parents, Harry and Joan Roselle, have been unflaggingly supportive. My daughters, Savannah and Olivia, encouraged me to finish this book, and brought joy to the process. My husband, Clyde Ellis, read every word many times and offered invaluable comments. He is a wonderful partner.

CHAPTER 1

Political Communication
and Policy Legitimacy:
Explaining Failure

Superpowers don't always win wars. This may seem to be a perfectly obvious fact, but it is really quite surprising in light of the focus on power capabilities—that is, military weaponry and personnel—in the study of international relations. This book examines superpowers and failure, focusing on the United States in Vietnam and the Soviet Union in Afghanistan. In both cases, superpowers withdrew short of victory against much smaller, less well-equipped third world countries. This work focuses less on why these superpowers failed to accomplish their stated military and political goals in Vietnam and Afghanistan,[1] and more on the factors that affected the way leaders explained these failures to their own people and to the world. How did leaders of powerful states present a lost war, and, in particular, how did they use television to tell the story? The answers to these questions involve understanding when and why leaders believe they have to explain anything at all, and how they shape the manner in which the story is told. Because a military defeat challenges superpower identity, this discussion directly addresses the literature on constructivism and international relations. What is particularly interesting about these cases is that dramatically different political and media systems produced remarkably similar stories. This book, therefore, addresses the literature on domestic policy legitimacy and the rhetorical presidency, and the international relations literature on identity, interests, reputation, and power. Domestic and international considerations are all involved in a complicated and multilayered way. This is, of course, a book about political communication and politics, and it argues that the study of political communication allows us to transcend dominant, and often artificial, segmentations in the fields of political science, communication, and international studies.

Many scholars have noted that political ideology and governmental structure significantly affect political communication.[2] In other words, democratic and authoritarian systems' media are structured quite differently and have different purposes. In a democracy the media are seen as an independent watchdog—the fourth estate acting as a protection against unrestrained power. In the authoritarian system media are depicted as a mouthpiece to disseminate the leadership's propaganda. Not surprisingly, scholars assume that these political systems will use media differently. For example, Soviet leaders predictably used state-controlled media to shape the coverage of Afghanistan in a way that was so pervasive that Soviet media did not even acknowledge the presence of Soviet combat troops in Afghanistan for five and a half years.[3] Conversely, American political and military leaders did not control media access and content to anything like the same degree, and journalists were relatively free to report what they saw.

Yet, if the differences in coverage are striking, it is equally striking to see how similar the leaders' stories of withdrawal were. In both cases, for example, the capabilities of allies were exaggerated. In the American case, Vietnamization—the process after 1968 by which the South Vietnamese political and military systems took over control of their own defense—was promoted as a logical and attainable step. Despite knowledge to the contrary, American leaders touted Vietnamization as the road to stabilization in the region. Because the South Vietnamese could take care of themselves, went the reasoning, there would no longer be any need for an American presence. In the Soviet case, confidence in their ally, the ruling government in Afghanistan, was expressed through the term "Afghan reconciliation," a rubric that suggested the imminent consolidation of power in the country under native-born leaders. As with Vietnamization, Afghan reconciliation would provide a plausible explanation for the withdrawal of Soviet forces secure in the knowledge that their ally was capable of defending its own homeland. Additionally, the resolution of conflict in both cases was framed to emphasize international negotiation. And, surprisingly, in both cases concern for the superpower's reputation was more important for convincing domestic audiences than it was for convincing international adversaries.

So, in light of the widely divergent political and media systems in the United States and the Soviet Union, how can we account for the similarities in the explanations of withdrawal? The work argues that difference in leadership communication strategies, including how leaders framed and explained the story of withdrawal from a failed war, can be understood to a great degree by focusing on differences in media and political systems. Similarities in explanations of withdrawal can be explained by understanding concerns about international identity and the ability to project power. This international identity is inextricably linked to <u>domestic</u> considerations involving policy legitimacy and coalition building. In both cases, leaders sought to legitimize withdrawal by linking it to perceptions of international identity. Soviet and American leaders, and much of their domestic audiences, believed or accepted that their states had special responsibilities related to interests and power in the international system. As Richard Nixon put it in 1970:

> "If, when the chips are down, the world's most powerful nation, the United States of America, acts like a pitiful, helpless giant, the forces of totalitarianism and anarchy will threaten free nations and free institutions throughout the world."[4]

Gorbachev, too, in spite of his "New Thinking" also felt distinctive responsibilities associated with the Soviet Union's superpower status, saying at a Politburo meeting in February 1987:

> Of course we could get out of Afghanistan, without another thought, and claim that we don't have to answer for the mistakes of the former leadership. But we have to think about our country's authority, about all the people who've fought in this war.[5]

Changes associated with glasnost in the Soviet Union created a political environment where policy legitimacy, linked to national identity, became important.

In both cases, leaders refused to acknowledge defeat, insisting that their allies were strong enough to defend themselves. In both cases, withdrawal was framed as the story of how a great power could not and did not lose, despite failing to secure either its stated political or military goals. Indeed, in a series of events fully expected by American leaders and the public, North Vietnam took over South Vietnam in 1975, only two years after the American withdrawal. In the Soviet case, substantial shifts in the basic ideas underpinning foreign policy behavior allowed more flexibility in explaining withdrawal. Still, some crucial ideas did not change, including those that emphasized great power status and the role of the Soviet Union in the international system. So, Soviet leaders declared their mission accomplished. In April 1992, three years after the Soviets withdrew, Afghan President Najibullah's government fell, an event that confirmed Soviet military predictions. This recurrent theme of superpower invincibility transcends the Cold War and has important consequences for subsequent foreign policy decisions and rhetoric in both the United States and the Russian Federation.

MILITARY FAILURE

This book focuses on Vietnam and Afghanistan as a subset of wars of the television age—failed wars. But what is failure in war? Losing in war implies that the state has been unable to use its military power to achieve political goals. Evidence of failure can vary; an armistice that identifies winning and losing parties is one example; the taking of territory is another. Less clear are those wars that produce negotiated settlements without an unconditional surrender. Here too, however, the losing side is that which has failed to accomplish its major objectives. Military forces from one side may withdraw while the other side remains in-country, for example.

The first question in assessing explanations of military failure is whether all "losers" behave similarly. That is, do all military losers claim victory? To answer this question, Correlates of War (COW) data were used to identify wars and their outcomes between 1960 and 2000.[6] The outcomes of all wars with clear state losers, as identified by COW, were reviewed to determine whether or not leaders publicly acknowledged failure, or claimed victory.[7] These data show that there were a number of responses to military failure, and that not all losers behaved similarly. See table 1.1.

Table 1.1 List of wars, dates, and losers derived from Correlates of War project, initiated after 1960 and through 2000.

War Name	Dates	Loser(s)	Outcome	Acknowledges Failure
Sino-Indian War	Oct. 20, 1962–Nov. 22, 1962	India	China takes territory in India along border and then withdraws.	India—no, but no claim that goals were secured.
Vietnamese War	Feb. 7, 1965–Jan. 27, 1973	USA	US withdraws its troops in 1973. North Vietnam takes over South Vietnam and unifies the country in 1975.	US—no and claim that goals are secured.[a]

Continued

Table 1.1 Continued

War Name	Dates	Loser(s)	Outcome	Acknowledges failure
2nd Kashmir	Aug. 8, 1965–Sept. 23, 1965	India	Fighting over Kashmir.UN brokered cease-fire.	India–no, but no claim of goals achieved.[b]
Six Day War	June 5, 1967–June 10, 1967	Egypt, Syria, Jordan	Israel takes Gaza Strip and West Bank.	Egypt—yes[c] Jordan—yes[d] Syria—no[e]
Football War	July 14, 1969–July 18, 1969	Honduras	Cease-fire under OAS threat.	Data inconclusive.
Bangladesh War	Dec. 3, 1971–Dec. 17, 1971	Pakistan	Bangladesh is formed.	Pakistan—yes[f]
Yom Kippur War	Oct. 6, 1973–Oct. 24, 1973	Saudi Arabia, Syria, Egypt, Iraq, Jordan	Great power sponsored cease-fire. Iraq did not accept cease-fire.	All—no and varying claims of goals achieved.
Iraq versus. Kurds 1974	March 18, 1974–April 3, 1975	Iran	Iran/Iraq agreement.	Iran—no.
Turco-Cypriot War	July 20, 1974–July 29, 1974	Cyprus	Turkey takes section of Cyprus, dividing it	Cyprus—yes. (Greece—yes)[g]
Vietnamese-Cambodian War	May 1, 1975–Jan. 7, 1979	Cambodia	Overthrow of Pol Pot—new government.	New govt.
Ethiopia versus Eritrean rebels	Dec. 5, 1976–May 28, 1991	Cuba	Cuba withdraws. Govt. fled, opposition took power.	Cuba—Insufficient information. Focus on Angola in Cuban press.
Ethiopian-Somalian War	Aug. 1, 1977–Mar. 14, 1978	Somalia	Somalia withdraws from Ogaden.	No, but no claim of goals secured.[h]
Ugandan-Tanzanian	Oct. 30, 1978–April 12, 1979	Uganda, Libya	Ugandan Leader Amin is overthrown.	New govt.

Continued

Table 1.1 Continued

War Name	Dates	Loser(s)	Outcome	Acknowledges failure
Sino-Vietnamese	Feb. 17, 1979–Mar. 10, 1979	Vietnam	China takes Lang Son and then withdraws.	Vietnam—no and claims China was defeated.[i]
Falklands	Mar. 25, 1982–June 20, 1982	Argentina	The British reclaim the Falkland Islands and Galtieri is overthrown.	New govt., but it does acknowledge failure[j]
Afghan War	Dec. 24, 1979–Feb. 15, 1989	Soviet Union	Soviets withdraw troops. April 1992 Afghan govt. falls.	No and claim that goals are secured.[k]
Gulf War	Aug. 2, 1990–Apr. 11, 1991	Iraq	Iraq, after attacking Kuwait, is forced to withdraw and must abide by United Nations resolutions and sanctions.	Yes, but vows to continue fight[l]

Notes:

Data on war comes from the Correlates of War Project (version 3). Data from both interstate and intrastate wars was used. Intrastate wars were used only if there was outside state intervention and the state that intervened was on the losing side. Only those wars with designated losers (rather than a draw) were used. Also, some cases were excluded because the intrastate war was caught up with interstate wars. (These include Lebanon versus Leftists [Israel], Iraq versus Kurds and Shiites 1980s [Iran], Bosnia versus Serbs [Yugoslavia]).

a. "Transcript of the President's Address Announcing Agreement to End the War," *New York Times*, January 25, 1973, 19.

b. "Shastri Welcomes Peace, Denounces Pakistan," *Foreign Broadcast Information Service*, September 24, 1965, 1–3.

c. "Text of Nasser's Speech Reviewing Course of War and Announcing his Plan to Resign as President," *New York Times*, June 10, 1967, 12.

d. "King Husayn Says Setback Worse then Expected," *Foreign Broadcast Information Service*, June 9, 1967, D1-D3; "Husayn: Setback Increases Determination," *Foreign Broadcast Information Service*, June 12, 1967, D1.

e. "Al-Atasi: Fight to Death Against Invaders," *Foreign Broadcast Information Service*, June 9, 1967, G1–G2.

f. "Yahya Khan Addresses Nation on Continuation of War," *Foreign Broadcast Information Service*, December 16, 1971, Q1–Q2.

g. David Holden and Steven Roberts, "Domestic Politics and National Pride Limit Their Options,"

New York Times, August 18, 1974, 157; Steven Roberts, "Caramanlis on TV," *New York Times*, August 18, 1974, 61.

h. "Government Issues Statement Announcing Ogaden Withdrawal," *Foreign Broadcast Information Service*, March 10, 1978, B6; "Education Minister Makes Statement to Muscat Radio," *Foreign Broadcast Information Service*, March 11, 1978, B4–B5.

i. "Nhan Dan Commentator Views PRC 'Strategic Defeat' in Vietnam," *Foreign Broadcast Information Service*, March 12, 1979, K2–K5.

j. "Defense Minister on Outcome of Falklands Conflict," *Foreign Broadcast Information Service*, June 17, 1982, B2–B3.

k. "Text of Gorbachev Statement Setting Forth Soviet Position on Afghan War," *New York Times*, February 9, 1988, A14.

l. "Saddam Hussein's Speech on the 'Withdrawal' of his Army from Kuwait," *New York Times*, February 27, 1991, A20.

The table shows that some leaders do, in fact, acknowledge failure. First, some losers are crushed by the opposing side in the conflict and new governments come to power (Cambodia in 1979; Uganda in 1979). Others are swept from office by their own colleagues who publicly recognize the failure (Argentina in 1982, for example). Some leaders stay in power and acknowledge failure, such as Pakistani President Yahya Khan who said in a speech to the nation after defeat in the Bangladesh War in 1971, "the enemy had greater weapons and had the support of a big power. Assisted by these factors, the enemy overcame us in East Pakistan."[8] Likewise, in August 1974 Greek Premier Constantine Caramanlis explained to his people that Greece could not challenge Turkey in Cyprus: "armed opposition to Turks in Cyprus was impossible by reason of distance as well as by the accomplished fact that Turkey had an overwhelming military advantage."[9] Finally, some leaders acknowledge military defeat but do not recognize a broader defeat as with Saddam Hussein in the First Gulf War in 1991.

A different rhetorical pattern is evident when leaders do not accept failure but do not claim victory either. For example, in March 1978 Somali Minister of Culture and Higher Education Omar Arteh Ghalib said that the decision to withdraw Somali troops from the Ogaden region of Ethiopia "was not made from a position of weakness but signified courage and was in response to the wishes of the big powers and African states which have exerted efforts to find a peaceful solution to Somalia's just cause."[10] Likewise, Prime Minister Shastri of India said of the cease-fire of the 2nd Kashmir War in 1965 that "although Pakistan's reply was a belated one, we are nevertheless glad that it did come after all. They wanted the cease-fire no doubt. Indeed they needed it. But as it is their practice, they wanted to put up a show of resistance until the very last moment."[11]

Finally, there are those states that do not acknowledge defeat and claim, in fact, to have achieved their military and political goals. The two most striking cases of this are the American war in Vietnam and the Soviet war in Afghanistan. Of the 1973 agreement to withdraw American troops from Vietnam, Nixon said on January 25:

> Now that we have achieved an honorable agreement let us be proud that America did not settle for a peace that would have betrayed our allies, that would have abandoned our prisoners of war or that would have ended the war for us but would have continued the war for the 50 million people of Indochina.[12]

And in his February 8, 1988 speech setting out his position on the withdrawal of Soviet troops, Gorbachev cited the heroism of the Soviet armed forces and the ability of the Afghan people to resolve their own conflict: "[S]uccess of the policy of national reconciliation has already made it possible to begin withdrawing Soviet troops from portions of the Afghan territory."[13] This very broad overview of how state leaders describe and explain failure in war suggests that not all losers behave similarly. The Soviet and American cases present an intriguing subset of the cases because of the distinctive parallels in such different political systems.

FACTORS THAT AFFECT POLITICAL COMMUNICATION

Identifying why leaders communicate is at the heart of understanding the factors that shape leadership communication strategies during war, including domestic, international, and communication considerations. Domestically, leaders may be concerned to one degree or another with securing support for withdrawal, or acquiescence to it from a variety of groups including elites, interest groups, and/or the public. International considerations include the perceived need to maintain superpower status despite a military loss, a scenario that leaders may believe would compromise reputation. Factors related to communication itself include the role of television, access to media, technique in crafting messages, and news values; each of these shape how leaders explain or frame withdrawal from a failed war. The cases of American withdrawal from Vietnam and Soviet withdrawal from Afghanistan provide a test for propositions about the role of domestic and international factors in political communication during a failed war.

Domestic Factors: Policy Legitimacy

Students of American presidential communication have long emphasized the importance of domestic policy legitimacy, and of elite and popular support for it.[14] Leaders use media to explain and justify policy decisions to their constituents because in a democracy leaders rely on the public for votes, a strategy that Alexander George calls policy legitimacy.[15] Although the study of politics is replete with work on political legitimacy, the focus here is on policy legitimacy—a slightly different concept.[16] George notes that achieving policy legitimacy is important to the president in the United States so that "the forces of democratic control and domestic pressures do not hobble him and prevent him from conducting a coherent, consistent, and reasonably effective long-range policy."[17] In the United Sates, policy legitimacy is tied to the role of political elites and public opinion because these forces play a powerful role in decision making and may act as a counterweight to leaders and their agendas. Therefore, policy legitimacy is important because it creates a "fundamental consensus" which eases constraints on policymaking.[18] Moreover, the media are central to shaping the context for elite discussion of the issues and for public opinion, a notion that ties into what Jeffrey Tulis calls "the rhetorical presidency":

> Today it is taken for granted that presidents have a *duty* constantly to defend themselves publicly, to promote policy initiatives nationwide, and to inspirit the population. And for many, this presidential "function" is not one duty among many, but rather the heart of the presidency—the essential task.[19]

This "essential task" is undertaken through the mass media. Mary Stuckey concurs, arguing that "[t]he president's function has moved from being one of administration to one of legitimation as the spoken word comes to dominate written text and as electioneering and governing move ever closer together."[20] As B. Thomas Trout asserts: "the process of shaping the image of the environment in support of a given policy at a given time is both politically significant and at the foundation of legitimation."[21]

According to George, policy legitimacy has two components. First, there is a cognitive component that establishes the feasibility of the policy. A leader "must convince people that he knows how to achieve these desirable long-range objectives."[22] Second, a leader must convince others in the administration, Congress, and the public that the policy is valid, or "that the objectives and goals of his policy are desirable and worth pursuing—in other words, that his policy is consistent with fundamental national values and contributes to their enhancement."[23] This seems closely related to Kenneth Burke's (1969) rhetorical view of identification: to persuade an audience one must argue that a particular policy "would enhance the general morality that they all share."[24] Likewise, in his study of European integration, Frank Schimmelfenning recognizes the importance of collective identity within a rhetorical action framework that emphasizes strategic behavior.[25]

National identity has been addressed in the literature as "a constructed *and* public national self-image based on membership in a political community as well as history, myths, symbols, language, and cultural norms commonly held by members of a nation."[26] Thus, national identity clearly shapes and often constrains the ways by which leaders will seek to legitimize policies. George suggests that because information about policies will be more detailed and sophisticated for elites, and less for the mass media, leaders' communication via the mass media will be more broadly consistent with dominant national values, myths, and identities. In his work on coalition building, Jack Snyder writes that because these "myths are necessary to justify the power and policies of the ruling coalition, the leaders must maintain the myths or else jeopardize their rule."[27] Moreover, these myths are not simply used strategically or cynically by groups as political instruments (although that certainly is true): "[o]ften the proponents of these strategic rationalizations, as well as the wider population," notes Snyder, "came to believe them."[28] Because these beliefs invariably affect future decisions, Snyder's work, like George's, directly addresses why international relations scholars should be concerned with the relationship between leadership explanations of policy and domestic political considerations.

But what about the Soviet Union? Is the concept of policy legitimacy applicable to the Soviet case even after glasnost? With a media system controlled exclusively by the political leadership, why would the Soviet leadership have had to explain anything to the population? Certainly prior to glasnost, Soviet leaders were less concerned with policy legitimacy than with policy acquiescence and compliance.[29] As Stephen Meyer has noted, Khrushchev, for example, <u>set the agenda</u>, made decisions with a small group of advisors (often cutting the military establishment out of foreign policy decisions), and used the media to inform citizens and elites alike about new policies. Brezhnev adopted an "institutional-consensus approach" in which ideas and policy options were presented by responsible organizations. Unlike the Khrushchev era, the Ministry of Defense had significant input, and Brezhnev used media for "post-decision <u>elaborations</u> of policy."[30]

Under Gorbachev, there were significant changes in political communication, even as the leadership maintained control of the state-owned television system that dominated the media landscape. Some aspects of policy <u>initiation</u>, for example, were brought into the open as the Soviet leadership moved closer than ever before to using media to pursue policy (and political) legitimacy. Glasnost— a term used to designate a different approach to information and ideas, meant openness, publicity, and coverage of events and issues in the mass media that were previously taboo.[31] Mickiewicz notes that prior to glasnost, the centralized control of mass media severely limited both critiques of Soviet policy and the ability of citizens to know of and comment on such conversations.[32] Greater coverage of the issues confronting Soviet society opened the space available for discourse and allowed a larger number of people to participate.[33] Glasnost called ordinary citizens to active participation in discussions of problems and policies, both in the domestic arena and in foreign affairs, at least in theory. Mickiewicz notes that Gorbachev, who remembered quite clearly what happened to Khrushchev and his reform attempts, claimed the "decisive mistake" occurred when the people were not involved in the process of reform.[34]

Glasnost was a means by which people could also serve as a power base for Gorbachev against entrenched political interests opposed to change. As Gorbachev wrote later in his memoirs:

> Freedom of speech made it possible to go over the heads of the apparatchiks and turn directly to the people, to give them the incentive to act and to win their support.[35]

This clearly echoes the concept of policy legitimacy because, although Gorbachev was not elected by the public, he had to consider his standing among the elite. This suggests that even in nondemocratic systems, selectorates (or specific groups) can be important for legitimizing policy. In addition, Gorbachev's decisions—even those which represented a substantial change for Soviet policy—had to fit within an understandable and accepted context. This does not mean that the Soviet media system changed to resemble the American model. There were limits to what the leadership considered acceptable, as suggested by the directives on the content of coverage on state-owned television, particularly in the foreign policy realm. But Gorbachev instituted a change as previously taboo subjects were tackled on television. People were more openly involved in policy discussions, and leaders considered television important for justifying and legitimizing new policies.

Television was absolutely essential to this process. Under this new policy, we might expect that Gorbachev, with new leadership and new policies, would simply blame previous leaders for Soviet involvement in the quagmire of Afghanistan. Doing so could have enhanced his own legitimacy, but Gorbachev and his advisors rejected this path. Why? As the following discussion suggests, Soviet leaders were motivated in part by the link between state identity and policy legitimacy, a fact that leads to an interesting discussion about the role of reputation and identity in international relations.

International Factors: Identity and Reputation

One way to understand why and how leaders communicate during war involves deterrence theory.[36] Deterrence, "[i]n its most general form, . . . is simply the persuasion of one's opponent that the costs and/or risks of a given course of action he might take outweigh its benefits."[37] Robert Jervis suggests that "[d]eterrence theory . . . assumes that states are—and should be—terribly concerned about their reputations for living up to their commitments."[38] If a state does not follow through on commitments, its reputation for resolve may be diminished, thereby encouraging adversarial threats. Jonathan Mercer, however, challenges the widely held assumption that reputation is central to international relations, and argues that adversaries "rarely get reputations for lacking resolve."[39] Ted Hopf's work supports this, arguing that the Soviets continued to view the United States as having resolve even after losses in the third world.[40]

The inability of states to achieve their political and military goals in non-proxy wars would seem to be the most damaging of all outcomes,[41] but the deterrence literature does not clearly address what happens when a great power is defeated. One might assume that leaders will focus on persuading international rivals that withdrawal does not signal weakness or a lack of resolve. Communication would be strategic, and Jervis suggests that getting out of a commitment involves decoupling, or destroying the link between the action and its previously understood meaning. This can be done "on any one of three points: *what* he said he would do to *whom* under what *conditions*."[42] This does not, however, address the broader context or normative component of why this change is valid.

Work on reputation and credibility raises the interesting issue of audience. As Patrick Morgan notes: "What is striking, then, about many occasions when officials acted to maintain the U.S. image for purposes of deterrence is that the target has often been friends and allies as much as opponents."[43] As Mercer and others suggest, third parties and allies are important to understanding reputation. Mercer, for example, argues that states should be more concerned about their reputation with allies than with adversaries. Some scholars assert that domestic costs will be important to international credibility, if only in democratic states.[44] Leaders may be held accountable by the electorate via the ballot box, therefore the argument is that democracies' threats are more credible. Hence, one should expect the Soviet and American explanations of withdrawal to be different because in the Soviet case, Gorbachev was not electorally accountable to the population. This suggests that explanations for particular audiences are relevant to understanding international behavior, and this ties domestic consider-ations to international behavior as well.

Another way to look at how leaders explain failure is to examine superpower identity in the construction of withdrawal narratives. In international relations theory, a burgeoning constructivist literature on the role of state identity argues that it affects foreign policy and international relations.[45] Identity, writes Marc Lynch, indicates "how each state understands the meaning and purpose of regional and inter-national organizations, the role the state should play in the world, and the kinds of interests worth pursuing."[46] This definition suggests that identities are complex and multifaceted, and must be (re)constructed over time; how this is accomplished in light of great power failure is not clear.

Wendt argues that "rhetorical practice," through "consciousness-raising, dialogue, discussion and persuasion, education, ideological labor, symbolic action, and so on" may affect identities and interests.[47] Scholars who address communication and identity [48] focus on com-munication among or between states, and argue against realists who "dismiss public justifications as empty talk, with no impact on the actual pursuit of policy."[49] This book shifts the focus by analyzing how leaders attempt to "filter identity discourses" within a state,[50] and how they frame policies "with public justifications which enact the identity and moral purpose of the state."[51]

Communication Factors: Television, Access, Technique, and News Values

The pervasive power of television to shape the story is not lost on polit-ical leaders. In the United States, the medium has "changed the way presidents govern and must govern."[52] Scholars argue that a leader's ability to "mobilize and wield public opinion" is more important in the age of television than in the past[53] because of television's vast reach. Moreover, this fact isn't limited to the United States. Work on Soviet political communication shows clearly that Soviet leaders believed that media, and television in particular, were absolutely central to power.[54] As Mickiewicz documents with compelling detail, "Politburo members watched television closely, noting how events were covered, how the news was presented, what other programs went out over the air, and how prime-time programming differed from late-night programming."[55] Why? Because "television reflected and conferred status. That applied not only to the top leadership, scrambling to be on the small screen, but also to the portrayal of state interests."[56] During the late 1980s, armed guards outside the central television building, checking all identification and passes, and, inside, stationed at the door of the news studio itself, testified to the importance of maintaining control over media and its messages.

The number of people who watch television is astonishing. In the United States during the late 1960s and early 1970s, 50 million people watched the nightly news on any given night. The pervasive nature of television was also evident in the Soviet Union, where 150 million people—more than 80 percent of the Soviet adult population—regularly watched the nightly news during the 1980s.[57] Moreover, during the conflicts discussed here, in both the Soviet Union and the United States television was the primary source of information about the world. According to the former head of *Gostelradio* (the State Committee for Television and Radio in the Soviet Union), during the 1980s, 90 percent of the Soviet population cited the nightly news program *Vremya* as their main source of information.[58] Surveys confirm that television has been the dominant source of mass information in the United States since the early 1970s.[59] As a result, television told the story of withdrawal in the cases of Vietnam and Afghanistan, and leaders paid particular attention to how it did so.

Leadership explanations of failure in war will depend, in part, on factors related to the medium of television itself. The two most important factors are access and technique. Access refers to how able a leader is to get a desired message on television. This ability is determined by a whole range of considerations, including the role of the media in the political system and the organizational structure of television. If leaders directly control media coverage they will rarely have to adjust television strategy due to considerations of access. In the Soviet case, the leadership could shape television coverage to a great extent even into the late 1980s during glasnost. In the American case, leaders' ability to control television output was much more limited. Even if leaders could get messages on television in the desired form, they had to understand what an effective message was. Communication technique entails the extent to which leaders can communicate their desired message effectively to their audience.

Leaders' ability to get their desired messages on television—here called access—is clearly influenced by the political and media systems in which they operate. For the most part, scholars have categorized media systems according to political systems,[60] arguing that political structures lead to specific kinds of operating procedures and media content. This approach, however, rests on assumptions that can create typologies of communication systems that are misleading and static. For example, characterizations of the Soviet media system often emphasized its commitment to extensive public saturation and an intense, unified message requiring obedience to the Soviet Communist Party. These typologies assumed that the Soviets would maintain the same goals over time, and that they would view as effective previous methods of achieving specific goals. The problem, of course, is that this description does not speak to the policy of glasnost.

What these models do accurately portray are the differences in how leaders in the US and USSR gained and used access to media. In the Soviet Union, for example, the television system was centrally controlled and the leadership could and did manipulate the depiction and interpretation of many subjects. Leaders set the tone for news stories on sensitive topics like Afghanistan by issuing written directives and paying close attention to broadcasts to confirm that coverage corresponded to official guidelines. A direct phone line from the desk of the Soviet leader to the head of *Gostelradio* suggests the degree to which Soviet leaders were involved in the state's use of media. In areas of especially high interest such as foreign policy and international relations, the connection between political leaders and television content was yet more pronounced, even under Gorbachev.

In the United States, however, media are not governmentally controlled. American media pride themselves on being the Fourth Estate, designed to fairly and impartially report events of the day. Yet despite the fact that the American government does not control media, American leaders have a great ability to get their message on television.[61] Michael Grossman and Martha Kumar note that there are basically three ways for the president to get on television.[62] The most effective method is the televised speech in which leaders speak directly to the American people. The second way leaders use television is by encouraging and allowing networks to cover news conferences. Finally, the president and members of the administration may try to appear on television news programs.

Leaders' ability to control coverage, however, is shaped in part by their responses to the organizational and institutional structures of media. Some scholars stress the importance of these factors and argue that in the American case "the combined efforts of the White House and the networks have made the President the single biggest continuing story on television news."[63] Shanto Iyengar and Donald Kinder write that "when the president speaks, the networks listen and so, therefore, do millions of Americans."[64] Richard Neustadt has written that "nowadays the medium itself is at the podium, another party to the whole transaction, molding presidential words and even events to its dimensions as an entertainer and to ours as spectators."[65] Others maintain that while news organization may have certain effects, the leader knows what these effects are and takes them into account. For example, David Paletz and Robert Entman argue that "because the president is so newsworthy, because the press is predictable, he can produce news of his own devising, knowing the media will cover him and it."[66] Regardless of which option prevails in a given situation, controlling the discussion is crucial: "Executive officials seek to confine the choice as much as possible to items that will be favorable to them."[67] For example, press conferences at which reporters can ask unscripted questions are not as easily controlled as a direct speech in which leaders address only those points they select.

The predictability of which Paletz and Entman speak is based on the organizational characteristics of media and news values. That is, "certain consistent directions in selecting, covering and reformulating events over long-term periods are clearly related to organizational needs" of the media.[68] Edward Jay Epstein's classic work on the media and politics, *News from Nowhere*, documented this for the period of the Vietnam War.[69] First, news budgets affected the number and extent of events covered. This was related, in part, to why high-ranking authority figures were more likely to "make news" than other people: "assignment editors tend to ration the camera crews among news makers that can be relied on with a fair degree of certainty to produce useable happenings."[70] The president, then, had an advantage in gaining access to television.

Still, leaders in the United States complain about their inability to get their message on television, and often claim that media are biased and/or antagonistic.[71] Leaders tend to dislike the fact that opposing views are given air time, and are irritated when information is released early enough for coverage on television but not early enough for full criticism or rebuttal. This has important implications for policy legitimacy because it suggests that if leaders already have public and elite support for or acquiescence to policies, they may be less likely to seek extensive coverage.

A second important characteristic of the American media system is its commercial nature and attachment to distinctive aspects of coverage. News organizations must be concerned with what makes "good" television—that is, coverage that attracts and keeps viewers, boosts ratings, and generates advertising income. News values that support common perceptions of what constitutes "good" television, then, shape leaders' access to, and use of, television. First, viewers are most likely to continue watching the news if images are easily recognizable. Second, conflict is both more interesting than peace and more easily understood if there are two distinct sides.[72] A third belief is that action is more appealing than static images. Finally, "good" stories need to be couched in a narrative form with a beginning, middle, and end.[73] As a result, leaders develop their media strategies to fit as comfortably as possible with these practices.

Technique refers to using media effectively. An effective message raises the probability that the audience receives, understands, and responds to the message as the leadership desires. If the leader is using media to secure policy legitimacy, the desired response is a "fundamental consensus," implying that the audience (or much of it) will accept the leader's explanation.[74] The degree of acceptance will depend, in part, on how credible the message is. Credibility, in turn, involves issues of timeliness, openness, and truthfulness. Some formats for the presentation of information are more credible than others. Timeliness is especially important, and research has shown that first accounts are believed to a greater extent than subsequently released information.[75] When leaders take the initiative to present information ahead of their rivals there is a greater chance of winning the audience's confidence. If leaders do not present information in a timely fashion, they may be forced to counter other descriptions of the event.

But timeliness is also often influenced by other factors, especially the need to balance openness with strategic imperatives of war-time secrecy. In his history of war reporting, Joseph Mathews maintains that timeliness in news has always been balanced against the sense that secrecy would help protect nations during war.[76] Interestingly, Mathews notes that there was a propensity for government to favor secrecy about war until World War I when Allied leaders became converts to the view that war could be waged more successfully with publicity than with silence. "There was even a growing belief in the Allied camp" Mathews concludes, "that victory could not be assured without the encouragement to morale that would presumably come with more news . . . . News had become a weapon in the arsenal of war, one that could not be ignored."[77]

Finally, Mathews stresses that presenting more information is complicated. While open and candid disclosures about war may enhance credibility, leaders are not always truthful. During World War I, for example, information deemed crucial to the war effort had to be shaped or framed in ways that balanced the legitimate needs of security against the public's right to know:

> There was easy, logical, and patriotic justification for giving the news a push in the direction believed to be the most helpful and open. . . . Under such circumstances the integrity of the news depended upon the conviction that truth rather than falsehood would promise the safest course. But truth and falsehood are elusive terms, capable of wide latitude in interpretation, and the motivation toward fact or fiction is complex.[78]

It is quite clear that leaders deliberately choose to release certain details and withhold others. Denton and Hahn have noted the "news or information favorable to the president is released from the White House whereas less favorable news is left unstated or released from other departments."[79] But what about the news that is left unstated? As Mickiewicz reminds us: "If stories go unreported, the events do not vanish."[80] Leaders run the risk of losing credibility if they do not present information about events or situations that people know to exist. This ties in directly to the notion of truthfulness. In the case of war, as time goes on, more and more soldiers return from the front with personal experiences of the war, and more families are touched by their own soldiers who were wounded or have perished. If people know information is false, credibility rests in the balance.

Clearly, the format or framing of information helps to influence its effectiveness. Is there a direct appeal from the leaders, or are others used to present information about the war? What backdrops or props are used?[81] With its mass audience, television requires information to be simply understood by the average person, but it must also be attractive, and plausibly presented. Complex issues and events must be boiled down into digestible but compelling pieces that do not appear to be mere propaganda. Balancing these needs will complicate leaders' communication during wartime, especially when the tide appears to have shifted against them militarily or politically.

The role of mass media is central to understanding the construction of international relations, and is useful to scholars interested in what Lynch calls "discursive structures and framing processes."[82] The literature on reputation highlights the importance of audience and the strategic nature of communication, if not the specifics on how costs are articulated and assessed, or the broader social context in which such decisions are made. Yet, most framing analyses in political communication and sociology have long emphasized that strategic and normative characteristics must be considered as a package, not independently. Frames are political instruments set within a broader social context, and they have purposes that extend beyond persuasion. This book argues that framing at the domestic level and through mass media is central to the construction and maintenance of state identities. Conversely, state identities also constrain the framing of messages meant to legitimize policy.

Framing is rooted in sociology at the individual level, and in the study of group dynamics and social mobilization.[83] In communication and political communication media are the foci.[84] Framing is also at the heart of work on the limits of rationality.[85] Those who study social mobilization focus on the role of groups and see framing as "conscious strategic efforts by groups of people to fashion shared understandings of the world and of themselves that legitimate and motivate collective action."[86] Political communications scholars' definitions have been broader, focusing less on groups and collective action. Entman defines framing as "selecting and highlighting some facets of events or issues, and making connections among them so as to promote a particular interpretation, evaluation, and/or solution."[87] Gadi Wolfsfeld defines an interpretive frame as "central organizing idea[s] for making sense of relevant events and suggesting what is at issue."[88] Most definitions of frame have in common the notion of an organizing principle that structures meaning, although this is less common in the work on limits of rationality. Entman applies "frame" to texts or messages, rather than to the "interpretive processes that occur in the human mind." This distinguishes framing from work focused more on cognition, including work on schemas and heuristics. As James Tankard argues, "[i]n both everyday and scholarly use, the term *frame* is sometimes used in an imprecise way, mostly as a metaphor."[89] Scholars who are more explicit about what constitutes a frame often use events, issues/subjects, and actors as components that establish definitions of problems, policies or issues, causal interpretations and proposed solutions, and convey affect or moral judgment. George's notion that leaders must explain how a policy is achievable and valid is, then, a description of framing.

It is also important to understand why and how leaders frame. Entman says that political leaders "peddle their messages to the press in hopes of gaining political leverage,"[90] while Robin Brown emphasizes that political actors use media to mobilize support.[91] This sounds much like George. Likewise, Zhongdang Pan and Gerald Kosicki suggest that "framing is a discursive means to achieve political potency in influencing public deliberation. It is an integral part of the process of building political alignments."[92] This sounds very much like Snyder. Leaders use framing strategically to gain support from public opinion and to build coalitions within the elite, but successful frames are tied directly to familiar, compelling and/or persuasive values, myths, or identities. Snow et al. refer to this as frame alignment.[93] Finally, Gaye Tuchman makes an important point when she says that frames "both produce and limit meaning."[94] So, an additional purpose of framing is to keep competing frames out of the discourse or to counter them. Leaders construct media messages for political ends, but these messages are shaped by ideational factors. This book seeks to understand the messages and the ends when a war is lost.

FRAMEWORK OF THE BOOK

This discussion sets the stage for an in-depth examination of leadership television strategies in the United States and the Soviet Union. Both Vietnam and Afghanistan were limited wars that lasted years and involved an escalation of forces followed by the reduction and withdrawal of forces without either superpower achieving its stated goals. This book focuses on how leaders explained withdrawal, but this is impossible to do without understanding how the wars themselves were explained. During those periods when leaders were engaged in policies guided by waging war, one might expect that television strategy reflected themes that uniformly stressed the validity of the effort and the ability to win the war. Surely leaders would rally the population by focusing on the war effort as essential to the state's interests. In fact, the Johnson administration downplayed U.S. involvement in Vietnam, and the Soviets did not allow coverage of combat in Afghanistan until mid-1985. During reassessment, when war-waging policy was questioned and reviewed, leaders found themselves in an awkward situation. Having committed themselves to war, they now had to explain how and why to get out. Yet, Lyndon Johnson did not prepare the American public for a change in policy, surprising even his closest friends and supporters with his announcement in March 1968 of de-escalation and his decision not to run for reelection. Conversely, Gorbachev did prepare the Soviet population, first changing television coverage to show the war, and then setting a new context for understanding the war. How do leaders explain such a significant change in policy? The answer to this question is the focus of the book.

The specific organization of the cases follows the general chronology of the larger war efforts. Chapter 2 covers war waging and reassessment by the United States. American involvement in South Vietnam began with the Eisenhower administration, continued under Kennedy, and peaked during the Johnson administration. The focus on American war waging looks at Johnson's escalation, or "Americanization" of the war in 1965. According to Robert Miller, during the 1950s and 1960s U.S. policymakers followed a strategy of incremental increases in aid "because they could not conceive of failure" and because a stable South Vietnam was a crucial part of the Cold War battle against the Soviet Union and China.[95] A major reassessment of American policy in Vietnam occurred between January 31, 1968 when the Tet Offensive began, and March 31, 1968 when Johnson ordered a partial bombing halt and announced his decision not to run for reelection. Chapter 3 covers withdrawal and its aftermath beginning with Nixon's inauguration on January 20, 1969 through the departure of the last American troops on March 29, 1973. The chapter also discusses leadership communication about the American experience in Vietnam in the year following withdrawal.

The Soviet involvement in Afghanistan is also broken down into periods corresponding to war waging, reassessment, withdrawal, and aftermath. Communication strategies during war waging and reassessment are set out in chapter 4. Bordering the Soviet Union, Afghanistan had long been important to Soviet policymakers, but became a higher priority after the April 1978 Marxist coup that installed a pro-Soviet regime. This conflict, too, was set in a Cold War context. The Soviets intervened militarily in Afghanistan in December 1979 due to concerns about the survival of the Afghan government. Soviet involvement escalated in 1984, and due to data considerations, the last three months of 1984 serve to illustrate the Soviet leadership's communication strategies during war-waging.[96] Soviet reassessment began with Gorbachev's rise to power in March 1985 and ended with his announcement on February 8, 1988 that Soviet troops would be withdrawn. Chapter 5 covers withdrawal from February 9, 1988 through the departure of the last Soviet soldier from Afghanistan on February 15, 1989.

Each chapter addresses leadership communication strategies. Leadership here refers to the top political leader and his immediate executive staff. Leadership framing was determined by analyzing official statements, memoranda, and directives on communication strategy, and, in the Soviet case, on the content analysis of Soviet television news broadcasts. In particular, the framing of withdrawal concerns the presentation of policy and the themes that placed policy within a broader context. In addition, the amount of detailed information provided by leaders and the tone of that information will be discussed. A process-tracing methodology was employed that addresses four areas of inquiry suggested by the theoretical discussion presented above.[97]

- First, do political leaders frame war policies as legitimate in cognitive and normative dimensions in both the democratic United States and the authoritarian Soviet Union? How is the policy presented as achievable and valid? How did great power and other identities fit into the story? How much information do leaders provide and what is its tone? This work hypothesizes that leaders in both countries shape communication strategies to legitimize policy in cognitive and normative dimensions.
- Second, each chapter addresses the impact of domestic politics on framing. How did coalition building, for example, affect the leadership's framing of withdrawal? What did leaders believe the role of public opinion to be? The literature suggests that leaders' communication strategies will reflect a concern with coalition building. But concerns about coalition building may cause leaders to minimize information released or increase the amount of information released. This depends on the specific dynamics of domestic politics.
- Third, what role did identity, reputation, and communication with superpower adversaries and third parties have in the framing of withdrawal policy? Constructivist works suggest that leaders' communication strategies will be constrained by beliefs about great power identity. Theories of deterrence imply that communication strategies will reflect a concern about international reputation and credibility. This work hypothesizes that identity will shape communication, and that leaders will be more concerned with reputation among allies, elites, and the public than with adversaries.
- Finally, how did access and technique affect leadership communication? The communications literature suggests that leaders and their staff understand and pay close attention to techniques involved in creating effective messages. In spite of this, they may not be successful in communicating, even when access is controlled.

A number of different sources were used to determine leadership strategy. In the American case there is extensive information on television strategy in the internal memos of the Johnson and Nixon administrations. In order to evaluate how the Johnson administration framed withdrawal, I examined the 11-reel microfilm collection from the Lyndon B. Johnson Library, *Vietnam, The Media, and Public Support for the War*. For the Nixon administration, I examined White House Special Files of Patrick J. Buchanan, Dwight Chapin, Charles W. Colson, John D. Ehrlichman, H. R. Haldeman, Herbert G. Klein, John A. Scali, Ronald L. Ziegler, and the President's Office Files containing annotated news summaries. In addition, I analyzed televised presidential speeches, as well as participants' memoirs.[98] In the Soviet case, I analyzed *Vremya* (nightly news) coverage because Soviet television framed media stories according to political directives drafted and approved by the top leadership. Samples of *Vremya* were taken from 1984 (under Chernenko) through February 1988 when Gorbachev publicly announced his intention to withdraw Soviet forces from Afghanistan.[99] Every *Vremya* newscast from February 8 to December 31, 1988 was analyzed; one week was sampled from both January and February 1989. In addition, I conducted interviews with Leonid Kravchenko, Former Chair of *Gostelradio*; Mikhail Leshchinskii, *Vremya* correspondent in Afghanistan from 1985 to 1989; Vadim Medvedev, a former Politburo member; Eduard Sagalaev, the former head of youth programming for *Gostelradio*, and former head of *Vremya*; and Aleksander Yakovlev, a Gorbachev advisor, and former member of the Presidential Council and Politburo. I also studied key directives and archival data.

The final chapter presents conclusions about the American and Soviet cases, and ponders the effects of maintaining great power identity, particularly during war. The conclusion also argues that the end of the Cold War did not change the underlying processes described here. Identity and domestic politics continue to shape how leaders explain foreign policy adventures and misadventures. The conclusion briefly addresses the questions begged in the cases of Russian involvement in Chechnya and American involvement in Iraq.

CHAPTER 2

War Waging and
Reassessment: Vietnam

The Vietnam War challenged the United States in unexpected ways.[1] Not only did the United States lose this war by withdrawing troops without securing a stable South Vietnam, it did so as television came into its own. The repercussions of the American failure in Vietnam are felt today, and continue to shape military strategy and media access to the battlefield. This chapter focuses on presidential explanations for waging war and asks whether or not these explanations changed when leaders reassessed the policy. The period for the baseline (war waging) is 1965, when Lyndon Johnson escalated and "Americanized" the war[2] and is marked by Johnson's desire to downplay the war. His reticence was caused by the inherent contradictions of superpower identity and a limited war, and by the political struggle at home for his domestic policy agenda. For the most part (and especially in the early years), Johnson, the political elite, and the public shared the belief that America's international reputation was at stake in Vietnam, and the broad explanations of American involvement fit neatly into the power politics lens of the post–World War II era. But, Johnson's particular way of dealing with the media and his discomfort with television contributed to communication strategies that would later contribute significantly to a perceived credibility gap.

The analysis of reassessment focuses on the events leading up to Johnson's March 1968 announcement of de-escalation and his decision not to seek reelection. North Vietnam's 1968 Tet Offensive, initiated on January 30, questioned the credibility of what Johnson had been saying about the war. In mid-March Robert Kennedy decided to challenge the president for the Democratic Party nomination. By the end of March Johnson's staunchest supporters had changed their views about the war, as had important members of Congress and the American public. When Johnson announced de-escalation it was a surprise to the American people and, according to Jane Holl, "marked the beginning of the end of the Vietnam war."[3] Both time periods show how domestic political imperatives and perceived great power identity shaped Johnson's explanations of war-waging and reassessment.

War Waging—1965

When Lyndon Johnson was elected president in November 1964, there were more than 16,000 advisors in Vietnam, but no American ground troops. During the first half of 1965, however, Johnson escalated American involvement by pursuing a policy of incrementalism and limited war, so that by the end of the year more than 180,000 combat soldiers were in Vietnam. His decision to escalate was driven by a deteriorating military situation on the ground and also by a commitment to Cold War ideology.

In August 1964 reports of North Vietnamese attacks on American ships prompted Congress to pass the Tonkin Gulf Resolution and give the president the authority to take all measures necessary in Vietnam. The February 6, 1965 Viet Cong attack on the U.S. barracks at Pleiku was answered with Operation Rolling Thunder which initiated the sustained bombing of the North. In a February 7, 1965 memo on Vietnam McGeorge Bundy set out this assessment of the situation:

> The stakes in Vietnam are extremely high. The American investment is very large, and American responsibility is a fact of life which is palpable in the atmosphere of Asia, and even elsewhere. The international prestige of the United States, and a substantial part of our influence, are directly at risk in Vietnam. There is no way of unloading the burden on the Vietnamese themselves, and there is no way of negotiating ourselves out of Vietnam which offers any serious promise at present. It is possible that at some future time a neutral non-Communist force may emerge, perhaps under Buddhist leadership, but no such force currently exists, and any negotiated U.S. withdrawal today would mean surrender on the installment plan.[4]

Audio tapes of White House conversations show that Johnson, too, was concerned with the reputation of the United States and believed that North Vietnamese military aggression had to be met with force. In a February 1965 discussion with Senate Republican leader Everett Dirksen, Johnson observed that:

> That we know, from Munich on, that when you give, the dictators feed on raw meat. If they take South Vietnam, they take Thailand, they take Indonesia, they take Burma, they come right on back to the Philippines.[5]

Yet even as Johnson made the decision to escalate, he confided his uncertainty to Secretary of Defense Robert McNamara in February 1965 about where this would lead the country: "Now we're off to bombing these people. We're over that hurdle. I don't think anything is going to be as bad as losing, and I don't see any way of winning."[6] The many decisions of this period are marked by the perceived certainty of the need to challenge North Vietnamese aggression, the fear that there was no end in sight, and the realization even at that early date that the war might not be winnable.

On March 6, 1965 as Johnson was finalizing his decision to send 500 Marines to Da Nang (but only for defensive operations), he consulted with his long-time mentor, Richard Russell. Johnson and Russell bemoaned the fact that escalation was the only choice, and both clearly recognized that this could lead to a quagmire:

> *LBJ:* I guess we've got no choice, but it scares the death out of me. I think everybody's going to think, "We're landing the Marines. We're off to battle." . . . Of course, if they come up there, they're going to get them in a fight. Just sure as hell. They're not going to run. Then you're tied down.[7]
>
> . . .
>
> *LBJ:* I don't know Dick . . . The great trouble I'm under—A man can fight if he can see daylight down the road somewhere. But there ain't no daylight in Vietnam. There's not a bit.
> *Russell:* There's no end to the road. There's just nothing.
> *LBJ:* The more bombs you drop, the more nations you scare, the more people you make mad, the more embassies you get—
> *Russell:* We're going to wind up with the people mad as hell with us that we are saving by being in there. It's just awful. . . . it's the worst mess I ever saw in my life.[8]

Despite the real possibility of a quagmire, Johnson and his advisors felt that American prestige was at stake, and that the only choice was to become more deeply involved in the war.

March was spent in what Robert Dalek calls a "fog of uncertainty"[9] as Johnson contemplated sending ground troops into Vietnam. In early April he approved the offensive use of the Marines, and in mid-April more Marines arrived in Vietnam. At the end of April, Secretary of Defense McNamara, General William Westmoreland, and Ambassador Maxwell Taylor recommended increasing the number of American troops on the ground in Vietnam and Johnson concurred.[10]

As the number of American troops rose, the domestic political situation in South Vietnam became increasingly unstable. In June 1965 Nguyen Cao Ky became the leader of South Vietnam after a military coup. The military situation was also deteriorating and Johnson began holding serious discussions with military commanders who wanted to increase U.S. forces to nearly 175,000. After much debate within the administration, in late July Johnson approved the use of American ground forces in battle "separately or in conjunction with South Vietnamese troops, as Westmoreland saw fit"[11] and he announced that troop numbers would increase from 75,000 to 125,000 with more later when requested. Still, in an early July conversation with Robert McNamara, Johnson was already worrying about the outcome of his decision:

> We know ourselves, in our own conscience, that when we asked for this [Gulf of Tonkin] resolution, we had no intention of committing this many ground troops. We're doing so now, and we know it's going to be bad. And the question is, Do we just want to do it out on a limb by ourselves? I don't know whether those [Pentagon] men have ever [calculated] whether we can win with the kind of training we have, the kind of power, and . . . whether we can have a united support at home.[12]

Yet, Johnson believed that America's reputation was on the line in Vietnam: "I was as sure as any man could be that once we showed how weak we were, Moscow and Peking would move in a flash to exploit our weakness."[13] In addition, Johnson felt that he was being personally tested as well, saying to Doris Kearns:

> For this time there would be Robert Kennedy . . . telling everyone . . . that I had let a democracy fall into the hands of the Communists. That I was a coward. An unmanly man. A man without a spine.[14]

During the remainder of 1965, American troop levels continued to rise and as they did Vietnam became an American war. By October, 184,000 troops had been deployed, a fact that compelled Johnson and the administration to explain how and why the United States was going to war in a country that most Americans could not locate on a map.

EXPLAINING THE WAR

Why are we in Vietnam?

Lyndon B. Johnson, "Annual Message to the Congress"[15]

Johnson was not especially comfortable using the media, a problem compounded by the fact that his speeches often suggested broad answers as to why the United States was in Vietnam. Invariably, he clung to standard Cold War rhetoric and explained American involvement as the obligation of a great power fighting Communism. The specifics of the policy, which were much more controversial than the notion that the United States had particular responsibilities in the international system, were not explained in great detail—a communication strategy called "minimum candor."[16] Hallin's research indicates that "from March through July [1965] the administration released information about increases in American involvement piecemeal, often on a not-for-attribution basis, presenting each additional step in the narrowest possible terms and refusing to comment on 'future operations.' "[17] Johnson used the first half of 1965 to debate and decide on the escalation of American involvement, but he did not seek to legitimize the escalation itself beyond the usual remonstrations about Cold War threats. So, when Johnson did address the American people about the war, he focused more on the normative reasons for American involvement in Vietnam and less on how U.S. objectives would be achieved. The answer to the question, "Why are we in Vietnam?" was simple: America's reputation as a superpower demanded it.

In his State of the Union message in January 1965, Johnson reminded his audience that:

In Asia, communism wears a more aggressive face.
    We see that in Viet-Nam.
    Why are we there?
    We are there, first, because a friendly nation has asked us for help against the Communist aggression. Ten years ago our President pledged our help. Three Presidents have supported that pledge. We will not break it now.
    Second, our own security is tied to the peace of Asia. Twice in one generation we have had to fight against aggression in the Far East. To ignore aggression now would only increase the danger of a much larger war.

Our goal is peace in southeast Asia. That will come only when aggressors leave their neighbors in peace.

What is at stake is the cause of freedom and in that cause America will never be found wanting.[18]

In early 1965 Johnson reiterated this theme in a February 4 press conference, again in a February 7 statement on the withdrawal of American dependents from South Vietnam, and once more on February 17 in remarks to a meeting of the National Industrial Conference Board.[19] In each case he repeated the same reasoning for an American presence in Vietnam—to help the South Vietnamese defend themselves against outside aggression.

Even as these statements consistently, but very broadly, spoke to the American involvement in Vietnam, there was no public statement at all when "Rolling Thunder" was initiated in February 1965. Concerned that "Rolling Thunder" would be interpreted as an escalation, Johnson did not want this to be presented as a new policy in any way, noting in a conversation with Secretary of State Dean Rusk on February 25, 1965:

> I want to be very careful that we don't show that we are desperate and dramatic and we are changing our policy. All of TV is trying to say that this is a [large] escalation, and that the B-52s yesterday are an entirely new policy. I've made clear to the people I've talked to . . . that [there is a] congressional resolution . . . It says that we will reply to any attacks and we will deter any aggression.[20]

The congressional resolution to which Johnson referred, introduced after the Gulf of Tonkin incident in 1964, authorized the president to use "all necessary measures" to respond to attacks against the United States and "to prevent further aggression." Yet, as Rolling Thunder began, the New York *Times* wrote that U.S. officials in South Vietnam were reporting that the president had "decided to open a continuing, limited air war."[21]

Still, the president continued to assert that American policy had not changed. In his March 20th press conference, for example, he made this point:

> Let me say this additionally on Viet-Nam. One year ago on March 17, 1964, I made this statement, and I quote: "For 10 years, under three Presidents, this Nation has been determined to help a brave people to resist aggression and terror. It is and it will remain the policy of the United States to furnish assistance to support South Viet-nam for as long as is required to bring Communist aggression and terrorism under control."

Our policy in Viet-Nam is the same as it was 1 year ago, and to those of you who have inquiries on the subject, it is the same as it was 10 years ago. I have publicly stated it. I have reviewed it to the Congress in joint sessions. I have reviewed it in various messages to the Congress and I have talked individually with more than 500 of them stating the policy and asking and answering questions on that subject in the last 60 days. In addition, I have stated this policy to the press and to the public in almost every State of the Union. Specifically last night I read where I had made the policy statement 47 times.[22]

His protests notwithstanding, Johnson's escalation of the war clearly Americanized it and represented a significant change. Some say that in February 1965 Johnson "made the war in Vietnam an American war."[23] The president's television strategy, however, was to maintain that the escalation was consistent with past Vietnam policy, and Summers notes that "efforts were made to make the change as imperceptible as possible to the American public."[24] Johnson was subsequently criticized for not being more honest about the situation in Vietnam, and rather than shielding him from criticism, minimum candor provided fertile soil for the credibility gap that would plague him later.

Johnson and his advisors discussed the need for a major speech on Vietnam during early 1965, and he finally decided to counter his critics and explain his policy in an April 7th speech at Johns Hopkins University. On the question of why America was in Vietnam, he answered:

We are there because we have a promise to keep. . . . over many years, we have made a national pledge to help South Viet-Nam defend its independence. . . . To dishonor that pledge, to abandon this small and brave nation to its enemies, and to the terror that must follow, would be an unforgivable wrong.

We are also there to strengthen world order. . . . To leave Viet-Nam to its fate would shake the confidence of all these people in the value of an American commitment and in the value of America's word. The result would be increased unrest and instability, and even wider war.

We are also there because there are great stakes in the balance. . . . The central lesson of our time is that the appetite of aggression is never satisfied. To withdraw from one battlefield means only to prepare for the next.[25]

These reasons for American involvement rested squarely on an understanding of the particular responsibilities of the United States as a superpower in the international system. Because the United States had the power, it was required to protect other nations and balance adversarial claims in the world lest those adversaries fail to be deterred.

Johnson made two major points in the Johns Hopkins address. First, he announced that the United States was willing to enter into negotiations with North Vietnam without preconditions. Heretofore the administration's position had been that the United States "would talk only after North Vietnam gave some sign of 'ceasing its aggression.' "[26] Johnson believed that a willingness to negotiate would counter critics on the left. Second, Johnson proposed a one billion dollar-aid program for Vietnam. This tied in nicely to his Great Society programs and spoke about how similar change might be accomplished in Vietnam.

Yet, even as he focused on a desire for peace and proposed a far-reaching aid program, Johnson was clear about his dedication to the cause:

> Our objective is the independence of South Viet-Nam, and its freedom from attack. . . .
> In recent months attacks on South Viet-Nam were stepped up. Thus, it became necessary for us to increase our response and to make attacks by air. This is not a change of purpose. It is a change in what we believe that purpose requires.
> We do this in order to slow down aggression.
> We do this to increase the confidence of the brave people of South Viet-Nam who have bravely borne this brutal battle for so many years with so many casualties.
> And we do this to convince the leaders of North Viet-Nam—and all who seek to share their conquest—of a very simple fact:
> We will not be defeated.
> We will not grow tired.
> We will not withdraw, either openly or under the cloak of a meaningless agreement.[27]

So, Johnson balanced a call for peace against a promise of war. He clearly recommitted the United States to the defense of South Vietnam and promised that the United States would not withdraw until South Vietnamese independence was assured.

After the Hopkins speech, Johnson continued to try and legitimize the American presence in Vietnam, if not the escalation. In press conferences on April 27, July 13, and July 28, 1965 he stressed that the United States was aiding South Vietnam due to aggression from the North,[28] and offered examples of North Vietnamese provocations which he said demanded American action. On April 27, for example, he said:

> Through the 7 [sic] months of 1964, both Vietnamese and Americans were the targets of constant attacks of terror. Bombs exploded in

helpless villages, in downtown movie theaters, even at the sports fields where the children played. Soldiers and civilians, men and women, were murdered and crippled, yet we took no action against the source of the brutality—North Vietnam.[29]

He went on to say that over time, the North's answer

was attack, and explosions, and indiscriminate murder. So it soon became clear that our restraint was viewed as weakness; our desire to limit conflict was viewed as a prelude to our surrender.

We could no longer stand by while attacks mounted and while the bases of the attackers were immune from reply. Therefore, we began to strike back.[30]

The conflict was placed within an international context that posed Communist North Vietnam as the aggressor committing acts of terrorism.

Hallin notes that as the decision to significantly increase America's commitment became apparent in June and July, administration leaders believed the public had to be prepared for the reality of a wider war. In Johnson's July news conferences he mentioned the possibility of increasing the number of U.S. troops,[31] commenting on July 13, 1965 that "it is quite possible that new and serious decisions will be necessary in the near future."[32] Johnson announced his decision to increase the number of U.S. forces in Vietnam in a July 28 televised news conference, but Hallin notes that because the public and press had been prepared for much worse, the announcement was anticlimactic.[33] Turner also emphasizes the low-key announcement.[34] Although televised, the news conference took place at noon. The specific decision to use ground forces separately or with the South was "undertaken with an absolute minimum of public announcement, as befitted Johnson's careful balancing of a limited war."[35] The escalation announcement in July was not presented as a new policy. Even the Department of Defense's Fact Sheet on the press conference, "The US Commitment to Freedom," made clear that "[t]hese remarks of President Johnson, significant as they are, mark no fundamental change in American foreign policy."[36]

Johnson began the noon press conference by referring to a letter from a mother whose son was in Vietnam, and he once again answered the question, "why are we in Vietnam?" by presenting the Vietnam War within a Cold War framework. The reason for the presence of American forces in Vietnam was that the North—the

Communist North—was threatening the existence of the *non-Communist* South.

> [t]his is really war. It is guided by North Viet-Nam and it is spurred by Communist China. Its goal is to conquer the South, to defeat American power, and to extend the Asiatic dominion of communism.
>
> There are great stakes in the balance.
>
> Most of the non-Communist nations of Asia cannot, by themselves and alone, resist the growing might and the grasping ambition of Asian communism.
>
> Our power, therefore, is a very vital shield. If we are driven from the field in Viet-Nam, then no nation can ever again have the same confidence in American promise, or in American protection.
>
> In each land the forces of independence would be considerably weakened, and an Asia so threatened by Communist domination would certainly imperil the security of the United States itself.[37]

The conflict in Vietnam was part of a larger conflict against Communism, and the United States, due to its abundance of power, was required to be a shield for the rest of the world. The importance of reputation, then, is not only important when dealing with adversaries, but with allies and third parties as well.

DOMESTIC POLITICS AND INTERNATIONAL FACTORS

By the end of 1965, Johnson and his staff insisted somewhat disingenuously that he talked about Vietnam all the time; media professionals and certain congressional critics, however, knew that the president was hiding information about American actions in, and plans for, Vietnam.

Johnson's "minimum candor" strategy was shaped by a number of factors. First, it is clear that domestic support for escalation was widespread among elites and the public. In fact, Hallin argues that "the continuing strength of the Cold War consensus [was] no doubt the most important reason the administration was able to contain the debate over Vietnam policy."[38] Kearns also stresses the importance of this consensus saying that "Johnson had inherited not only an office but a world view: criteria of American responsibility, principles of action, necessities of leadership, established standards for determining threats to American freedom and to our greatness as a nation. Beside him were advisers who shared that view."[39] In early 1965 the public supported Johnson's policies: In January 67 percent approved of the action taken by the United States in Vietnam,[40] in October 58 percent approved.[41] Johnson's explanation for why the United States was involved in Vietnam aligned with the dominant beliefs held by most of the population.

In addition, because the war was limited in scope, Johnson felt that it would be harder to legitimize in light of the very different American experiences in World War II and Korea. Turner writes that "Americans in overwhelming numbers enthusiastically endorsed wars 'to end all wars' and 'to make the world safe for democracy.' "[42] Korea and Vietnam were not such wars. In June 1965 Senator Wayne Morse said:

> It would be a very serious mistake to think the American people would support a stalemated ground war in Vietnam for a period long enough to force the Communists into negotiating. They refused to support that kind of war in Korea. It became a choice between going all out to win, or ending it on almost any terms.[43]

Polls showed that Americans felt the United States had made a mistake in fighting in Korea, and some Democrats attributed Truman's 1952 defeat, in part, to Korea.[44] Korea could not be used to legitimize the Vietnam conflict.

Johnson did see the need to tie Congress to the deployment of additional forces in Vietnam. When Johnson increased the number of Marines in Vietnam in April 1965, for example, he followed with a military appropriation request in early May for $700 million and made clear that a vote for this money was a vote to continue the effort in South Vietnam.[45] Johnson knew full well that Congress was not likely to vote against money for the troops:

> To deny or to delay this request means you're not giving a man ammunition he needs for his gun. You're not giving him gas he needs for his helicopter. You got him standing out nekkid and letting people shoot at him. And we don't want to do that.[46]

Even those who questioned Johnson's Vietnam policy supported the appropriation request: the vote was 408 to 7 in the House and 88 to 3 in the Senate with no debate and no amendments. In June 1965, Johnson was again concerned about congressional representatives who were challenging his Vietnam policy: "We've either got to do one of two things. We've got to tuck tail and run, or we've got to have somebody . . . tell us that 'the Indians are coming' and protect us. . . . That puts [Congress] in the position of either tucking tail and running or giving us what we need".[47]

This congressional support points to another factor sustaining a minimum candor policy: Johnson did not want to open a debate with anyone who questioned his Vietnam policies from either the right or the left. This was imperative because of the importance he attached to his domestic agenda, and particularly to his Great Society programs.[48] He did not want attention diverted to Vietnam, and noted that "History provided too many cases where the sound of the bugle put an immediate end to the hopes and dreams of the best reformers."[49] He feared that opponents of his domestic agenda would use the war as an excuse for not funding domestic priorities. If he could mute the discussion on Vietnam, he could continue to push for civil rights and antipoverty measures at home.

But, as Johnson increased the number of American troops in Vietnam throughout 1965, congressional leaders, foreign leaders, and the public began to pay more attention to the war. In spite of widespread support for his policy, important voices were expressing concern about the administration's strategy. Senators Frank Church, George McGovern, and Mike Mansfield became increasingly disaffected. Students at the University of Michigan held the first teach-in against the war in March 1965. On the other side, there were many who supported the president and called for more aggressive action, not less, so "in ordering the air strikes on North Vietnam . . . Johnson faced criticism for doing both too much and not enough."[50] In fact, after his well received Hopkins speech, there were indications that those further on the right and left remained unsatisfied. Johnson felt caught between the two sides, even agonizing to his friend Tex Goldschmidt over the telegrams he received after his speech:

> Let me show you what they're saying. Atlanta, Georgia: "People are sick and tired of your lies about Vietnam. Bring these troops home." Lubbock, Texas: "We'll back down in Vietnam, as we have everywhere else under your position.". . . "Your speech made me sick. Why bomb? Negotiate!" "Your Vietnam backdown is [an] insult to US men who died in the cause."[51]

His explanation for a limited American involvement in Vietnam could not please everyone and so by minimizing information Johnson sought to avoid public statements that would "hem us in."[52]

Johnson was frequently asked about domestic opposition to his Vietnam policy, and his response recognized the difficulties in legitimizing support for a limited war. Asked about partisanship, for example, during his August 25, 1965 press conference, Johnson replied:

> So, I would say that we welcome expressions of viewpoint from the
> leadership in both parties. There will be times when we don't see every-
> thing alike, but that may contribute strength to our system. I don't
> think that Hanoi should ever for a moment entertain the illusion that
> the people of this country are not united in the work of this
> Government.[53]

Concern that opposition would be understood by the enemy as weakness or indecision was typical during war and Johnson was very sensitive
to it. The Cold War consensus and the domestic situation combined
with Johnson's discomfort with television led to a contradictory,
deliberately veiled, and politically driven communication strategy.
And we can now turn to a look at Johnson and TV.

Dealing with the Media

*[C]ontrolling the national consensus is not the same as controlling
the legislative majority.*

Palmer "Ep" Hoyt in Turner, *Johnson's Dual War*[54]

Television in 1965 was still in its infancy in the United States. CBS
and NBC had expanded their nightly news programs to half an hour in
length only in 1963, and the networks' reports relied to a great degree
on wire service reports for stories and video of official statements.[55]
A great many people watched television and Lyndon Johnson paid
attention to how he and his policies were covered. Indeed, for a man
famously reticent about using the media, he was often preoccupied by
press relations.[56] He had three television sets set up in the White House,
for example, so he could watch all three networks simultaneously.

In spite of Johnson's preoccupation with media coverage, he did
not heed recommendations from staff, family, and friends on how to
deal with the media.[57] For example, aide Douglass Cater urged
Johnson to hold two televised news conferences a month, plus commit
to four television programs a year in order to get his message out.[58]
Johnson refused. Early in 1965, advisors urged Johnson to go directly
to the American people via television to gain support for his Vietnam
policy. McGeorge Bundy prepared material for a speech to explain the
escalation but "the president insisted on his low-profile approach."[59]

Assistant Secretary of State for Public Affairs James Greenfield supported a greater release of information to the press.[60] Suggestions also came from friends outside the government as when Palmer "Ep" Hoyt, editor of the Denver *Post*, advised Johnson to hold regular televised press conferences (but adroitly noted that "controlling the national consensus is not the same as controlling the legislative majority"[61]).Television, Hoyt observed, allowed direct contact with the people that was vital to presidential control.[62] Johnson, however, had a different strategy in mind. As Hallin notes, "For Johnson the basic purpose of public and press relations policy on Vietnam was to keep the war off the political agenda."[63] For example, when the decision was made in March 1965 to send Marines to Da Nang, McNamara assured the president that he would "handle it in a way that will minimize the announcement."[64] As a result, the announcement was released late on Saturday, thereby missing the late Saturday afternoon papers.

American political leaders do not have unlimited access to television and they must take into account the organizational and structural characteristics of media as well as its appeal to the masses. Johnson was not comfortable with this; his political style was intensely personal.[65] This is not to say that he did not understand the structure of news organizations and the power of television. Turner sums it up this way:

> He wanted to communicate successfully over television, and he wanted members of the media to love him and to treat him well; but he resented that *he* might have to accommodate *them*, especially since he was, as he often noted, "leader of the Western world." Consequently, . . . he seesawed back and forth between courtship and rejection, and between soliciting advice and ignoring it.[66]

As a result, Johnson exercised firm control over the administration's media strategy, often doing so in ways that irritated his staff. George Reedy, Johnson's press secretary until July 1965, noted that:

> He [Johnson] was thinking of the press office as a place that produces stories for the press. I thought of the press office as a point of contact between the press and the White House. . . . And the two concepts just didn't jell . . . He thought I was pampering the press. I wasn't. I was just trying to set up rational procedures so that the press could cover him.[67]

Johnson also tended to show little concern for relationships with the press. Journalists were often surprised by Johnson's frequent changes in plans or travels, and Turner points out that while Johnson probably thought of himself as flexible when deciding at the last minute to travel (or not to travel) to his Texas ranch, correspondents saw this as annoying.[68] News organizations had to have at least some time for planning and logistics, but Johnson made himself available when it suited him, making it difficult for journalists to anticipate important briefings, news conferences, or last minute meetings. Increasingly, media professionals saw Johnson as secretive and duplicitous, to paraphrase Evans and Novak.[69]

By mid-1965 and despite Johnson's attempt to explain his Vietnam policy, his advisors recognized that they had a Vietnam "information problem." Bill Moyers replaced George Reedy as press secretary in July and there was a reassessment of media coverage of the administration's policy. Over dinner on August 3 and then lunch the next day, a group met to discuss the nature of the problem and how to address the issues involved. Aide Douglass Cater set out the problem:

> Our public posture is fragile; we rely too much on the President and too much on specific facts. There seems to be no basic understanding of the broader aspects on the part of the American people. And with this situation, we are extremely vulnerable to rumor, gossip, and quick reverses.[70]

Others set out a range of problems including that this war was different from previous wars with John Chancellor saying that "perhaps we have, for the first time in our experience, a non-packageable commodity."[71] Bundy noted that the American people didn't understand how the United States got into Vietnam, but then candidly suggested that there might not be a way to explain this: "this particular piece of exposition [how the United States got in] might simply not be manageable. Our best posture may be to say simply that somehow we are there and that we have to stay."[72]

In response to these concerns, the president created the Public Affairs Policy Committee for Vietnam, an ad-hoc group chaired by Mac Bundy and asked to focus on two issues: "the problem of educating the American people on the nature of the . . . war," and "broadening the President's image as a man who has other things on his mind besides Vietnam."[73] The agenda and minutes of the committee's meetings do not reflect a coherent or consistent communication strategy, but focus on select issues or problems as they arise. This group met weekly and discussed topics ranging from whether administration officials would attend teach-ins,[74] the distribution of the pamphlet "Why Vietnam?"[75] and how to approach "hard liners."[76]

Interestingly, certain characteristics of news organizations helped Johnson's messages about Vietnam get out.[77] In his analysis of television coverage of Vietnam, Hallin shows that Johnson got much of what he hoped for. The Vietnam story during this period was presented as the good—South Vietnam and the United States—versus the bad—North Vietnam, China, and the Soviet Union. Themes that were important included "war as a national endeavor," "war as an American tradition," "war as manly," "winning is what counts," and "war is rational."[78] Television presented a simple story of the virtuous United States and South Vietnam battling against the threatening North, and Hallin shows that, for the most part, until 1967 television supported Johnson's policy in Vietnam.[79]

The president's policy in 1965 was one of escalation, but his media strategies reflected the difficulties of pursuing such a policy, within the framework of great power identity. He was often secretive about decisions related to Vietnam and he was uncomfortable using television to legitimize his policy. Johnson felt that the American people would be less likely to support a war that was limited in scope, but he did not want to expand the scope of the war for fear of Chinese involvement. His communication strategy was to set the increases in American involvement within the context of a continuing but limited policy. South Vietnam had asked for American help; the United States had in the past, and would in the future, support the South against the Communist North. But as the war dragged on, it became increasingly apparent that a communication strategy designed to minimize bad news would lead to a credibility gap that Johnson could not overcome.

Reassessment—January 30, 1968– March 31, 1968

Tonight I want to speak to you of peace in Vietnam and Southeast Asia.

Johnson, Public Papers[80]

Fighting continued in Vietnam throughout 1966, 1967, and into 1968; as the number of American troops rose and the military's claims of control became less and less persuasive, Johnson nonetheless maintained his positive assessments. On January 1, 1968 he said that "we feel that the enemy knows that he can no longer win a military victory in South Vietnam."[81] In his January 17, 1968 State of the Union address, he told the American people that there were signs of progress in Vietnam and that that United States would persevere. Elections had been held, "the enemy ha[d] been defeated in battle after battle," and more South Vietnamese were living in areas under government protection.[82] After three years of combat, the challenge Johnson saw was "that it is our will that is being tried, not our strength."[83] Still, he recognized that there was opposition to his policies, and questions about the extent of progress, but he confidently assured his audience of America's resolve: "[The enemy] continues to hope that America's will to persevere can be broken. Well—he is wrong. America will persevere. Our patience and our perseverance will match our power. Aggression will never prevail."[84]

In March 1968, in the wake of the Tet Offensive and the military's request for an additional 206,000 troops, the administration began a serious reassessment of its policy that culminated in the report of the Senior Advisory Group on Vietnam, or the Wise Men—a group of Johnson's most trusted advisors—who ultimately advised that the United States seek de-escalation. At home he was challenged within his own party for the Democratic presidential nomination as the election year heated up. In the midst of all of this, American policy was reassessed quite quickly, and the public was not prepared for what Johnson would say in his March 31 televised speech to the nation when he announced that de-escalation would begin shortly, saying, "We are reducing—substantially reducing—the present level of hostilities. And we are doing so unilaterally and at once."[85] He then stunned the country by announcing that he would not seek or accept the Democratic Party's nomination for presidency. The popular perception was that Vietnam had beaten him. The quick reassessment of the policy left little time or planning for legitimizing de-escalation in either cognitive or normative dimensions. The questions of how to achieve de-escalation without losing the South, and how to reconcile it with the promises of a great power would be left to the next president.

By early 1968, the United States had approximately 500,000 troops in Vietnam, and there was growing dissatisfaction about the war at home. While Small writes that reassessment had three major stages, beginning with Johnson's nomination of Clark Clifford as Secretary of Defense on March 1,[86] it had already begun in the wake of the Tet Offensive, launched by the North on January 30. Most scholars agree that Tet was a military victory for the United States and South Vietnam, but this was not, however, the image presented by American media.[87] The massive offensive was covered extensively, and because it reached right to the American embassy in Saigon, the war came to the journalists' hotels. Television news showed gun fights and reporters running for cover at the American embassy. The apparent strength of the North Vietnamese reinforced the notion of Johnson's credibility gap. How could the United States be making progress if the pictures from Vietnam looked so grim? Hadn't Johnson emphasized progress in Vietnam? The immediate fallout from Tet was a shift in public opinion. In February confidence in Johnson's Vietnam policy was 35 percent while disapproval was 50 percent.[88] In March these numbers were 26 percent approval and 63 percent disapproval.[89]

Administration officials remained preoccupied with the reassessment of Vietnam policy through February and March, and on March 25 and 26, Johnson reconvened the Wise Men.[90] The group had last met with Johnson in November 1967 and had supported the administration's Vietnam policy, but by the end of March, the committee's views had begun to change. The majority, according to Bundy, were "in agreement with Dean Acheson that we could no longer do the job we set out to do in the time that American opinion would permit us."[91] Most supported de-escalation, a conclusion also reached by a small group of friends and advisors with whom Johnson had met as he drafted his March 31 speech. Johnson was surprised by the turn around of some long-time supporters of his Vietnam policy, but within a few days made the decision to de-escalate the war.

Johnson may not have intended to change American policy to one of withdrawal but that is what happened. Schandler's assessment is that Johnson's March 31 speech presented a real change in U.S. policy. He writes:

> Did these decisions announced by Johnson on March 31, 1968, constitute a turning point, a "fork-in-the-road" in the Vietnam policy and strategy theretofore pursued by the United States? The answer is "yes," although it was not intended or foreseen by most of the principal participants in the making of those decisions that such a result would occur.[92]

Whether or not Johnson sought this turning point or recognized it as such, his speech on March 31 marked the end of American reassessment.

TELEVISION DURING REASSESSMENT

Television was no longer an asset to him, he had done his television thing.

David Halberstam, Powers That Be[93]

In the beginning of this reassessment period, Johnson attempted to counter the image of Tet as a major victory for the North Vietnamese and he also tried to maintain the previous posture on the administration's commitment to holding the line against the North. General Westmoreland, for example, was ordered to issue a statement to the press at least once a day in which he underscored the administration's message of progress.[94] A cable sent on January 31 put it this way:

> We are facing, in these next few days, a critical phase in the American public's understanding and confidence toward our effort in Vietnam . . . Nothing can more dramatically counter scenes of VC destructiveness than the confident professionalism of the Commanding General. Similarly, the dire prognostications of the commentators can best be put into perspective by the shared experience and wisdom of our Ambassador. . . . Appearances by you, in the immediate situation, will make a greater impact here at home than much of what we can say.[95]

To refute the image of a crisis for the U.S. policy in Vietnam, the military was asked to present facts about enemy casualties and military action to show the success of American forces in rebuffing North Vietnamese attacks.

In addition to appearances by Westmoreland, Johnson's advisors appeared on major news programs to echo his positive assessment of the war.[96] In his February 2 news conference, the president said that because American leaders had expected a winter-spring offensive, Tet was hardly a surprise. But while asserting that the offensive had been a military failure, Johnson recognized that the North sought a "psychological victory" as well. He reviewed the basic facts of the attacks, including the known casualty figures and loss of materiel, and observed that the stated purposes of the general uprising have failed."[97]

National Security Advisor Walt Rostow urged Johnson to give a major speech to the nation to amplify the administration's position, and believed that "the president still could rally the nation behind him with a strong speech."[98] Johnson declined and David Halberstam argues he did so because he felt he could not contain television coverage and was wary of it:

> As 1968 opened, even the President was on the defensive. Television was no longer an asset to him, he had done his television thing. . . . The war had played too long, the glib predictions of White House officials had been put on once and then twice too often. Now television was about to start aiding the other side.[99]

This is overly dramatic—after Tet Johnson was simply unsure how to respond because he was in the midst of a policy reassessment during February and March.

Instead of following Rostow's advice, the administration pursued a different tack. The State Department worked on media strategy by compiling a briefing book that addressed, once again, why the United States was fighting in Vietnam. However, Turner notes that

> Johnson was reluctant to involve himself in these efforts to make members of the media understand his position, as he was assessing the military and political situation in Vietnam himself amid debate within the administration about the best ways of responding to the major offensive.[100]

Reassessing Vietnam, lacking a clear policy, Johnson did not use television extensively during this period to secure support for a policy of de-escalation. Once the decision was made, Johnson simply announced it to the American people without preparation:

> It had been quite a month, [March 1968] but now the wheels were turning; the decisions had been made. Only the announcement of those decisions remained.[101]

Still, in speeches during this period, and without extensive media coverage, Johnson continued to support the broad American commitment in Vietnam according to the Cold War rhetoric he had long embraced. In remarks at the National Rural Electric Cooperative Association Convention in Dallas on February 27, for example, Johnson said

> Our answer here at home, in every home, must be: "No retreat from the responsibilities of the hour and the day."
> We are living in a dangerous world and we must understand it. We must be prepared to stand up when we need to.
> There must be no failing of our fighting sons.
> There must be no betrayal of those who fight beside us.
> There must be no breaking of America's given word or America's commitments. When we give our word it must mean just what it says. America's word is America's bond. Isn't that the way you feel about it?[102]

Likewise, in remarks at the Conference on Foreign Policy for Leaders of National Nongovernmental Organizations on March 19th, Johnson said, "We must not break our commitment for freedom and for the future of the world."[103] So even as he reassessed policy, Johnson continued to legitimize American involvement in Vietnam by emphasizing the importance of American credibility.

Nonetheless, by late March 21 Johnson was shifting American policy objectives from an independent, free South Vietnam to peace.[104] Indeed, the president began his March 31 televised address to the nation by saying "Tonight I want to speak to you of peace in Vietnam and Southeast Asia."[105] Johnson announced a unilateral bombing pause, called for negotiations, and sought to legitimize these policy changes to the American people, albeit weakly. For example, Johnson emphasized the progress made by the South Vietnamese, including their victory during the Tet offensive. He reported positively on the numbers of volunteers for military service in South Vietnam, and he repeated President Thieu's recently made statement that "We must make greater efforts and accept more sacrifices because, as I have said many times, this is our country. The existence of our nation is at stake, and this is mainly a Vietnamese responsibility."[106] Johnson reported that the South had begun drafting nineteen year-olds and would begin drafting eighteen year-olds by May and sought to reassure the American public that the South Vietnamese could, with American help, defend themselves. Combined with a negotiated settlement, these measures would allow de-escalation to succeed without the abandonment of American goals. In addition, President Johnson reemphasized the broader commitment to freedom from Communism that Vietnam represented by stressing the special, even providential, role of the United States as a great power protecting freedom: "[o]f those to whom much is given, much is asked."[107] Quoting President John F. Kennedy's famous words that America would "pay any price, bear any burden, meet any hardship, support any friend, oppose any foe to assure the survival and the success of liberty," Johnson addressed the normative component of policy legitimacy by emphasizing values that resonated with many Americans.

Finally, recognizing the domestic strife then plaguing the United States, Johnson called for unity, saying "[I]n these times as in times before, it is true that a house divided against itself by the spirit of faction, of party, or region, of religion, of race, is a house that cannot stand," and asked the American people to "guard against divisiveness."[108] Stressing the need for unity, Johnson concluded the speech by noting that his time should not be taken up by electoral partisanship, and he made his now famous announcement that he would not run again.

DOMESTIC FACTORS

Although he was reluctant to admit it, Johnson's policy of incrementalism did not work. The North was not deterred from the fight, the

South had not consolidated a viable government, and more and more American lives were being lost in a faraway war whose merits were increasingly unclear. The nation was divided, as the hawks sought greater commitment and the doves sought less. Polls showed that Johnson's policy in Vietnam was supported by most Americans until July 1967.[109] This was after key congressional leaders had spoken out against the war and Senate hearings were held in August 1966. By early 1968, the Congressional leadership was divided, and some very influential representatives—and particularly Democratic representatives—were questioning Johnson's policy and calling for an end to the war. Moreover, Johnson faced challenges from Robert Kennedy and Eugene McCarthy for his party's nomination. Johnson noted: "The thing I feared from the first day of my Presidency was actually coming true. Robert Kennedy had openly announced his intention to reclaim the throne in the memory of his brother."[110] All of these domestic factors were kindling opposition to the administration's handling of Vietnam. After Tet, Johnson's ability to contain criticisms was badly eroded.

As Hallin convincingly shows, opposition had moved into the sphere of legitimate controversy.[111] Even Walter Cronkite, the beloved anchor of the CBS Evening News, questioned American policy in Vietnam during his February 27 broadcast:

> We have been too often disappointed by the optimism of the American leaders, both in Vietnam and Washington, to have faith any longer in the silver linings they find in the darkest clouds. . . .
>
> To say that we are mired in stalemate seems the only realistic, yet unsatisfactory, conclusion. . . .
>
> But it is increasingly clear to this reporter that the only rational way out then will be to negotiate, not as victors, but as an honorable people who lived up to their pledge to defend democracy, and did the best they could.
>
> This is Walter Cronkite. Good night.[112]

Elite views on the war had changed over time and television reflected it. Combined with Johnson's reticence to use television, it now came to rely less on administration officials and instead facilitated coverage of the opposition.

Johnson had kept secret the full extent of the war in Vietnam and years of empty predictions of victory had drawn down his credibility. Ironically, when Tet occurred and he told the truth, the country would not believe him. The credibility gap created serious repercussions for

Johnson and the administration. Writing later he observed:

> Looking back on early 1968, I am convinced I made a mistake by not say-
> ing more about Vietnam in my State of the Union report on January 17,
> 1968. In that address I underscored how intensely our will was being
> tested by the struggle in Vietnam, but I did not go into details con-
> cerning the build-up of enemy forces or warn of the early major com-
> bat I believed was in the offing. I relied instead on the "background"
> briefings that my advisers and I, as well as the State and Defense depart-
> ments, had provided members of the press corps for weeks. In those
> briefings we had stressed that heavy action could be expected soon.
> This was one of those delicate situations in which we had to try to
> inform our own people without alerting the enemy to our knowledge
> of its plans. In retrospect, I think I was too cautious. If I had forecast
> the possibilities, the American people would have been better prepared
> for what was soon to come.[113]

While it is unclear whether Johnson could have effectively prepared
the American public for the scale of the North's attacks, it is true that
his past secrecy in some areas and buoyant optimism in others lessened
his credibility once the Tet crisis peaked. This also points out that a
perceived failure may be just as potent as a "real" failure. Tet simultaneously strengthened domestic opposition to the war and prompted a
major reassessment of U.S. policy. Detailed examinations of the opposition to the Vietnam War exist elsewhere,[114] but what is crucial during
this period is that many of Johnson's advisors changed position on the
war in Vietnam, citing the opposition of the American public to the
status quo.

This analysis of Johnson's Vietnam policies and his communication
strategy speak to the research questions set out in chapter 1. First,
how did Johnson seek to legitimize policy? In both periods discussed
here (1965 and 1968), Johnson underscored the validity of his
Vietnam policy (the normative component). Overall, his messages
were focused on answering the question: "Why are we in Vietnam?"
This was tied to American identity as a great power engaged in a Cold
War with Communism. Perhaps the most important fact here is that
President Johnson sought to curtail information about and public
debate on the specifics of his Vietnam policy (the cognitive component).
This ties into this study's second question, about domestic politics.
Johnson wanted Congress to focus on his domestic agenda, and
in 1965 most of the public and elite were strongly supportive of
Vietnam policies. Too much attention from the president might
encourage more vigorous opposition. By 1968, however, Congress

and the American public were divided on Vietnam, and television covered the opposition as well as the supporters. Tet and subsequent challenges for the Democratic Party presidential nomination caused Johnson to seriously reassess Vietnam policy. Still, in 1968, as in 1965, Johnson was concerned about foreign perceptions of American resolve and this speaks to this study's third question, about reputation. Johnson keenly felt that the United States, as a great power, had to triumph in Vietnam so that American credibility would be bolstered both at home and abroad. Finally, and related to this study's fourth question about access and technique, much of Johnson's communication strategy was shaped by his uncomfortable relationship with the media itself. His overly optimistic pronouncements on some issues combined with a deceptive silence on others, were mirrored by his seeking coverage at some times and leaving journalists out at other times. This, inspite of the fact that he paid close attention to television coverage of his policies. When Johnson called for peace and announced that he would not run again, he left a set of problems for the next president.

The stage is now set for the focus of the American case: President Nixon's television strategy during withdrawal from the Vietnam War. Johnson left office without thoroughly preparing the American public for the end of the war. With no clear understanding on how withdrawal could be achieved, Richard Nixon faced the dilemma of securing this goal and developing a television strategy to explain the process without acknowledging failure. His attempts to control and intimidate media would only serve to exacerbate his own credibility problems as he pursued "peace with honor."

CHAPTER 3

Withdrawal and Aftermath: Vietnam

Richard Nixon was elected in 1968 in part on the strength of his promise to withdraw American forces from Vietnam and end the war on favorable terms. Knowing that a decisive military victory in Vietnam was unlikely, Nixon's goal became withdrawal conducted in stages as the administration simultaneously undertook negotiations with the North to secure a final settlement. At its heart, Nixon's story of American withdrawal from Vietnam depicted the United States as a superpower that could not and would not be defeated. "Peace with honor," the rubric for ending the war, was clearly and consistently linked in public communication to the policy known as Vietnamization. But bringing North Vietnam to a final settlement that reflected the administration's anxieties about maintaining American prestige and reputation was not an easy venture.

Nixon and Secretary of State Henry Kissinger felt strongly that the North Vietnamese would come to a settlement only if faced with strong U.S. military action, but such action also strengthened antiwar sentiment and seemed to contradict a policy of withdrawal. Domestic opposition to the president's policy grew more adamant, yet the need to resolve the situation was so dire that Nixon and Kissinger pursued withdrawal knowing that the South Vietnamese were not prepared to defend themselves. And while Kissinger acknowledged this in private discussions with Soviet Ambassador Dobrynin, the administration's messages to the American public repeatedly emphasized the importance of maintaining American credibility according to the Cold War rubrics of Great Powers. Keenly aware of the need to shape the tone and content of news coverage, Nixon was very concerned about controlling media messages. He believed if he could get television to cover *his* message, the American people would understand and accept that message. But because Nixon could not control what the networks covered, or how they interpreted it, the White House developed an elaborate system to influence television coverage. While the strategy covered many fronts, at its heart it was a plan to orchestrate attacks on the media that at the time were unique in their scope and ferocity. Designed to intimidate the media and gain control over access to information and how it was used, the administration adopted a hostile posture toward the press from the very beginning.

WITHDRAWAL 1969–1973

In June 1969 Nixon and South Vietnamese President Thieu met on Midway Island in the Pacific to discuss the situation in Vietnam and announce the withdrawal of 25,000 American troops. Subsequently, Nixon wrote of the meeting that:

> Early in the administration we had decided that withdrawing a number of American combat troops from Vietnam would demonstrate to Hanoi that we were serious in seeking a diplomatic settlement; it might also calm domestic public opinion by graphically demonstrating that we were beginning to wind down the war.[1]

Between 1969 and 1973, Nixon regularly reduced the number of American troops in Vietnam. On September 16, 1969 he announced that the troop ceiling would be dropped from 540,000 to 484,000 by December 15, 1969. Nixon's official statement, parts of which were taped for television broadcast, was interesting because he gave no explicit justification for the withdrawal. The statement simply noted that "after careful consideration with . . . senior civilian and military advisers and in full consultation with the Government of Vietnam" Nixon had made the decision to withdraw the troops.[2] Clearly giving the impression that withdrawal was a signal to the North Vietnamese to negotiate seriously, the statement reads: "The withdrawal of 60,000 troops is a significant step. The time for meaningful negotiations has therefore arrived."[3] Moreover, speaking to the American people in a live televised address, Nixon set out a fixed schedule for troop withdrawals; this was a new tactic as a set schedule had always been avoided for fear that it would reduce the incentive for the North Vietnamese to negotiate an end to hostilities. At the end of 1968 there were 540,000 American troops in Vietnam; by the end of 1970 the number dropped to 280,000. One year later it was 140,000. The last combat troops left on March 29, 1973.[4]

Holl argues that a set schedule was finally given due to domestic opposition. Kissinger's memoirs support this view.[5] In his memoirs,

Kissinger focuses on withdrawals as a tool for appeasing domestic political opposition, saying withdrawals would "help . . . win public support so that the troops which remained and our enhanced staying power might give Hanoi an incentive to negotiate seriously."[6] Alternatively (and far less likely), Kissinger also hoped that if the South Vietnamese could be sufficiently strengthened, the United States might be able to end its involvement without a negotiated settlement.[7] Holl argues, however, that domestic considerations prompted the decision, and there was a very weak case for claiming that American withdrawals would encourage the North Vietnamese to negotiate. Why would they want to negotiate if America was leaving anyway?[8]

Explaining Withdrawal

[W]e have instituted a Vietnamization program which envisages South Vietnamese responsibility for all aspects of the war.

Kissinger, "Action Memos"

As noted earlier, withdrawal was tied to hopes for a negotiated peace, one that would signify that the United States was not being forced out of the war. It also worked the other way around, and Holl writes that Nixon used negotiation to legitimize withdrawal.[9] In fact, as Nixon later wrote: "I was rather less optimistic than Kissinger regarding the prospect of a breakthrough in the . . . negotiations, but I agreed that at the very least they would provide an indisputable record of our desire for peace."[10] Yet, over time it became clear that the North Vietnamese had little reason to seriously negotiate, especially after American troop withdrawals had begun.

Between October and December 1969, the administration's explicit media strategy stressed progress in ending U.S. involvement. In October 1969 a coherent legitimation strategy emerged in the fact sheets compiled by Kissinger and sent to television news directors by Herbert Klein, the White House Director of Communications. A typical example compared the situation in October 1969 to the one the Administration faced when it took office on January 20, 1969.[11] In assessing the military and political situations, several general legitimizing themes were apparent. First, the fact sheet emphasized progress in withdrawal. In January 1969, prior to Nixon's assumption of the presidency, the number of troops had continued to increase, despite Johnson's announcement of de-escalation. Under Nixon, withdrawal became a mainstay. But, the administration could use the theme of negotiations to legitimize withdrawal only when there was some prospect for progress, and there was little evidence of it in 1969. An internal White House memo from late 1969 describing presidential objectives, for example, stated that media strategy should focus on:

> Progress toward peace in Vietnam evidenced by troop withdrawals, a sixth month comparison of casualty list, [*sic*] and draft reduction, [*sic*] rather than being judged on the success and negotiations.[12]

In addition to touting progress in both withdrawal and negotiations as a legitimizing theme, Nixon used Vietnamization to justify American withdrawal from Vietnam. The plan for Vietnamization was generally credited to Secretary of Defense Melvin Laird. (Klein pointed out that the "credit given Laird by the media bothered the President, and more, it irritated Kissinger."[13]) Announced in the spring of 1969, Summers writes that Vietnamization became the focal point, and that "resisting aggression and nation building were to become a responsibility of the South Vietnamese government."[14] This would in turn become the rationale for a complete U.S. withdrawal. Put another way "Vietnamization was actually 'the model or paradigm of a new strategy of retreat.' "[15] If the South Vietnamese could defend themselves, American withdrawal would not mean the loss of South Vietnam.

The theme of Vietnamization became increasingly important as peace negotiations dragged on. Kissinger's October 1969 fact sheet said that:

> [W]e have instituted a Vietnamization program which envisages South Vietnamese responsibility for all aspects of the war—coping with both Viet Cong insurgency and regular North Vietnamese forces—even if we cannot make progress in the political negotiations.[16]

The crucial problem however, was that there was no negotiated peace settlement in sight in 1969, and under no circumstances would Nixon unilaterally withdraw forces from Vietnam without a settlement. This would amount to an acknowledgment of failure in Vietnam, and Nixon believed that this would constitute a serious blow to the nation. His alternative was "peace with honor," and the administration's strategy focused on developing a framework that allowed the United States to claim that it had kept its commitment to South Vietnam (even as that commitment was severed).

Because Vietnamization was touted as a strategy that would prepare South Vietnam to successfully defend itself, withdrawal was framed as being inherently achievable. It was also firmly set within the context of the United States as great power, particularly in light of the Cold War. Presidents Eisenhower, Kennedy, and Johnson clearly explained Vietnam within a Cold War context by asserting again and again that American forces were in Vietnam because the *Communist* North was threatening the existence of the *non-Communist* South.[17] Nixon did the same. As a great power, the United States would defend allies, democracy, and capitalism in pursuit of Cold War promises to deter Communist aggression. If Vietnamization was successful in fulfilling those promises, the United States could claim to have fulfilled its responsibility and withdraw from Vietnam secure in the knowledge that it had not violated its pledges.

On November 3, 1969, Nixon addressed the nation in a speech designed to counter domestic opposition to the war and reassert the identity of the United States as a superpower. Deeply angered by the October 15 Moratorium on the War that had attracted 125,000 protesters to Washington, DC, Nixon later blamed the event for destroying his hopes of ending the war in 1969, but used it at the time to bolster support by appealing to mainstream ideas of patriotism, honor, and prestige. Commonly known as the Silent Majority speech, it rallied American public opinion around the president and his policy. Nixon began the speech with uncharacteristic candor:

> I believe that one of the reasons for the deep division about Vietnam is that many Americans have lost confidence in what their Government has told them about our policy. The American people cannot and should not be asked to support a policy which involves the overriding issues of war and peace unless they know the truth about that policy.
>
> Tonight, therefore, I would like to answer some of the questions that I know are on the minds of many of you listening to me.[18]

Explaining why he felt the United States could not unilaterally withdraw from Vietnam, Nixon stressed the consequences of such a decision for a world divided by Cold War fault lines:

> Our defeat and humiliation in South Vietnam without question would promote recklessness in the councils of those great powers who have not yet abandoned their goals of world conquest. This would spark violence wherever our commitments help maintain the peace—in the Middle East, in Berlin, eventually even in the Western Hemisphere.[19]

This speech reiterated the three principles of the Nixon Doctrine, first set out in Guam in July 1969.[20] First, the United States would keep its treaty commitments. Second, the United States would provide a nuclear shield for vital allies threatened by another nuclear power. Finally, the United States would supply military and economic assistance as per treaty commitments, but expected that any nation directly threatened would ultimately assume the primary responsibility for its own defense. Logically extending the doctrine to southeast Asia, Nixon explained Vietnamization and assured his listeners that the South Vietnamese had gained strength and were beginning to assume combat responsibilities from American troops.[21]

Five months later, on April 20, 1970, Nixon again spoke to the nation and claimed that Vietnamization had exceeded original expectations:

Tonight I am pleased to report that progress in training and equipping South Vietnamese forces has substantially exceeded our original expectations last June.

Very significant advances have also been made in pacification.[22]

Ten days later, however, on April 30, Nixon announced his fateful decision to send U.S. troops into Cambodia.[23] Describing the threat to South Vietnamese security caused by increased North Vietnamese military activity, especially in Cambodia, Nixon used a map and pointer to indicate what and where he was talking about.[24] He showed where the countries were located—North Vietnam, South Vietnam, Cambodia, and emphasized that the South Vietnamese would bear the major responsibility for the operations with the United States providing air and logistical support.[25] Notably, and in a bit of logic that seems counterintuitive, Nixon tied U.S. actions in Cambodia to withdrawal, saying: "To protect our men who are in Vietnam and to guarantee the continued success of our withdrawal and Vietnamization programs, I have concluded that the time has come for action."[26] He also legitimized the decision with normative arguments:

If, when the chips are down, the world's most powerful nation, the United States of America, acts like a pitiful, helpless giant, the forces of totalitarianism and anarchy will threaten free nations and free institutions throughout the world.[27]

This explanation was clearly tied to superpower identity and the role Nixon perceived the United States should play in world affairs. The stakes were clear: unless the United States fulfilled its role as a super-power, anarchy would result and the forces of evil would win.

The administration put its best face on the decision to go into Cambodia, but some staff members were anxious. Herbert Klein, Nixon's Director of Communications for the Executive Branch, writes that "on the night Nixon announced that we were moving into Cambodia, I felt genuine fear in the bottom of my stomach."[28] His fear had a lot to do with how this decision could be legitimized within the context of withdrawal:

> Here we were facing a public sentiment to limit the war or get out of it, and our policy was to decrease American involvement—yet suddenly we were enlarging the theater of action. The President felt this was the way to end the war more quickly, and I think he was right; but if I was scared, what about the public? What we were lacking on the presidential staff, and what is lacking on most, was the ability to coordinate major strategic decisions with an evaluation of how this affected a very disturbed American citizenry. A President cannot act by studying public opinion polls, but he should consider how the public will react and how best to deal with the reaction when making any major decision. The President incorrectly felt he could go public via TV and that would suffice.[29]

Klein and adviser Bryce Harlow believed that a more hands-on approach was necessary, and they accompanied a small group of governors and congressional representatives on an inspection trip to South Vietnam and into the incursion areas of Cambodia in the hope of "generat[ing] support for the President's decision to send troops into Cambodia."[30] On June 3, Nixon again used television to report that the Cambodian operation had been an unqualified success. Showing a film of captured war materiel, ammunition, and weapons, the president pledged that American combat forces would leave Cambodia within a month, and once again linked the Cambodian affair to broader war aims: "We have a program for peace—and the greater the support the administration receives in its efforts, the greater the opportunity to win that just peace we all desire."[31] The emphasis on withdrawal and Vietnamization continued, and on April 7, 1971 Nixon reported that "Vietnamization has succeeded."[32] He repeatedly emphasized its success in speeches in 1972 even as the North attacked the South in the spring, American troop withdrawals continued, and the United States mined Haiphong Harbor and intensified bombing of the North.[33]

Domestic Politics and Television

The public . . . wanted to get out of Vietnam and yet did not want defeat.

Kissinger, *White House Years*[34]

The importance of maintaining great power identity in the Nixon administration was often linked to concerns about the domestic audience. For example, a 1969 White House memorandum reported: "If we are defeated in Vietnam, the US people would never stand firm elsewhere. The problem is the confidence of the American people in themselves, and we must think in domestic terms."[35] Kissinger admitted the intractable nature of the dilemma when he said that "The public . . . wanted to get out of Vietnam and yet did not want defeat."[36] Nixon assumed that a majority of the public accepted America's great power identity, but he and others also held that media had to be used to bolster this identity, especially in light of the problems he encountered in Vietnam after 1969. Without American domestic confidence, Nixon believed the United States could not use its material power to effect the kind of change that he and many others believed the nation was uniquely obligated to undertake.

Domestic elites and public opinion were extremely important to the administration from January 1969 to March 1973, when opposition to the conduct of the war existed on both the left and the right. Nixon was quite concerned about domestic protests and he took deliberate steps to blunt criticism. As noted earlier, Nixon felt that he could counter the opposition by gaining support from the "silent majority." Indeed, in his November 3, 1969 speech, Nixon explicitly asked for this support:

> Let us be united for peace. Let us also be united against defeat. Because let us understand: North Vietnam cannot defeat or humiliate the United States. Only Americans can do that.[37]

This speech emphasized the importance of supporting the president's policy, implicitly criticized the opposition, and stressed the role of the United States as a world power incapable of being defeated by enemies.

The November 3 speech struck a chord with many Americans and it emboldened the president to stay the course. Nixon considered the speech one of his finest moments, noting later that it had "a direct impact on congressional opinion."[38] Writing in his memoirs, he remembered:

> I had never imagined that at the end of my first year as President I would be contemplating two more years of fighting in Vietnam. But the unexpected success of the November 3 speech had bought me more time, and bolstered by Sir Robert Thompson's [Special advisor on pacification to President Nixon] optimistic estimate that within two years we would be able to achieve a victory—either in the sense of an acceptable negotiated settlement or of having prepared the South Vietnamese to carry the burden of the fighting on their own—I was prepared to continue the war despite the serious strains that would be involved on the home front.[39]

Public opinion polls revealed significant support for Nixon in the wake of the speech. Before the speech, on November 2, 1968 Gallup reported that 58 percent of respondents approved of Nixon's handling of Vietnam.[40] When Nixon appeared on the Today Show on November 5, he heard Barbara Walters report that a subsequent Gallup Poll registered 77 percent approval of the president's Vietnam policy.[41]

The Cambodian invasion notwithstanding, Nixon continued to withdraw troops from Vietnam in an effort to defuse domestic opposition and encourage the North to negotiate. On October 7, 1970, he called for a cease-fire, a halt to U.S. bombing, expanded peace talks, and the release of POWs.[42] On October 12, the White House announced that another 40,000 troops would be withdrawn. Kissinger—concerned with the war's domestic consequences, wrote that the decision to speed up withdrawals was based on the need to quell domestic opposition to the war.[43] Holl notes, however, that this was a forlorn hope. "By the fall of 1971, it was clear that the President could not keep the costs of the war down to acceptable levels in order to achieve an acceptable negotiated settlement because, to the vocally antiwar partisans, no costs were acceptable."[44]

Moreover, troop withdrawals did not lead to the breakthrough in negotiations for which Nixon hoped, and at the end of 1972 he resorted once more to military force in an attempt to speed up negotiations. Nixon wrote that his first priority after his 1972 reelection was to end the war,[45] but significant progress had eluded him. When talks stalled in early December, Alexander Haig and Kissinger advised breaking off the talks and a resumption of bombing. The secretary of state also suggested the president go on television to explain the situation, but, according to Kissinger, Nixon "had a horror of appearing on television to announce that he was beginning his new mandate by once again expanding the war."[46] Nixon, for his part, remembered that:

> Expectations were raised so high prior to the election and since the election that to go before the American people on television and say that we have been tricked again by the Communists, that we were misled by them, and that now we have to order resumption of the war with no end in sight and no hope, is simply going to be a loser.[47]

On December 13, 1972 the talks were recessed and Nixon decided to significantly step up the bombing in a campaign called Operation Linebacker II, but popularly known as the Christmas Bombing.[48] Rather than explaining the decision himself, Nixon directed Kissinger to conduct a briefing to explain the impasse in the negotiations.

Media coverage of the Christmas Bombing was extensive, and Nixon was irritated by its tone and content:

> On the negative side, the columnists and the media broke down about the way they had during the election and on all the Vietnam decisions previously.
>
> The record of the liberal left media on Vietnam is perhaps one of the most disgraceful in the whole history of communications in this country. I am not referring to the honest pacifists who have been against the war from the beginning, but to those in the media who simply cannot bear the thought of this administration under my leadership bringing off the peace on an honorable basis which they have so long predicted would be impossible.
>
> The election was a terrible blow to them and this is their first opportunity to recover from the election and strike back.[49]

On December 26th the North Vietnamese signaled that they were ready to resume negotiations, a decision that Nixon attributed to the bombings. Kissinger concurred, saying Nixon's "decision speeded the end of the war and saved lives."[50] In a comment that reflected his disdain for the media, Nixon commented that the media did not understand how successful the bombing had been: "most of them [reporters] indicated that it was not clear whether the return to negotiations was the result of the bombing, or whether the bombing halt was the result of the enemy's agreement to return to negotiations."[51] Talks resumed in January, and an agreement was initialed on January 23rd. Formal ceasefire agreements were signed in Paris on the 27th. Even as a settlement was reached, Klein wrote that there was a staff discussion about the president's critics:

> Haldeman raised the question about how the opponents of the President, those who had followed Senator McGovern, would greet the announcement. Would they question publicly why we had not accepted terms like these earlier? Was this the peace with honor the President had constantly reiterated as his goal?[52]

Klein reported that Kissinger saw three main lines of attack by opponents. The first was that this settlement could have been reached long ago. The second was that a settlement could have been gotten in October before the election. The third was that it was only the pressure of the doves that made the administration pursue peace.[53] Klein commented that Patrick Buchanan, special assistant to the president, had prepared a paper on how the administration should respond to its critics. Utterly unwilling to make any concessions, Buchanan called for direct attacks on the administration's critics while maintaining that the administration had achieved its goals and satisfied its commitments. Quoting Buchanan, Klein writes that "This was a victory for the Silent Majority, which had stood strong with the President against 'relentless, harsh, and vitriolic attack from the left.' "[54]

The importance of domestic considerations was plainly evident even as the final agreement was announced in early 1973. Tellingly, a White House planning group convened to establish and communicate themes, the most important of which was the perception of President Nixon as "Peacemaker": "We should have our short-term and long-term 'media-plans' formulated, aimed at limiting the media's own inclinations and initiatives, whether conscious or willy-nilly, to form and direct the reportorial and emotional context of the event."[55] The first stage involved a short and simple announcement of the negotiated peace itself, and Nixon made a brief address on January 23 in which he said:

> Now that we have achieved an honorable agreement let us be proud that America did not settle for a peace that would have betrayed our allies, that would have abandoned our prisoners of war or that would have ended the war for us but would have continued the war for the 59 million people of Indochina.[56]

The second stage was to set out "a story of the war that they [the public] can understand and live with" because, as Nixon advisor Dwight Chapin wrote "the people are neither really interested in nor capable of assessing and assimilating the tortuous processes of diplomatic negotiations."[57] The core of this approach was that President Nixon had achieved peace with honor. Moreover, in a memo to Haldeman, Chapin reiterated that domestic opposition was not only dangerous, it represented unacceptable solutions to the war:

> Had the president's opponents in Congress prevailed—instead of the president—Americans would today be witnessing a bloodbath, on an unprecedented scale, the victims of which would be those Vietnamese who placed their confidence in the word of the United States. The difference between what the president has achieved, and what his opponents wanted is the difference between peace with honor, and the false peace of an American surrender.[58]

Above all, the administration's version of events needed to be established quickly: "Whether or not we succeed in the first few days of peace in framing such a context will largely determine the direction taken."[59] All in all, the evidence suggests that strategy succeeded; the Nixon administration gave most people a story they could "understand and live with." Most Americans polled believed the United States had achieved "peace with honor" (58%).[60] This, despite the fact that 54 percent of the American public did not believe the South Vietnamese could withstand Communist pressures, 70 percent thought it likely the North would try to take over the South, and 79 percent thought if this did, indeed, occur, the United States should not send troops to help.[61]

INTERNATIONAL ACTORS AND REPUTATION

If the Vietnamese can agree among themselves on a reasonable compromise, and if thereafter, war breaks out again between North and South Vietnam, that conflict will no longer be an American affair.

Kissinger to Dobrynin in Kimball, *Vietnam War Files*[62]

From the beginning of American involvement, the war in Vietnam had always been placed squarely within the framework of the Cold War, and American assistance to the South Vietnamese was routinely justified as a necessary counterweight to communist aggression. The normative argument used by Nixon for American involvement in Vietnam and gradual withdrawal was that communist threats to world security had to be halted. Yet even as he was making these statements, the Cold War status quo was shifting in dramatic ways. In mid-July 1971, for example, the administration announced that Nixon would go to Communist China for high level talks. In May 1972, Nixon visited Moscow and signed the first SALT agreement. Here was the president of the United States strengthening ties with China and the Soviet Union, a fact that at the very least called into question the clarity of Cold War rhetoric. Given these developments, casting Vietnam as a case study in Cold War containment was problematic.

While public statements typically suggested that rival superpowers would take advantage of American weakness, a strikingly different message was conveyed through high level diplomatic channels. Soviet Ambassador to the United States Anatoly Dobrynin reported that in his first meeting with Henry Kissinger after Nixon's inauguration, Kissinger said that the administration was not prepared for an immediate shift in the South Vietnamese government, "although they had no objection to a gradual evolution,"[63] but could not accept a settlement that looked like a military defeat. Dobrynin characterized these secret meetings as particularly important to Kissinger because they avoided congressional and public scrutiny, and kept the media out of the discussions.

Kimball argues that by the fall of 1970, the administration clearly favored a policy of unilateral withdrawal, delinking American and North Vietnamese withdrawal from South Vietnam. Moreover, Kissinger was not at all sure that the South was or would ever be strong enough to counter aggression from the North, and said so to Dobrynin:

> If the Vietnamese can agree among themselves on a reasonable compromise, and if thereafter, war breaks out again between North and South Vietnam, that conflict will no longer be an American affair; it will be an affair of the Vietnamese themselves, because the Americans will have left Vietnam. It will be beyond the scope of the Nixon administration.[64]

Tapes of White House conversations from the time also support this, suggesting that the plan was to seek a "decent interval" between the withdrawal of American troops and the coming battle between North and South. According to Kimball, by early 1971 "[t]he 'game plan' was to hurt the North Vietnamese in Laos, get Thieu reelected in October 1971, then meet with the North Vietnamese in Paris and propose a total US withdrawal within twelve months, accompanied by a cease-fire and a release of POWs."[65] For his part, Nixon was determined to keep to his timetable, even if it meant throwing the South Vietnamese to the wolves. In March 1971, for example, an oval office recording of the president's comments revealed this: "I'm not going to allow their weakness and their fear of the North Vietnamese to, to, to delay us."[66]

In his public statements, however, Nixon repeatedly emphasized America's promises and commitments to third parties and allies. In his opinion, Vietnamization not only validated withdrawal, it confirmed American resolve for third parties, especially in Asia.[67] In October 1969 Nixon addressed this point:

> What was at stake now . . . is not only the future peace of the Pacific and the chances for independence in the region, but the survival of the US as a world power with the will to use this power. If South Vietnam were to go, after a matter of months countries such as Thailand, the Philippines, and Indonesia would have to adjust because they believe they must play the winner. In fact, the domino theory would apply.[68]

In his June 3, 1970 speech, Nixon again explicitly tied the bombing of Cambodia to the maintenance of credibility with third parties in "Latin America, Europe, the Mideast, or other parts of Asia."[69]

So, while it publicly reiterated the success of Vietnamization, privately administration officials took a less optimistic and more self-serving view of matters when they adopted a "decent interval" strategy, planning to leave the South Vietnamese to their own devices after American withdrawal. Moreover, this change they shared with their Soviet and Chinese counterparts, but *not* with the American people, allies, or third parties.[70] Interestingly, the decent interval policy is at odds with what Kissinger wrote later about Vietnam and serves as a reminder of the painfully hypocritical position taken by the Nixon administration: "No serious policymaker could allow himself to succumb to the fashionable debunking of 'prestige' or 'honor' or 'credibility.' For a great power to abandon a small ally to tyranny simply to obtain a respite from its own domestic travail seemed to Nixon—and still seems to me—profoundly immoral and destructive of efforts to build a new and ultimately more peaceful pattern of international relations."[71]

CONTROL OF TELEVISION

In the modern presidency, concern for image must rank with concern for substance.

Nixon, *Memoirs of Richard Nixon*[72]

In the United States, media are not owned by or directly controlled by the government. Since the nation's founding, media professionals have, for the most part, prided themselves on being the watchdogs of society. To the degree that this position can be maintained, political leaders cannot therefore completely control the media's coverage of war. Klein notes that "Vietnam provided the toughest of the problems in seeking favorable, or at least balanced, coverage from the media. Emotions ran as high within the news corps as they did with the public."[73] Nixon certainly could not control all that was broadcast about Vietnam (a point he repeatedly reiterated during and after his presidency). So he went on the offensive and attempted to directly shape television's coverage of the American experience in Vietnam. Nixon routinely used the veiled (and sometimes not-so-veiled) threat of cutting off reporters whose stories were unfavorable to him or his policies, attempted to muzzle his critics, and was very deliberate about intimidating media outlets he accused of pandering to his critics. Vice President Spiro Agnew's attacks on the media, discussed below, were explicitly designed to put the media on the defensive and force journalists to consider more carefully how they covered the administration's policies on Vietnam.

Nixon had had a long and complicated relationship with the media prior to his inauguration as president in January 1969. Two crucial events helped shape his view of what constituted the effective use of television: the September 23, 1952 Checkers speech, and his September 26, 1960 televised presidential debate against John Kennedy. The lessons that Nixon learned were that in the postwar world, television could make or break a politician and his policies, and that he should speak directly to the American people and avoid media filtering his messages.

The Checkers speech was prompted by allegations in 1952 that Nixon had used a private fund to pay for personal expenses and had never reported it, a breach serious enough to threaten his place on the Republican ticket with Eisenhower. Convinced that he could stem the criticism by going directly to the American people via television, Nixon appeared on national television in an emotional and now famous speech known afterwards as the Checkers speech for his reference to the family pet. His performance was persuasive, and ever after Nixon used direct television appeals to the American people at crucial junctures.

Nixon did not enjoy the same success during the debates with Kennedy; he refused make-up, and a heavy five o'clock beard showed through the light powder he did allow. Dressed in a baggy suit, Nixon sweated heavily during the debate, and <u>looked</u> terrible. Later Nixon paraphrased Soviet leader Khrushchev who said, "One TV picture is worth ten thousand words."[74] The Checkers speech and the debates with Kennedy reinforced Nixon's belief in the importance of television, and Klein said that Nixon's first instruction to him after winning the 1968 election was, "I want you to do a lot more television."[75] A March 1969 memo reiterated this message:

> In developing the weekly game plan for the President, it is extremely important that major emphasis be given to TV coverage as well as general news releases. In other words, the game plan should look specifically at stories that are slanted to TV and that will be given major television play.[76]

As much as he appreciated television's power, Nixon was also distrustful of it and felt that he could not get a fair hearing when his views and policies were filtered through the nightly news or were discussed in commentaries. He bore a peculiar animus against reporters whom he believed were little more than liberal patsies, and rather than allowing them to dictate how events would be covered and interpreted, he believed that leaders had to shape the news:

> Since the advent of television as our primary means of communication and source of information, modern Presidents must have specialized talents at once more superficial and more complicated than those of their predecessors. They must try to master the art of manipulating the media not only to win in politics but in order to further the programs and causes they believe in; at the same time they must avoid at all costs the charge of trying to manipulate the media. In the modern presidency, concern for image must rank with concern for substance—there is no guarantee that good programs will automatically triumph.[77]

He believed that the media, and particularly television, could be used to legitimize policy, but the process had to be carefully controlled, or in his own words, manipulated. Klein wrote:

> Nixon understood the needs of the press for new leads, excerpts issued in time for deadlines, sidebar features, and filing and broadcast time. Our scheduling reflected this. He fully understood the importance of the press, and, as the years went on, he recognized and perhaps overemphasized the importance of television.[78]

Nixon felt that television was important for a number of reasons, but perhaps the most salient was that he believed "if the public hear[d] his own words directly, the chances of effective distortion by newsmen diminished."[79] He particularly felt this way with regard to

American policy with Southeast Asia generally and in Vietnam specifically: "I must say that without television it might have been difficult for me to get people to understand a thing."[80] Nixon believed that television coverage of the Vietnam War had seriously weakened American resolve:

> More than ever before, television showed the terrible human suffering and sacrifice of war. Whatever the intention behind such relentless and literal reporting of the war, the result was a serious demoralization of the home front, raising the question whether America would ever again be able to fight an enemy abroad with unity and strength of purpose at home. As *Newsweek* columnist Kenneth Crawford wrote, this was the first war in our history when the media was more friendly to our enemies than to our allies. I felt that by the time I had become President the way the Vietnam war had been conducted and reported had worn down American's spirit and sense of confidence.[81]

Nixon was careful to use television strategically so that when he appeared, viewers would assume that his message was important. Over time this raised expectations about each live televised prime-time speech. In addition, many in the news media expected Nixon to make major policy statements only or primarily on television, and in prime time. A White House news summary of a September 1969 Nixon press conference, for example, noted that:

> Sevareid said it was hard to see what the President's conference added to the sum total of human knowledge but that shouldn't be surprising. If he had wanted to make a major statement, he would have gone for prime time.[82]

In the margin Nixon wrote, "H[aldeman] & Ziegler—Note—You can't win when you try to please the writing press."[83]

The structure of the administration's communications office was directly related to Nixon's desires to control access to information and shape the story of Vietnam. There was a large White House public relations and communications staff, and much of its work was centralized under Haldeman, a practice that allowed for great control by the president. Nixon decided, for example, there would be no press secretary as had been the tradition under recent presidents. Ehrlichman wrote that:

> Nixon wanted Ron Ziegler to run the press office, but it would be a far less important place than in the past. Ziegler would conduct the

ministerial aspect of the office—the routine postings and announcements and press logistics—but he would have not discretionary functions. The President would hold his own press conferences from time to time to deal with policy matters. And in between, Ziegler would say what Nixon told him to say at regular press briefings.[84]

Herbert Klein was enlisted as Director of Communications in which capacity he was to organize and "coordinate activities of the information officers of various executive departments . . . reduce the overall staff."[85] According to Porter, "the new structure was as much designed to expedite the movement of information within the government as to serve the media."[86] Memoirs of administration officials and records in the Nixon archive clearly indicate that there were many people involved in public relations. Klein later observed that:

> It seemed to me that half of the President's staff considered themselves experts on press and public relations. The President himself spent a disproportionate part of his time complaining about the press and our dealings with it.[87]

Moreover, Klein recalled, the administration's concern about the media led to bad decisions:

> From the President on down, an amazingly excessive amount of time was spent worrying about plans to conjure up better and more favorable coverage. In striving for coups with the news media, many self-designated White House experts forgot the simple fact that direct and honest dealings with the press work best, as was evident in the initial months of the Nixon administration.[88]

Nixon came into office clearly prepared to take on the media. Although Klein announced a policy of "openness,"[89] this deteriorated quite rapidly:

> [T]he White House did not accept the concept of openness and gradually we drifted from an atmosphere of mutual working arrangements to an unproductive bully attitude toward the news media. The problem stemmed not from a lack of attention to the media, but more from obsession with it.[90]

This obsession helped shape Nixon's views on media coverage of his Vietnam policy, and it certainly fueled his often hostile reactions. Klein sought a more moderate position, and noted "an effort to discredit the networks was not going to change bias in reporting on Vietnam. We were better off to develop a stronger case for the President's side of the issue and to use our best spokesmen frequently."[91] However, as this chapter will show, attempts to legitimize withdrawal were deeply connected to a broader attack on the media itself, and to an attempt to silence the administration's critics.

The administration's stand on the media came under review in July 1969 when Haldeman sent a memo to White House staffers Patrick Buchanan, Raymond Price, William Safire, James Keogh, Richard Moore, Ron Ziegler, Herbert Klein, Charles Colson, Dwight Chapin, Robert Finch, and Donald Rumsfeld requesting an "analysis of the strengths and weaknesses surrounding our whole approach and relationship with the press and media."[92] Specifically Haldeman asked for views on the balance of administration use of television versus print media, the administration's relationship with television, radio, and press, and recommendations "as to what we should be doing."[93] The responses of Moore (Attorney General's office), Finch, Rumsfeld, Keogh, Colson, Price, and Klein are in the White House Special Files of the Nixon Project. Two unidentified responses are also in these files, most likely from Buchanan, Ziegler, or Chapin. A response from Safire was not found and a reference to such a response is not present in the summary of these memos written to Haldeman by Gregg Petersmeyer.[94]

The responses represent a variety of views. Some advocated a hard line and firm stand against the press. Colson, for example, wrote:

> I think . . . that our posture of being somewhat aloof and not trying to cater to the press is absolutely correct. They can't be won over on a personal or philosophical basis. We have to force them to print our line and we have to make them respect us.[95]

Others were less confrontational and took a more conciliatory approach as when Klein said that personal contacts with network executives were quite important for positive coverage. The hard-liners clearly won the day.

The president paid close attention to how the media were covering him and his policies, and he ordered a daily news summary from Buchanan and his staff. His extensive underlining and marginalia on the summaries show that Nixon read them quite carefully. In fact, Nixon said, "I get my news from the news summary the staff prepares every day and it's great; it gives me all sides. I never watch TV commentators or the news shows when they are about me. That's because I don't want decisions influenced by personal emotional reactions."[96] Buchanan and his staff, then, had the opportunity to shape Nixon's view of the media. And while Nixon claimed he wanted to avoid emotional reactions, the news summaries could be quite emotionally loaded.[97]

These news summaries were used both to check on how the president and his policies were being covered, and to develop strategies for countering news coverage which Nixon perceived as defying his goals. Nixon's notes on the news summaries were followed up with action memoranda to appropriate staff members. Haldeman wrote in a March 1969 memo, for example, "He [Nixon] wants to be sure, first of all, that we _are_ auditing the television news and, secondly, that we are getting our oar in when we should."[98] Nixon also focused on television programs that reached wide audiences. Responding to a July 1969 report on "Washington Week in Review," Nixon wrote in the margin, "Buchanan—I don't consider this program worth so much time. It is really a rehash of the columns—What we need is more emphasis on the shows with big listening audiences."[99]

Nixon wanted a structure built into the communication system that would counter coverage perceived by the White House as negative. In September 1969, for example, in marginalia on a news summary which noted the lack of the coverage of what Buchanan described as the president's "excellent and well received remarks," Nixon wrote: "H[aldeman]—See that NBC gets a hard kick from Klein on this and _again_ when are we going to have a system where this is automatically done and reported to me?"[100] A September 1969 summary's suggestion that "the voice of the hawk is barely heard in the land" prompted Nixon to write: "H & K—correct—But I thought we had a program where Buchanan was supposed to talk to some of the right wing on this—and what happened to Harlow and Nofziger on this."[101] This focus was also evident in Nixon's comments about the content of coverage, at least as presented in the news summaries. For example, an October 1969 summary reported that the networks noted the increasing support of the antiwar demonstration called the Moratorium, but only briefly mentioned Senator Robert Dole's resolution of support for the administration that had been signed by 33 senators. Nixon circled the section about the scant coverage of Dole and wrote in the margin: "H & Klein—give them hell for this inadequate coverage and give me a report."[102] In another example, Nixon noted in the October 7th news summary that NBC had a three minute sequence based around an antiwar song, "Don't Take Your Love to Town." Nixon's marginalia said, "What has been done to complain?—Give me a report."[103]

Nixon also moved aggressively to create lists of media leaders who were categorized as friendly to or antagonistic to the administration. In June 1969 a list of commentators for and against Nixon was drafted,[104] and by December 1969 a list of television White House correspondents and their network affiliations noted whether they were friendly, neutral, or unfriendly. Typical entries included these:

> Tom Jarriel ABC Neutral: <u>Jarriel</u> is a new man who tries to be objective—his reports have been mixed, some off target.
> Dan Rather CBS Neutral: <u>Rather</u> tries to be objective, but in this effort tends to feel his obligation to point out negative rather than positive in a story. He checks facts frequently, however, and can be turned off a negative slant and turned onto positive.[105]

Journalists who were described as hostile could expect pressure from the White House. A December 1970 news summary stated that there was a "very, very negative commentary by Bill Lawrence the thrust of which is that RN and his Administration are following the same path to Credibility Gulch taken by LBJ although the paths are clearly marked."[106] Nixon circled Lawrence's name and in the margin wrote, "H—I believe some hard cracks at him would be useful."[107] A particularly mean-spirited December summary reported that NBC's Sander Vanocur would shortly be changing positions, a move that prompted Nixon to write: "<u>An upgrade</u>—H—an <u>absolute</u> freeze on him—<u>anyone</u> who violates will be fired—Inform our top staff and cabinet."[108]

Not only did Nixon see daily news summaries and demand analyses of reporters, he also ordered more extensive analyses of television's coverage of his policies. One specific example from late 1969 gives a good sense of the tone and substance of these reports. On September 28, 1969, Buchanan wrote a long memo for Nixon on television coverage of the president during the summer of 1969 in which he noted:

> The one network where, on a controversial story, the chances are greatest that we will come off badly, is without question <u>NBC. There is a strong and visible bias against the ABM-military</u>-industrial complex, which comes through in all stories touching on it; there is always a market here for the Saigon-Washington rift type story and the "weakness of ARVN" theme; they do as much or more than any network on the Administration "confusion" over a desegregation policy. [Nixon underlining, marginalia: "H & Klein—Note and act accordingly."]
> <u>John Chancellor, we would estimate,</u> is negative toward the Administration and the President's position <u>90 percent of the time.</u> Because of his frequency on the tube, and because of the time he

commands on Huntley-Brinkley, we consider him perhaps the most offensive commentator on the air. A close second is Daniel Schoor, who specializes in the Finch splits with the Administration. [Nixon underlining, marginalia: "H & Klein—Tell them."]

Huntley and Brinkley take a chunk out of us with some regularity but this seems more or less their style; they do it to us but they do it to others also; more perhaps to us because the President and the Administration command more of the news than anyone else. From our point of view, Chancellor and Schoor do more damage to us in the public mind than do Huntley and Brinkley.

As for ABC, Bill Lawrence is rough at times as is Frank Reynolds— but for the most part ABC (Reynolds-Smith) has given us the best deal over the summer. CBS is a close second as both Pierpont and Rather give us as objective a coverage of the White House as we get. One reason for ABC's lead over the other networks in coverage is Howard K. Smith's hawkishness and no-nonsense attitude on law and order and student disorder. Smith does hit two themes repeatedly however which affect us directly—he is critical of both Congress and the Administration for lack of action on legislation; he will refer time and again to the need for the President to speak out in a State of the Union address; or for the President to go to the people with a Presidential explanation of Vietnam. One gets the impression he would want to see the President as more of an advocate, and more of an outspoken leader.

. . .

One final note. The President's critics Fulbright and Harriman, [Senator J. William Fulbright and W. Averill Harriman], get a disproportionate amount of coverage in our view; considering their ranks vis a vis a President, they get a good deal more than their peers of "equal time," [Nixon underlining, marginalia, "Get this changed—Z & Klein."] especially when you consider Mr. Harriman has no official rank at all. For a while there, Harriman was trotted out regularly by the networks to comment on this or that Vietnam or Paris decision—or what he would have done. Invariably, Harriman feels what we have done is not enough, or we have missed some opportunity or other which he has seen.[109]

There are a number of interesting points about this memo. First, Nixon's marginalia show that he expected his staff to confront television news professionals when their coverage was considered antiadministration, a tactic that continued throughout his presidency. Second, there is obvious concern with the amount of time afforded to administration critics. Nixon and his staff were particularly concerned with Harriman's criticism of the administration's Vietnam policy.

Vice President Spiro Agnew's attacks on the media addressed both of these issues and fit within a communication strategy deliberately designed to intimidate journalists. The attacks on television began in earnest on November 13, 1969 in Des Moines. Keogh has written that there was a general anger with the media inside the Administration, especially after negative reactions to Nixon's November 3rd speech on Vietnam, and that Agnew's remarks reflected this anger. Klein told *Newsweek* that the speech "came as a result of a lot of discussion after the letters about November 3 came in."[110] In his memoirs, Nixon observed that

> One result of the unexpected success of the November 3 speech was the decision to take on the TV network news organizations for their biased and distorted "instant analysis" and coverage. Unless the practice was challenged, it would make it impossible for a President to appeal directly to the people, something I considered to be of the essence of democracy.[111]

Nixon wrote that Buchanan drafted the speech and that Nixon and Agnew toned it down,[112] but there is debate about this.[113]

Saying it was time to take a hard look at television and its news presentation, Agnew criticized what he called the networks' "instant analysis and querulous criticism" after Nixon's November 3rd speech. What was shown on television, Agnew argued, had been decided by a handful of network executives who were not elected and were not held responsible for their decisions. Agnew compared the Vietnam situation with World War II and the Cuban Missile Crisis:

> When Winston Churchill rallied public opinion to stay the course against Hitler's Germany, he didn't have to contend with a gaggle of commentators raising doubts about whether he was reading public opinion right or whether Britain had the stamina to see the war through.
> When President Kennedy rallied the nation in the Cuban missile crisis, his address to the people was not chewed over by a roundtable of critics who disparaged the course of action he'd asked America to follow.[114]

To Agnew the issue was one of national security: the president must have the ability to protect the nation's interest without having to deal with criticism by media. Less partisan observers countered that in a democracy, the media have a responsibility to present a number of different opinions on issues of the day so that citizens can be informed and participate as they see fit. In early 1970 there were renewed efforts to hone strategies for using media to legitimize the administration's Vietnam policy. Chuck Colson, for example, developed a proposal to use the Citizens' Committee for Peace with Freedom in

Vietnam (also known as the Douglas Committee) to generate "articles, press and TV reports in support of Vietnamization policy" and to demand "equal time from any network or publication that presents a major attack of Administration policy on Vietnam."[115]

There was also a clear strategy to intimidate the media into providing more favorable Vietnam coverage. The February 15, 1970 news summary noted the coverage of the Foreign Relations Committee Hearings on Vietnam:

> Footage on all networks of Foreign Relations Committee Hearings on Vietnam. ABC said they began quietly but didn't end so. Kalb said it was one bipartisan group of VN doves interviewing another such group. Fulbright conceded that most Americans agree with the President's policy for getting out of Vietnam. Goodell charged that Vietnamization is not working and is an illusion. Hughes said that the Administration has created a mood of "national euphoria" by commandeering the national media. Hughes was rebutted by the Vice President on CBS and ABC film saying that the opposition put all their eggs in the Vietnam basket and that they are again trying to find something with which to attack the Administration. Marvin Kalb said the doves "fear" that the VP's earlier comments have pistol-whipped the media to such a degree that hearings will only receive minimal attention. Frank Reynolds said that the President had indeed effectively quieted debate and criticism of Vietnam and that the hearings were not likely to raise the decibel level. [Nixon underlining.][116]

Nixon marked the last two sentences above and wrote: "K & Z—Be sure this is our strategy. Make no comment whatever on V. Nam (in any context) except to refer to them to RN's statements."[117] In this marginalia Nixon clearly showed that he wanted to intimidate the media into reducing coverage of opposition views, halting coverage of criticism and debate. Agnew's speeches, as well as the many other intimidation techniques pursued, were intended to control access to television, yet the White House vehemently and disingenuously denied that intimidation was part of its strategy.

The administration continued its hard line toward the media, and particularly toward television, especially when events seemed to challenge its hopes for controlling the media. When CBS President Frank Stanton announced a new series of programs called "The Loyal Opposition," for example, the White House was appalled. In addition, Morley Safer, an insistent critic of the administration, had returned to Vietnam where he would, presumably, begin filing reports critical of the administration's handling of Vietnam. In a July 7, 1970 memo to Haldeman and Magruder, Mort Allin stooped to a new low when he lamented not begin able to leave Safer "in a rice paddy somewhere":

> Morley Safer of CBS has returned to SVN, as noted in TV reports. He is, without a doubt, among the most negative observers of our effort there. As long as he can't be left in a rice paddy somewhere, it might not be a bad idea to remind Defense of Safer's leanings and urge a minimum of cooperation with his reports.[118]

Challenges also appeared on other fronts as when the Democratic National Committee chair appeared on CBS on July 7 to blast Nixon. Patrick Buchanan wrote a memo to the president calling for firm action:

> We ought to go after this thing right now—with no delay and with firmness; let us face facts; the networks, after the Vice President's speech are deathly afraid of this Administration and increasingly pro-Democratic in their national orientation. But they are <u>vulnerable</u> nationally; their credibility has been eroded; their support among the national public has receded drastically. Instead of trying to coddle and cozen the likes of Stanton—who has been downright splenetic in his criticism of the Administration, we ought to treat in the same manner that an angry and impatient Cabinet member once suggested to Henry Adams that the White House treat Congressmen:
> "You can't use tact with a Congressman! A Congressman is a hog! You must take a stick and hit him on the snout!"
> Finally, the President—<u>as the only elected national leader of the American people</u>—has a right to address the people on a matter of national monument without having his policies at once challenged by a partisan opposition. Any President. If the address is partisan in nature, they should get equal time; if not, then not.
> . . .
> This is only the first incursion—Mr. Stanton is testing the water on this—we ought to move on it at once. As Ceasar said, don't give up the first inch of the empire.[119]

Administration officials also schemed for ways to get more favorable coverage of the president. In July 1970 Haldeman sent a memo to Klein that said, in part:

> As you know we have raised the point over and over why we can't get out a column on how remarkable it is the President even survives in view of the opposition of the press, Congress, etc.

Since, apparently at least, we have completely failed to get anything out on this, we now have to have one of our people write this column—Buchanan might be the best—and have it put together and mark it at his boiler plate somehow.

This could be written in terms of the television controversy now underway. In other words, the Democrats have the press, the network commentators, the Congress and all the media of communications basically on their side, and now they are trying to block the one chink in their armor, which is the President's ability to get through direct to the people on television. The point is we make points by fighting the press, and we've got to do it.[120]

While some staff members wrote memos and reports on media strategy, others analyzed the specifics of media coverage and met with media executives. In an attempt to prove network bias, for example, Colson produced a report showing that during August 1970 there had been 35 appearances by 8 senators making negative comments about the conduct of the war in Vietnam. Only 12 senators, appearing once each, had been on to support President Nixon's policy.[121] In addition, when Colson met with network executives in September, he described them as "extremely nervous" and "the more I pressed them (CBS and NBC) the more accommodating, cordial and almost apologetic they became."[122] He concluded:

These meetings had a very salutary effect in letting them know that we are determined to protect the President's position, that we know precisely what is going on from the standpoint of both law and policy and that we are not going to permit them to get away with anything that interferes with the President's ability to communicate.[123]

Colson suggested that the networks be called each and every time the administration determined there was slanted coverage. In addition, he would follow-up with Dean Burch of the Federal Communications Commission on the issue of time for opposing views.[124]

Other actions designed to influence television coverage included speeches on the Senate floor, antitrust suits brought by the Justice Department, FBI investigations of journalists, and FCC and IRS intimidation.[125] In an especially interesting move, officials also considered purchasing a network. In September 1970 Haldeman wrote to Colson to ask about this:

As you know a number of people have been dabbling around with the idea of trying either to purchase one of the television networks or to set up another network—Billy Graham, Tom Dewey, etc., have been talking about this.

Would you please run a hard check on this to see if there is any possibility of pulling this off. I would like your analysis and recommendation in this regard.[126]

The only reply in the Nixon Archive is a preliminary memo from Colson to Haldeman on September 25, 1970 stating:

In response to your memo of the 21st, I will determine the precise ownership situation of each of the networks. CBS and NBC are subsidiaries of larger companies, and therefore, could only be purchased from the parents, a very unlikely prospect. ABC has been for sale from time to time (Remember the ITT situation) but I don't know its current status. It wouldn't do us much good to buy ABC since their coverage has been reasonably fair. Although, of course, I would love to have one of the networks in very friendly hands and ABC is probably the only possible target.

I know nothing about starting a new network other than the fact that in most markets there is not a good fourth outlet. I gather that this is the basic problem.[127]

While Colson and Buchanan expressed the most extreme views on the media, Nixon's staff members were also taking direction from the president himself. On a September 1970 news summary Nixon wrote:

H—E—Finch

I can't emphasize too strongly my concern that our Administration team—including W.H. staff has been affected too much by the unreal atmosphere of the DC press, social and intellectual set. Perhaps Cambodia and Kent State led to an overreaction by our own people to prove that we were pro-students, . . . , left—

We must get turned around on this before it is too late— Emphasize—anti crime—anti demonstration—anti drug—anti obscenity—get with the mood of the country which is fed up with the Liberals.[128]

Nixon clearly set the tone that allowed Colson and Buchanan to flourish, and as events unfolded Nixon turned more and more to Colson. Nixon wrote, "When I complained to Colson I felt confident that something would be done, and I was rarely disappointed."[129]

Internal White House reports on the media continued to stress what officials perceived as anti-American reporting. However, within the administration not all agreed with the Colson-Buchanan depiction of the media and its role. In an April 14, 1971 memo, John Scali criticized an administration report that characterized network stories according to the level of their support of policy. Responding to the comment that ABC had been "loaded with anti-Administration spokesmen in recent weeks," Scali wrote, "I fail to be impressed by the log attached to the memo, since it includes many stories (some of mine) which I know were not anti-Administration in intent or content."[130] Scali also noted that ABC had conducted studies of the news and found more pro-administration coverage than antiadministration coverage. He closed the memo to Colson, saying, "if anyone can come up with a conclusion based on the evidence presented that ABC News is being unfair, I suggest a new evaluator or judge is needed."[131]

Nixon and his staff understood the techniques of effective television very well. Many staff members came from the media, advertising, or public relations. Still, the fact that the administration could not completely control access to television created the perception within the White House that there were serious problems in getting television to frame withdrawal as desirable and achievable. This broader context of control led to measures that can only be seen as extreme in a democratic society.

Aftermath

POWs began to return to the United States in February 1973 and the last American combat troops left Vietnam on March 29 of the same year. The American people turned their attention away from Vietnam to the domestic repercussions of Watergate which had changed the American political landscape. Of course, the aftermath of the withdrawal from Vietnam came at one of the most difficult times in American political history. Watergate crippled the Nixon administration throughout 1973 until Nixon's resignation in August 1974. On May 1, 1973 Bob Haldeman and John Ehrlichman resigned. Klein left in August 1973. The media were increasingly preoccupied with Watergate and, in fact, at news conferences on October 3 and October 26, 1973 and February 25 and March 6, 1974, there were no questions about Vietnam at all.

On February 26, 1974 Nixon signed a proclamation honoring Vietnam veterans and establishing March 29 as Vietnam Veterans Day.[132] On March 29th Nixon spoke at these ceremonies and said:

> To those who have served, I can imagine that sometimes they are
> discouraged as they read and hear the postmortems on this very long

and very difficult war. But the verdict of history, I am sure, will be quite different from the instant analysis that we presently see and sometimes hear.

Those who served may be discouraged because it seems sometimes that more attention is directed to those who deserted America than those who chose to serve America. They may be discouraged because they read and hear that America becoming involved in Vietnam was wrong, that America's conduct in Vietnam was wrong, that the way we ended the war was wrong.

I would say to all of those who served and to all of my fellow Americans that not only was it not wrong but I think it is well for us to put in perspective on this day why we went there, what we accomplished, and what would have happened had these men not served their country as bravely and as courageously as they did in these difficult times.[133]

Five months later he resigned as president of the United States. In his memoirs, Nixon wrote:

In hindsight I can see that, once I realized the Vietnam war could not be ended quickly or easily and that I was going to be up against an anti-war movement that was able to dominate the media with its attitudes and values, I was sometimes drawn into the very frame of mind I so despised in the leaders of that movement. They increasingly came to justify almost anything in the name of forcing an immediate end to a war they considered unjustified and immoral. I was similarly driven to preserve the government's ability to conduct foreign policy and to conduct it in the way that I felt would best bring peace. I believed that national security was involved. I still believe it today, and in the same circumstances, I would act now as I did then. History will make the final judgment on the actions, reactions, and excesses of both sides; it is a judgment I do not fear.[134]

If we turn to the first question set out in chapter 1, Nixon's communication strategy during American withdrawal from Vietnam did attempt to address both normative and cognitive components of policy legitimacy. His emphasis on great power responsibility and credibility spoke to why the United States <u>had to</u> achieve "peace with honor." His emphasis on Vietnamization explained how the United States could leave as the South Vietnamese took control of the situation. The specific details of his communication strategy were shaped by domestic politics, great power identity, and his negative view of the media. There was a large and vocal opposition to the Vietnam War, calling for withdrawal. Yet much of the American public accepted

Nixon's argument that the United States would lose credibility and dishonor those who had given their lives if it withdrew without a negotiated settlement on "honorable" terms. What is interesting in this case is that Nixon claimed that credibility was at stake even as Kissinger approached the Soviet Union for help in getting out. This raises important questions about to whom credibility matters. Finally, Nixon's stark hostility to media contributed greatly to undermining his message. His administration's optimistic assessments, like Johnson's, seemed disingenuous and his antipathy toward the media fueled a substantial credibility gap.

Years later, the leader of another great power, Mikhail Gorbachev, would also seek to withdraw his country's forces from a protracted, limited war, and it is to this case we now turn.

CHAPTER 4

War Waging and
Reassessment: Afghanistan

The Soviet Union entered into its war in Afghanistan in December 1979 following months of debate about the advisability of such a course of action. After committing troops, however, Soviet leaders did not publicly acknowledge the active engagement of its forces in combat, insisting that Soviet specialists were simply aiding the Afghan people in the development of their country. And when Soviet leaders finally acknowledged a presence in Afghanistan, they framed it within the larger Cold War context. News stories and television broadcasts about Afghanistan, for example, reflected the leaders' characterization of Soviet specialists in Afghanistan as "internationalists" fighting for a socialist victory against Western aggression perpetuated by the United States and Pakistan. The leadership strategy was clearly to portray outside forces as the cause of conflict in Afghanistan.

When Mikhail Gorbachev came to power in March 1985, however, he set out to reassess Soviet involvement in Afghanistan[1] and as a result he changed the way the Afghan War was shown on Soviet television. Under his leadership, the Soviet television format shifted to reflect a more sophisticated understanding of effective television, and the content of war coverage was broadened to include coverage of Soviet combat. These changes in policy and political communication were part of a major shift in Soviet security doctrine. On one level, a new understanding of Soviet identity in the international system developed as Gorbachev sought "normal" status for the Soviet Union as an active player in European and world politics. What some analysts missed, however, was that old characteristics of Soviet identity remained, primary among them the identity of the Soviet Union as a super- or great power. Gorbachev's explanation for the withdrawal of Soviet troops from Afghanistan took this into account and he used this to mitigate conflicts about the policy within the political and military elite. This chapter begins with Soviet Afghan policy and political communication under Konstantin Chernenko in 1984, before Gorbachev's rise to power. This will serve as a baseline against which to compare Gorbachev's reassessment of Soviet policy from March 1985 to February 1988.

WAR-WAGING OCTOBER 1984–DECEMBER 1984

And if we lose Afghanistan now and it turns against the Soviet Union, this will result in a sharp setback to our foreign policy.

Gromyko, "CC CPSU Politburo session"[2]

There is a large body of work on how and why the Soviet Union moved troops into Afghanistan in 1979.[3] In April 1978 a Communist-led coup established a new government in Afghanistan with Hafizullah Amin as prime minister and Nur Mohammad Taraki as president. The new government did not consolidate its rule during the next year, and in fact, encountered opposition in many regions of the country. Throughout 1979 the Afghan leadership asked for more and more Soviet aid, including the introduction of Soviet military personnel.[4] The Soviets, for their part, supplied aid and advisors, as the Americans had in Vietnam, emphasizing the importance of keeping Afghanistan in the Soviet camp. When uprisings occurred in March 1979 in Herat, the Politburo met to discuss the Soviet response.[5] Minister of Foreign Affairs Andrei Gromyko stated, and KGB Chairman Yuri Andropov and Prime Minister Alexei Kosygin reiterated, that under no condition should Afghanistan be lost. Gromyko said:

> In my opinion, we must proceed from a fundamental proposition in considering the question of aid to Afghanistan, namely: under no circumstances may we lose Afghanistan. For 60 years now we have lived with Afghanistan in peace and friendship. And if we lose Afghanistan now and it turns against the Soviet Union, this will result in a sharp setback to our foreign policy.[6]

It is clear that this is set within the competition between socialist and capitalist camps and that Soviet leaders regarded the issue as a zero-sum encounter.

For a time, however, the Soviets resisted Afghan requests for military intervention, clearly recognizing the potential problems. At the March 18 meeting, for example, Kosygin reported on his telephone conversations with Taraki, who had asked the Soviets for reinforcements in the form of tanks and armored cars.

> I then asked him, will you be able to muster enough tank crews to place the tanks into action? He responded that they have no tank crews, and therefore he requested that we dispatch Tajiks to serve as crews for tanks and armored cars, dressed in Afghan uniforms, and send them here. I then stated again, Comrade Taraki, there is no way you will conceal the fact that our military personnel are taking part in battle operations; this fact will be immediately uncovered, and press correspondents will broadcast to the whole world that Soviet tanks are engaged in a military conflict in Afghanistan.[7]

After discussing the situation, Politburo members ruled out Soviet military intervention. Kosygin summed up the meeting:

> I completely support Comrade Andropov's proposal to rule out such a measure as the deployment of our troops into Afghanistan. The army there is unreliable. Thus our army, when it arrives in Afghanistan, will be the aggressor. Against whom will it fight? Against the Afghan people first of all, and it will have to shoot at them. Comrade Andropov correctly noted that indeed the situation in Afghanistan is not ripe for a revolution. And all that we have done in recent years with such effort in terms of détente, arms reduction, and much more—all that would be thrown back. China, of course, would be given a nice present. All the nonaligned countries will be against us. In a word, serious consequences are to be expected from such an action. There will no longer be any question of a meeting of Leonid Ilych with Carter, and the visit of [French President] Giscard d'Estang at the end of March will be placed in question. One must ask, and what would we gain? Afghanistan with its present government, with a backward economy, with inconsequential weight in international affairs. On the other side, we must keep in mind that from a legal point of view too we would not be justified in sending troops. According to the UN Charter a country can appeal for assistance, and we could send troops, in case it is subject to external aggression. Afghanistan had not been subject to any aggression. This is its internal affair, a revolutionary internal conflict, a battle of one group of the population against another. Incidentally, the Afghans haven't officially addressed us on bringing in troops.[8]

But the situation deteriorated further when Amin and Taraki clashed. The Soviets chose to support Taraki, whose murder in early October 1979 may have influenced General Secretary Leonid Brezhnev to support intervention in December.[9] The decision to invade was made in December 1979 by a small group of individuals within the leadership—Andropov, Minister of Defense Dmitrii Ustinov, Gromyko, and Brezhnev—and was intended to stabilize the military situation after forcibly removing Amin and replacing him with Barbrak Karmal.[10] This group believed that Amin was not trustworthy and saw evidence to suggest that Amin was reaching out to the West, in particular to the United States. There is also evidence that some military leaders objected strenuously to the deployment of Soviet troops in Afghanistan, but were overridden by the political leadership with support from the KGB.[11] By 1981, there were 110,000 Soviet troops in Afghanistan.[12]

The Soviet leadership's belief that the situation could be "stabilized" was quickly crushed. The United States and Pakistan, among others, supplied the opposition with money and weapons and the Soviet Union soon found itself mired in its geographically difficult and politically fragile neighbor to the south. High-level conversations about withdrawal took place as early as 1980,[13] but according to Aleksandr Liakovskii, in 1980 Ustinov, Andropov, and maybe Gromyko were against withdrawal, believing that it would be perceived as a concession to American aggression and would hurt Soviet prestige in the international system.[14] They also feared that withdrawal would destabilize the Afghan government and increase Islamic fundamentalism in the Soviet Union proper. Still, in June 1982 indirect talks were begun under the auspices of the United Nations, and in October 1982 a rough draft of a proposed UN settlement was sent to Gromyko, "who did not respond."[15] During this period, the Soviet government was going through serious succession issues: Brezhnev died on November 10, 1982, Andropov took over until February 9, 1984 when he died, and Chernenko lasted only until March 10, 1985 when he too died in office. As a result much of Soviet policy proceeded in an incremental manner as no leader had enough power, health, or time to promote major policy shifts. But one policy directive was clear: by 1984, under Chernenko, the Soviets were fighting to a victory against "counterrevolutionaries" in Afghanistan and had escalated their participation in the war, conducting several major offensives.[16]

During this time, of course, the Soviets were engaged in the Cold War with the United States, and, in fact, the Soviet invasion of Afghanistan fueled Cold War antagonisms. Cold War ideology according to the Soviets explained the structure of the international system as bipolar in nature. The imperialist powers, associated most prominently with the United States, were seen as challenging the very existence of the Soviet Union. The Brezhnev Doctrine, articulated after the Soviet invasion of Czechoslovakia in 1968, stated that the USSR would "lend 'fraternal assistance' to any member of this [Socialist] commonwealth in order to protect the 'gains of socialism.' "[17] So, it was in this context that the Soviets undertook the intervention in Afghanistan and this contributed substantially to how the Soviets explained the war.

Domestic Politics and Television

In order to understand the Soviet leadership's television strategy in telling the story of Afghanistan, it is important to examine the role of television in Soviet society. Television came onto the scene in force in the Soviet Union in the 1970s. Unlike in the American system, however, it was not independent of government. During this time the production of television sets increased substantially, and satellite technology developed during the 1970s and 1980s allowed television signals to reach a large percentage of the vast country. Historically, the role of television in Soviet society was patterned on the role of all other media and the leadership believed that it could be used with great effect in socializing Soviet citizens.

Controlled from above, television presented the official line. There was no norm of fairness, or presentation of opposing sides, as in the United States. The State Committee for Television and Radio (*Gostelradio*) coordinated the communication of ideological messages through directives sent down from above, and the Chairman of *Gostelradio* was directly responsible to the General Secretary of the Communist Party and the Politburo. TASS (the Telegraph Agency of the Soviet Union) functioned "as a centralized source of authoritative information for media organizations as well as for many agencies of the party and government."[18] The State owned all equipment, paid all salaries and monitored all broadcasts. As a consequence, television presented the leadership's views and agendas and did not cover events they preferred to suppress. Under Soviet control, for example, citizens were unlikely to view stories about crime, accidents, policy failures, or other bad news. There were two main networks (or programs, as they were called), Program One and Program Two. *Vremya*, the evening news show, was broadcast on Program One every evening at 9:00 p.m. and was viewed by 150 million people on any given night. One reason for this was that no local broadcasts were allowed to preempt *Vremya* and it was shown on all networks, across all eleven time zones.[19] *Vremya* was so important that an armed guard was stationed outside the studio.

Given the state's control of the media, one might expect that the Soviet leadership would use the media to rally the people in support of the Afghan War, yet this was not the case. We saw in the American case that Johnson chose to diminish the perceived importance of the Vietnam War effort by not disclosing all actions to the American people. In the Soviet case the strategy was not simply to diminish the importance of the effort, but to hide it altogether. The Central Committee of the Communist Party established action steps on Afghanistan that included plans for media coverage.[20] The instructions for propaganda activities directed media to say that the Afghan government had requested help against internal aggressors from the Soviet Union and that Soviet personnel would help and assist the Afghan people—no other goals were permitted to be discussed. Media were also directed to rebuff claims that the Soviet Union was interfering in Afghanistan's internal affairs.[21] Hence, reflecting direct orders from above that no Soviet personnel be shown in combat on Soviet television, there were no stories about active Soviet involvement in the war.[22]

This also meant that Soviet media were not permitted to acknowledge the deaths of Soviet soldiers in Afghanistan.[23] In fact, Major-General Aleksander Liakovskii,[24] included in his history of the Soviet war in Afghanistan an excerpt from a July 31, 1981 Politburo meeting in which memorials to the dead were discussed.[25] Politburo member Mikhail Suslov brought up the question of whether or not the government could give each family that had lost a son in Afghanistan 1000 rubles to cover the cost of a tombstone, but he noted that this would mean publicly acknowledging the war. Andropov and Politburo member Andrei Kirilenko said that it was not appropriate to recognize the dead at that time and the idea of payments for tombstones was scrapped.

TELEVISION COVERAGE

As we don't have detailed archival data or extensive memoirs on the Soviet war in Afghanistan, it is necessary to look at other sources for information on leadership communication strategy. Due to the strict leadership control of television, it is possible to look more deeply at Soviet pronouncements on Afghanistan during war waging by analyzing *Vremya*, the official nightly news broadcast. Every *Vremya* broadcast during a three month period, from October 1984 to December 1984,[26] was coded for the number and length (in seconds) of stories, format, countries portrayed, newsmakers, and themes. The number and length of stories tells us something about how important the leadership felt the story was for elite and domestic audiences alike. Heavy emphasis on and a media campaign surrounding the decision to intervene in Afghanistan would support the idea that policy legitimacy was important to the leadership.[27]

The coverage tells us about how Afghanistan was seen on Soviet television. For example, was there footage of events? Were stories simply presented by readers in the studio, or did correspondents report from the field? Research has shown that viewers more readily believe filmed reports from the field than stories read in the studio,[28] and as Soviet leaders came to understand and believe this, a change in the format of news stories occurred. The countries covered on Soviet television also suggest something about the perceived context of the conflict in Afghanistan. Was the conflict depicted as a civil war, as a conflict in which Afghanistan was beleaguered by outside forces, as a multilateral or regional conflict, or as a Cold War conflict? How does this contextualization of the conflict in the international system contribute to the desired legitimation of policy? Newsmakers refer to those who are either cited in the story or who speak for themselves in the story. Those who speak for themselves may or may not be named. By coding for newsmakers we can see who made news about Afghanistan. Was the Afghan story presented by the military? By politicians? What was the role of intellectuals and ordinary citizens in Afghan stories?

Finally, the subjects covered in the Afghan stories on Soviet television tell us something about the legitimation strategy of the Soviet leadership. Here the subjects were broken down into five major groups. The first was political and included political or diplomatic meetings between leaders in the various countries involved in or concerned about the war in Afghanistan. The second subject was war, including reports of damage, casualties, weapons, and actions of belligerents. Third, Afghan domestic issues included the economy, social issues, and education. Stories that specifically address the Soviet experience in Afghanistan were included in the fourth subject group. Soviet-Afghan nonmilitary cooperation makes up the last subject group. The full list of subjects under subject group is included in the Appendix.

Between October and December 1984, *Vremya's* broadcast time was 37 hours and 13 minutes.[29] There were only 22 stories on Afghanistan during this period, and they totaled 15 minutes and 33 seconds, meaning that they comprised only .7 percent of the total news time. Clearly, the Soviet leadership did not make the Soviet war in Afghanistan a priority for its viewers. It did not seek to legitimize the war, it sought to hide it.

It is striking that only three stories in this sample mentioned any Soviet presence in Afghanistan at all, and when they did it was to portray the Soviets as involved in Afghanistan only to supply material and technical aid. One of these stories was reported by *Vremya* correspondent Leonid Zolotarevskii on November 14, 1984. In a special report on Soviet transport aid in Afghanistan, Zolotarevskii commented that counterrevolutionaries in Afghanistan had made transportation complex and dangerous. Similarly, a December 28 story showed Soviet specialists helping the Afghan people with "economic development."[30] Soviet specialists, it was reported, had jobs in all parts of Afghanistan. Some, for example, were building the largest clinic in Afghanistan—shown in the story, successfully completed.

While Soviet television did not cover Soviet involvement in combat, it did cover violence associated with the acts of what were called "bandits" or "counterrevolutionaries." Sixty-eight percent of the news stories on Afghanistan in the period under review covered some aspect of the conflict. These stories were primarily TASS stories, read by the anchor (called "readers" in the Soviet context) sitting behind a desk with a map of Afghanistan or picture of Kabul in the background. For example, in early October there were reports on the bombing of Kabul airport, and about the arrest, trial, conviction, and sentencing of the "bandits" responsible for the attacks. Zolotarevskii reported on October 9 on the trial in a story that showed the accused in the courtroom, heads hanging low as they stood before a special tribunal. The camera panned over the faces of those in the room who had "come to see justice done." Zolotarevski reviewed the crime, saying that "from reports in the press" viewers knew that at the end of August there were crimes at the airport, including the bombing which left 14 dead and many wounded. The background film showed bombed-out buildings and injured civilians. Zolotarevski emphasized that the process was open, would be broadcast on television, and that citizens would be allowed in the courtroom. "Justice," he declared, "will decide their fate."[31] On November 5th, the anchor read a 25-second-long TASS report announcing that the special tribunal had condemned the convicted to death. These stories acknowledged the violence in Afghanistan, but not the presence and role of Soviet combat troops. The conflict was presented as serious clashes provoked by the "bandits" trying to undermine the Afghan government. But why?

The Soviets had intervened militarily in neighboring countries in the past to control political situations. The most important examples occurred in Hungary in 1956 and Czechoslovakia in 1968. However, the Eastern European countries were seen as firmly within the Soviet camp; the invasion of Afghanistan was "the first time the Soviets had sent combat forces into a country that was not a part of the Soviet bloc."[32] This divergence from previous policies created problems for the Soviets. Most of the world was stunned by the invasion of Afghanistan, and there were negative reactions not only in the West, but in Moslem countries as well. Moreover, unlike other interventions, the Soviets had got bogged down and had not achieved their goals quickly. The terrain, lack of a Communist infrastructure, and Western aid to the rebels contributed to the quagmire. A protracted, limited war was a new experience for the Soviet Union. Worse, it came at a time of intense global competition with the United States. By 1984 President Ronald Reagan was engaged in a serious defense buildup and had described "Soviet communism as 'the focus of evil in the modern world.' "[33]

When Soviet leaders did acknowledge the presence of Soviet troops in Afghanistan, it did so within the larger Cold War context. In fact, during the three month period under review here, the United States and Pakistan were mentioned more often in stories on Afghanistan than the Soviet Union. Many of these stories reported protests of Pakistani actions by the Afghan government. All were TASS reports, broadcast on October 12, 24, November 2, 15, 20, 22, and 30. In many of these stories, there was also mention of the United States as interfering in the internal politics of Afghanistan.[34] The leadership clearly portrayed outside forces as instigators of the conflict in Afghanistan. There was one story during this time on the United Nations, but it was not presented, as it would be later, as an organization that could help resolve regional conflict.

A word must be said about support for and opposition to the Soviet policy within the Soviet Union itself. Chernenko, perhaps unlike Andropov, supported the policy of war waging in Afghanistan. Many within the elite supported the war effort, particularly within the military and the KGB.[35] Little data are available to ascertain the level of public support for the war in Afghanistan. In 1984, a New York *Times* columnist Seth Mydans could not find anyone in Moscow, young or old, who opposed the war.[36] But being unable to find some-one who would say that he or she disagreed with the war did not mean there weren't those who believed exactly that. But the penalties for expressing opposition could be quite heavy. Those who spoke out faced prison or exile, as Andrei Sakharov had in 1980. As a result, public opposition to the war was effectively muzzled. The leadership did not acknowledge opposition to the war and it certainly was not covered on Soviet television. But, by 1984 Soviet soldiers had been in

Afghanistan for five years and many thousands of citizens had been touched by the experiences of loved ones in combat. How could the Soviet leadership think they didn't have to address this?

Part of the answer to this question involves how Soviet leaders and media personnel understood the media system and its effectiveness. The hypodermic model asserted that media messages would be received, understood, and accepted as with the medicine from a hypodermic needle. Because they believed media messages directed from above would transform the masses, early Soviet leaders did not perceive a need to ascertain the degree to which the masses understood or accepted these messages. Under Stalin, for example, research on public opinion was prohibited. (This is not to say that there were no feedback mechanisms in place; letters to the newspapers and write-in polls were used, but they were hardly representative.) The lack of knowledge about the public's perceptions changed slowly with the development of social science inquiry and the analysis of public opinion.[37] By the 1960s and 1970s, Soviet specialists and scholars began to study public opinion and the effect of mass media messages on the public and found that the commonly accepted hypodermic model of media transmission was seriously flawed. Public opinion research told a different story. Contrary to the leadership's hopes, audience members did not necessarily understand or place credence in the party's political messages. For example, people were suspicious of the media when it ignored disasters, crashes, and other crises known to have occurred. This gap between what was experienced and what was reported was profound, and contributed to the skepticism with which many citizens viewed the media. Audiences also desired more than domestic political fare and wanted more human interest stories, entertainment, and international programming. The lack of timeliness also eroded the effectiveness of media messages. Ironically, despite enormous attention to the control of the media and the suppression of sources and ideas that contradicted the official line, rumor was very important as a means of communicating information.

The leadership's lack of understanding about effective communication was demonstrated in the formatting of Soviet news. The dominant format for television news was what might be called the TASS-Reader approach. During the three-month period studied here, 81 percent of stories on Afghanistan were presented by the reader in the studio. In addition, 77 percent of the stories contained no film while 68 percent were TASS stories supplied by government officials promoting the official line. In addition, television stories dealt with countries rather than individuals. In fact, during the period under review, only eleven people were cited or spoke directly in Afghan stories. Lacking a human face, Washington, Kabul, Moscow, and Karachi were the actors. Overall, then, one is left with the epitome of controlled and uninteresting reporting that characterized the Soviet use of television.

Leaders can hide information about war from the country's citizens for a limited period, but over time stories will inevitably come from other sources to a greater or lesser degree. Soldiers will return home and share their own view of events. Families will know when they bury their own. If television coverage does not reflect the larger reality of the war, the leaders' credibility will suffer. After all, we know that personal experience will carry greater weight in most cases than television reports. The Soviet case was even more problematic for the leadership because the coverage of Afghanistan was visually dull. Although Soviet research had shown media to be ineffective in many ways, the Soviet leadership either did not believe in or did not understand the power of the visual nature of television. This changed considerably under Mikhail Gorbachev.

The Soviet leadership, then, did not attempt to legitimize war waging in Afghanistan. During this period Chernenko (like Brezhnev and Andropov) controlled coverage via the centralized and state-run *Gostelradio*. Organizational factors associated with the production of news broadcasts had much less influence than in the American case. Events that happened far away were not reported, and there were few ways that the Soviet public could systematically and reliably get that information. Those who might oppose the war effort were effectively silenced through coercion and fear. The limited information given to the Soviet population explained the conflict in Afghanistan as one in which the Soviets were supplying material aid to the Afghan people to fight the imperialist aims of the Americans and Pakistanis. But, even though the leadership could control the story, this did not guarantee that the people believed what they were told. The issue of credibility would be taken up by the new, young leader, Mikhail Gorbachev, when he allowed the broadcast of more information about the Soviet involvement in Afghanistan.

REASSESSMENT MARCH 1985–FEBRUARY 1988

The goal which we raised was to expedite the withdrawal of our forces from Afghanistan.

Gorbachev, "Meeting of CC CPSU Politburo"[38]

When Gorbachev became general secretary of the Communist Party in March 1985, he immediately began a reassessment of the Afghan

War.[39] Some maintain that Gorbachev wanted to get out of Afghanistan when he became general secretary.[40] Aleksandr Yakovlev, Gorbachev's advisor and a member of the Presidential Council and Politburo, told me this was true. Mikhail Leshchinskii, *Vremya* correspondent in Afghanistan from 1985–1989, said he knew that Gorbachev and Yakovlev wanted to get out of Afghanistan in 1985 but Leshchinskii didn't know if it could be accomplished. In fact, he said, because there was significant support within the military for the war effort, he remained unconvinced that all of the troops would be withdrawn until the last Soviet soldier, General B. V. Gromov, actually left Afghanistan.[41]

During 1985 and 1986 Gorbachev tread lightly, pursuing two separate tracks. First, he ordered a military build-up in Afghanistan and by the summer of 1986 the number of troops reached 130,000.[42] Mendelson notes that one explanation for this is that Gorbachev was giving the military one last chance to win the war.[43] If, despite increased support and personnel, the military failed to stabilize the situation, Gorbachev would be in a much better position to push for withdrawal. Second, he sought to convince the political and military elite that Soviet policy should change—that withdrawal should be agreed upon and implemented. In October 1985 the Politburo discussed the need to settle the Afghan situation, and Gorbachev later said that the group had "determined upon a course of settling the Afghan question. The goal which we raised was to expedite the withdrawal of our forces from Afghanistan and simultaneously ensure a friendly Afghanistan for us. It was projected that this should be realized through a combination of military and political measures."[44] In February 1986 at the 27th Communist Party of the Soviet Union (CPSU) Congress, Gorbachev described Afghanistan as "a bleeding wound," clearly signaling his desire for a reassessment of policy. Three months later, in May 1986, Babrak Karmal was dismissed, a move that signified "a new flexibility in Moscow's definition of an acceptable post-intervention Afghan government."[45]

Gorbachev reminded Politburo members of the goal of withdrawal as discussion continued in late 1986 and Soviet goals shifted from winning in Afghanistan to securing an acceptable withdrawal.[46] Notes from the November 13, 1986 Politburo meeting indicated that others were also pushing for withdrawal. Gromyko, for example, said "[o]ur strategic goal is to make Afghanistan neutral, not to allow it to go over to the enemy camp. Of course it is important to also preserve that which is possible in the social arena. But most important—to stop the war."[47] Marshal Sergei Akhromeev, Chief of Staff of the Armed Forces, acknowledged that the

Soviet military would not be able to secure a victory:

> Military actions in Afghanistan will soon be seven years old. There is no
> single piece of land in this country which has not been occupied by a
> Soviet soldier. Nevertheless, the majority of the territory remains in the
> hands of the rebels. . . . The whole problem is in the fact that military
> results are not followed up by political [actions]. At the center there is
> authority; in the provinces there is not. We control Kabul and the
> provincial centers, but on occupied territory we cannot establish
> authority. We have lost the battle for the Afghan people.[48]

Gorbachev, for his part, pushed for withdrawal:

> We must operate more actively, and with this guide ourselves with two
> questions. First of all, in the course of two years effect the withdrawal
> of our troops from Afghanistan. In 1987 withdraw 50 percent of our
> troops, and in the following [year]—another 50 percent. Second of all,
> we must pursue a widening of the social base of the regime, taking into
> account the realistic arrangement of political forces.[49]

In December 1986, "Gorbachev promised Najibullah that the
Soviet Union would not desert him but he made it clear that it was
time for change."[50] In January 1987, Eduard Shevardnadze and
Dobrynin went to Afghanistan for further discussions on the imple-
mentation of withdrawal. Early 1987 also saw the call for Afghan
national reconciliation which emphasized the ability (and necessity) of
the Afghan government to deal with the opposition.[51] In July 1987
Gorbachev told Najibullah that Soviet troops would be withdrawn.[52]
The Soviets pushed the Afghans to broaden their base of support and
consolidate power. In January 1988 Shevardnadze went to
Afghanistan where he informed Najibullah that the United States had
agreed to stop aiding the opposition (mujahedeen) and the Soviet
Union could, therefore, withdraw troops. The formal announcement
of the Soviet intent to withdraw came in February 1988.

New Thinking and International Reputation

Gorbachev's new ideas about international politics and the role of the
Soviet Union in the international system were set out under the rubric
called New Thinking.[53] New Thinking was a set of beliefs about the
nature of the international system, how it should work, and desirable
policies and procedures. At its core, New Thinking on international

affairs referred to understanding the international system not as a competition between capitalism and socialism, but as interdependent and requiring a cooperative framework for interaction. These ideas about the international system were used to support changes in the definition of national interests, particularly in foreign policy. In addition, these ideas implied a new identity for the Soviet Union as a member of the community of nations, as a "normal" country.[54] Withdrawal from Afghanistan fit squarely within the tenets of this new understanding of Soviet international behavior.[55] Of traditional Soviet behavior, Gorbachev noted:

> Our diplomatic style was toughness for toughness' sake. The main thing was to demonstrate an unyielding spirit and an attitude of arrogant pride which was justified neither by political nor practical considerations.[56]

While New Thinking is clearly evident in the Soviet case, another set of beliefs about the international system represented continuity rather than change. The international system was still depicted as one in which power mattered considerably. Soviet leaders clearly anticipated a continued competition with other states in the system, and the expectations associated with what great powers should do shaped how the story of Afghanistan was told during the reassessment of the policy. These stories began as the Politburo was struggling to find a way to explain Soviet withdrawal without appearing to surrender power. The notes of Gorbachev's foreign policy advisor Anatoly Chernaev from the February 1987 Politburo meeting show that Gorbachev himself wrestled with this question:

> The reaction to our decision to withdraw is not simple. We did enter, how do we leave now? We can leave quickly, without thinking about anything: say that the former leadership was to blame for everything. But we cannot do so. We hear from India, and from Africa that if we just leave, it would be a blow to the authority of the Soviet Union in the national-liberation movement; imperialism would start its offensive in the developing countries if we leave Afghanistan.
> Another issue. A million of our soldiers went through Afghanistan. And we will not be able to explain to our people why we did not complete it [i.e. the war]. We suffered such heavy losses. And what for? We undermined the prestige of our country, brought bitterness. What for did we lose so many people?[57]

Thus, an identity as a "normal" country within the international system did not preclude an identity as a great power. In addition, as in the

American case, credibility with allies around the world and the public at home was stressed.

TELEVISION AND DOMESTIC POLITICS

As the political and military elite debated a policy of withdrawal during this period of reassessment, Gorbachev used television to push his case. Importantly, he needed to do so without suggesting that the Soviets were losing the war. A June 7, 1985 directive from the Central Committee of the Communist Party of the Soviet Union ordered a change in the coverage of Afghanistan and a full explication of specifics was drafted in mid-June and approved the next month.[58] The document directed media at all levels to report on the activities of Soviet forces in Afghanistan, including their participation in battle, the care given to soldiers who had served and been wounded, their awards or decorations given by the state, and recognition and aid of the families of those who had been killed in Afghanistan.[59] In light of opposition to withdrawal, the directive was careful to order television to highlight the heroism of the troops and limit the direct coverage of Soviet soldiers. Coverage still had to be approved by military censors, and the directive limited stories on soldiers hurt or killed to one a month.[60] As a result of this directive, in June 1985 Chairman Sergei Lapin of *Gostelradio* called *Vremya* correspondent Leshchinskii in Kabul and ordered him to show Soviet soldiers. Leshchinskii said that this order came directly from Yakovlev, via Lapin.[61] Leshchinskii's understanding of this change in coverage was that it was ordered to prepare the Soviet population for withdrawal.[62]

Gorbachev, then, used television in an instrumental manner to prepare for withdrawal and to counter those in the elite who opposed it. Recognizing the debate on withdrawal, Leshchinskii made a distinction between those who had served in Afghanistan and those who had not.[63] Those who had been in Afghanistan wanted the Soviets to get out; those in Moscow, particularly General Dmitriy Yazov, were against withdrawal.[64] There is still debate about who supported withdrawal and who did not.[65] In a television interview in 1991 with Politburo member Alexander Yakovlev, who prompted and supported Gorbachev's policy of glasnost, Leshchinskii stated:

So there were two sides, two opposing teams. On the one side was the military, the KGB, and so on. On the other side were people who had a fresh approach—Shevardnadze, you [Yakovlev] and Gorbachev. There were these two forces opposing each other.[66]

Yakovlev said, "yes, that was absolutely obvious." Yakovlev also addressed the specific order to show the war on television:

> The difficulties, the maneuvering in the commission and the Politburo increased. You could only guess what people were really thinking. They would say one thing and clearly be thinking something completely different. This had to be read between the lines, so to speak. Suddenly, somebody had the idea of actually showing what was really happening. This put pressure on . . .
> Ada Petrova [reporter] interjects: Who did this idea come from?
> Yakovlev continues: The idea came from—it's difficult now to say whose idea it was. But of course it came from us, the ones who wanted to speed up all these processes. But I remember that Mikhail Sergeyevich came down firmly on our side. Why not show it, he said. Why keep it all secret? Let's show it. On the whole, this process of glasnost—applied to the war—helped us a very great deal in bringing closer the withdrawal.[67]

Yakovlev believed that showing the war would increase support for withdrawal.[68] Leshchinskii also maintained this to be the effect of showing the war. When asked if war coverage might have inspired the Soviet people to fight to a victory, he replied, "Absolutely not, the results are never such."[69] Georgii Shakhnazarov, a member of Gorbachev's personal staff, has written that glasnost and the media were used to promote an "antimilitarist" mood.[70] For his part, Gorbachev has said of glasnost in general:

> I placed particular value on glasnost when I realized that the initiatives coming from the top were more and more obstructed in the vertical structures of the Party apparatus and administrative organs. Freedom of speech made it possible to go over the heads of the apparatchiks and turn directly to the people.[71]

TELEVISION COVERAGE

A closer look at the Soviet story of Afghanistan during this period of reassessment was done by analyzing 19 full weeks of coverage—four weeks in 1985, seven weeks in 1986, seven in 1987, and one in 1988. The total amount of time in the sample was 86 hours and 52 minutes. Of this time 1 hour, 58 minutes, and 20 seconds was spent on Afghanistan. So while more time (as a proportion of the total) was spent on Afghanistan than during the war waging sample, this is still only 2.2 percent of total *Vremya* coverage in the sample. Eight-two percent of the Afghan stories were done by the husband and wife team of Mikhail Leshchinskii and Ada Petrova, who lived in Kabul from 1985 until the final soldier left Afghanistan in 1989.[72] Their film was sent via satellite to Moscow and text was sent via telephone; editing was done in Moscow where the material was censored according to political directives. Leshchinskii got most of his information from the Soviet military, KGB, and Afghan government and he grew close to many in the military.[73]

In the second half of 1985 and throughout 1986, Soviet television coverage of Afghanistan reflected the directive of June 1985. There was an amplified theme of Soviet military support or help to the Afghan people, and *Vremya* covered the deaths of Soviet soldiers in Afghanistan. In a typical story of this type, broadcast on July 8, 1986 viewers saw Soviet troops and tanks, and Leshchinskii interviewed a young soldier who commented that he was doing his internationalist duty. A shot of a memorial to Soviet soldiers killed in Afghanistan highlighted the reality of the war effort. This in a country where after six years of combat, according to Doder and Branson, burial markers for soldiers killed in Afghanistan made no reference to that fact, emphasizing instead that they had died "fulfilling their internationalist duty."[74]

Yet, even as some of the reality of war was brought home through *Vremya* broadcasts, many stories continued to highlight nonmilitary assistance with a rather saccharin approach. For example, in December 1985, Petrova reported with film from a classroom where Afghan children were learning Russian from a teacher who had come from the Soviet Union.[75] Petrova asked the children, "What is the first word you learned?" The children replied, "mama." "Who has friends in the USSR?" All of their little hands went up and Petrova gasped, "Oh, so many!" She concluded the story by commenting that in this new republic the important words for these children were *mama, khleb* and *mir* [mother, bread, and peace].

In the wake of the June 1985 directive, television's coverage of Afghanistan increasingly reflected the leadership's desire to withdraw. On December 11, 1985 a TASS report quoted Shevardnadze as supporting a "realistic, constructive program for the resolution of the situation in Afghanistan," with Shevardnadze adding that this depended on noninterference in Afghan internal affairs.[76] By October 1986, there was an increase in the coverage of diplomatic activity as calls for an agreement on Afghanistan became more frequent. In December, Soviet television covered meetings between Gorbachev and the head of the Afghan government, Mohammad Najibullah. On December 12, 1986 *Vremya* quoted Gorbachev as saying Soviet troops would be withdrawn as soon as there was an agreement on regularization of the Afghan situation, something about which Gorbachev was said to be optimistic. Soviet television presented political negotiations as a viable means for achieving withdrawal, a story line that echoed the broader theme giving precedence to political solutions over military solutions. Along these lines, Soviet television increased coverage of the United Nations and highlighted its ability to facilitate a negotiated settlement. Included in these were reports about United Nations representative Diego Cordovez and his talks with Afghani and Pakistani representatives, and meetings between Foreign Minister Shevardnadze of the Soviet Union and Foreign Minister Shaq Muhammed of Afghanistan.

In the baseline sample of Soviet television taken from 1984, there was a heavy emphasis on American and Pakistani "interference" in Afghanistan. This lessened during the reassessment period, especially after 1985, but did not disappear. For example, in a March 20, 1985 story, Fadaev reported on a protest of U.S. interference in Afghan internal affairs, during which workers carried signs that depicted Pakistanis as carrying out American imperialist objectives.[77] On September 9, 1985 a commentary by Genrikh Borovik suggested similarities between American intervention in Nicaragua and Afghanistan.[78] Leshchinskii followed three days later with a filmed report from Kabul of a meeting of leaders from all over the Afghan countryside during which one older man commented on the interference of outside forces supplying weapons through Pakistan and Iran.[79]

During this reassessment period specific references to interference by the United States in Afghanistan decreased. In 1986 there were no reports that complained about American interference until December. Of the twenty stories in the December 1986, February, and March 1987 samples, only three made reference to American interference, but there was no change in tone. The United States was still to blame for the supply and training of the counterrevolutionaries, and the Soviet Union was obliged to support and help its Afghan neighbor. Towards the end of 1987 there was another shift as Soviet coverage frequently noted that the American involvement in Afghanistan was preventing a Soviet withdrawal. A number of stories on Soviet television tied American aid to the "counterrevolutionaries" and drug trafficking, saying that the opposition brought drugs to use against the people of Afghanistan or to transport to Asia, Europe, and America in exchange for hard currency to buy weapons. One story showed bags of heroin piled high as Petrova explained that what appeared at first glance to be a storehouse full of goods, was actually full of confiscated drugs. This drug traffic, she explained, helped the opposition obtain arms for fighting the Afghan people.[80]

Soviet leaders knew that American intelligence monitored Soviet media and that the American government was very wary of what the Reagan Administration considered propaganda, rather than a significant shift in Soviet ideas about international relations. As a result, the Soviet leadership may have also used media to try and signal the West that the Soviet Union was serious about withdrawal from Afghanistan. In October 1986, for example, Soviet television devoted almost all of its Afghan coverage to stories about the return of six Soviet regiments from Afghanistan. Leshchinskii said that the coverage was constructed as a "show" for the West, signaling the Soviets were willing to seriously negotiate for a total withdrawal.[81] On four days during one week, the stories included shots of Soviet soldiers either parading in Kabul before they left, or triumphantly returning to the Soviet Union. In a brief story that aired on October 25, the news reader said that there was hope that the decision by the Soviet leaders to bring home some of the troops would lead to a normalization of the situation. In addition, Leshchinskii suggested that Soviet viewers would understand the stories to mean that a full withdrawal was coming.[82]

Stories that covered the arrival of the soldiers back home carried a dual message. On the one hand, the heroism of the troops was lauded, and one story broadcast on October 23, 1986 compared them to the heroes of World War II. On the other hand, stories also reflected the desire to celebrate the power of the Soviet state. Parents expressed their pride with sons who had done their internationalist duty, and soldiers said that they had gone to Afghanistan because of the Afghan request for help. Others said they wanted peace. One story covered a parade of Soviet soldiers through the streets of Kabul and reported that thousands and thousands of people had turned out to thank the Soviet troops by holding signs that said *spacibo*, [thank you], "which is a Russian word, but one they know."[83]

Despite these changes in the nature of coverage, Soviet leaders still faced the task of explaining why, exactly, withdrawal was the best strategy. The answer to this question emerged most forcefully in early 1987, when the subject of Afghan national reconciliation became an important story on Soviet television. Emphasizing the ability of the Afghan government to deal with the opposition justified the withdrawal of Soviet troops from Afghanistan. *Vremya* covered the processes involved in national reconciliation, including meetings of various groups with the Kabul government, amnesty for those who fought against the government, and the return of refugees to Afghanistan. In March 1987, for example, Borovik reported from Afghanistan that national reconciliation was designed to connect the Democratic Party of Afghanistan to the masses:

> I want to say a few words about the situation in Afghanistan. At the beginning of this year the Afghan government began a policy of national reconciliation. A political solution to the Afghan problem is wanted. Already 35,000 have returned to their people and country. More than 10,000 who had fought against the government brought weapons and themselves back. The Afghan government is talking with others but still children keep getting hurt. Everyday more go to the hospital. The United States is still supplying weapons and money—more than before, including Stingers. The Committee for the Defense of Peace [of which Borovik is a member] turns to its friends in the United States—writers, journalists, scientists, actors and religious leaders to ask their government to stop supplying the bandits.[84]

Borovik implied that if the United States would cooperate, the Afghan government would be able to take care of itself when the Soviets withdrew.

Vremya continued to report on national reconciliation throughout the rest of the reassessment period. In October 1987 Leshchinskii reported on the second General Conference of the Communist Party in Afghanistan and interviewed two delegates to the Conference. One was a man more than 100 years old; the other was a young man of 20 who had fought for the government. Leshchinskii reported that both the very oldest and the youngest supported the policy of national reconciliation.

During this reassessment period, the goals of the Soviet leadership were changing and this is illustrated with a comparison of the March 21 Islamic New Year celebration stories from 1986 and 1987. In March 1986, Leshchinskii covered the holiday as the camera panned children laughing and people celebrating. He reported that the people were happy with the progress made in the country and that they wanted *freedom* in the future. The story from March 1987 looked much the same—children dancing and people congratulating one another. However, there was a shift in the message as Leshchinskii noted that it was spring in Afghanistan and the only hope that the people had for the new year was *peace*. There was no mention of the revolutionary struggle for freedom as in the past. Leshchinskii declared that spring brings a newness and that this was a new day for peace.

Television and Glasnost

Lenin said that an illiterate person is outside politics, but now we have an educated people.

Gorbachev, "Gorbachev Exhorts Media on Restructuring"[85]

While the reassessment of Afghan policy was underway, Gorbachev also instituted a concurrent and monumental change in the understanding of the role of media and their use in the Soviet system. His policy of glasnost reflected an understanding of the deficiencies of the previous approach to media; glasnost would remedy many of these problems and create new ones of its own. Clearly, Gorbachev was not the first to recognize deficiencies in how media were used. Mickiewicz has shown that there was a growing concern with the effectiveness of television even before Gorbachev came to power.[86] However, Gorbachev gave momentum to the process of changing television's coverage of domestic and foreign affairs. In December 1985 he appointed a new Chairman of the State Committee for Television and Radio, Alexander Aksyonov.[87] Some scholars trace the beginning of change in television, particularly in format, to the 27th Party Congress in 1986,[88] but his changes clearly began earlier. The changes in formatting reflected a greater understanding of audience and of what constituted effective television in the wake of revelations confirming that audiences were neither understanding nor believing what Soviet media offered them.[89]

Specific changes in format during the reassessment period were dramatic. First, the number of correspondent reports increased dramatically. In the period sampled, 45 percent of all Afghan stories during this period were correspondent reports. In addition, the relative importance of TASS and filmed stories reverses in comparison with the 1984 period. In the reassessment sample, almost 80 percent are not TASS stories and 63 percent contain filmed footage in the story. These changes reflect the leadership's understanding that filmed footage and visual imagery are effective television tools.

Under Gorbachev a new understanding of the importance of the visual nature of television prompted significant changes. There were more reports from correspondents in the field with film of events. Graphics began to improve as Soviet television used computer generated images to present a slicker look. There was greater coverage of press conferences during which political and military leaders answered questions from reporters. In addition, more foreigners were covered who could and did present opinions contrary to the official Soviet position.[90] The Soviet leadership also recognized the importance of timeliness for effective political communication. Finally, the realization that Soviet media were hardly the only sources of information led to the conclusion that television "operates with less credibility if it either fails to cover events which are known about and taken seriously or covers them in a superficial or unrealistic way."[91] Gorbachev said:

> When we shone a "rosy" light on life, the people saw everything and lost interest in the press and in public activity. They felt that they were simply humiliated and insulted when a "fake" was palmed off on them: After all, they knew what real life was, what actually existed. Lenin said that an illiterate person is outside politics, but now we have an educated people: The way we acted in recent years meant keeping them outside politics. This was disrespect for the people. It was a kind of elitism. Now we must put everything in its proper place through the democratic process . . .[92]

Under both Gorbachev and Chernenko, Soviet television was centrally controlled, yet Gorbachev's television strategy was significantly different from Chernenko's. With support from Yakovlev and Shevardnadze, Gorbachev decided to use television to push for withdrawal from Afghanistan. They also changed significantly the role of television in the Soviet Union, seeking to use it more effectively in both domestic and foreign policy spheres. In addition, Soviet citizens were getting information about Afghanistan from sources other than the central press. So, the Soviet leadership had its own credibility gap with which to deal. More had to be reported about the role of the Soviet Union in order for television to have any sort of credibility in its reports on Afghanistan. This, coupled with a greater understanding of the importance of visually interesting television stories, structured the changes in the content of Soviet television news.

The themes associated with Afghanistan reveal the legitimation strategy of the Soviet leadership and address this work's central questions. First, Soviet involvement was justified by the interference of the United States and Pakistan and was set within a Cold War framework during war-waging under Chernenko. This normative argument became more nuanced under Gorbachev as Western interference was presented as the reason why withdrawal could not be accomplished immediately. Hence, the story of Afghanistan during reassessment addressed how withdrawal would be achieved—the cognitive dimension of policy legitimacy. As withdrawal became more likely, Soviet television stressed national reconciliation, and the ability of the Afghan government to deal on its own with the opposition. In addition, news stories emphasized the political negotiations surrounding Afghanistan. While these changes were evident in the leadership's communication strategy, there was no change in the affect surrounding the Soviet presence in Afghanistan. Television showed Soviet soldiers as brave men doing their internationalist duty and there was no questioning of the official reasons for intervention in Afghanistan. As the political leadership reassessed Soviet Afghan policy during this period, the population was prepared for withdrawal, even before it was announced in February 1988.

Traditionally Soviet leaders' concerns about television were about the message, not about whether audiences received or even believed that message. Television did not show bad news or news that was not approved. For five and a half long years, Soviet political officials ordered television not to show military combat. Gorbachev changed this in 1985 soon after he came to power. In part he did this for domestic political reasons. Gorbachev felt that he could use television to solicit support from the domestic audience and to demonstrate a change from above. Glasnost became a hallmark of the new Soviet regime and ties into our questions about domestic politics and television technique. New and more effective communication methods were used—correspondents in the field, for example. And all of this fit within Gorbachev's broader reform program, associated with New Thinking. Great power identity was not lost, but New Thinking presented a fresh set of ideas about the international system and set out a new normative context for the conduct of Soviet foreign policy.

Chapter 5 sets out how the Soviet leadership explained the withdrawal itself, and examines events in the year that followed.

Withdrawal and Aftermath: Afghanistan

The official Soviet announcement that they were willing to withdraw troops from Afghanistan came on February 8, 1988. Both Gorbachev and Najibullah called for progress in negotiations so that an agreement could be signed by March 15, 1988. In reality the Geneva Accords on Afghanistan were signed on April 14, 1988 a month later than the target day. Withdrawal was completed ten months later on February 15, 1989. During withdrawal Gorbachev continued to use television to legitimize his policy, placing it within the context of New Thinking and great power identity. These were balanced carefully, taking into account domestic political considerations. In addition, as in the American case of withdrawal from Vietnam, the Soviet leadership communicated a more sophisticated message to its superpower rival than it did to its own population and allies. The Soviets were also looking for a decent interval of calm before a likely Afghan collapse. After withdrawal was completed, television all but ignored the Soviet experience in Afghanistan and its effect on Soviet society.

FINAL NEGOTIATION FEBRUARY 8, 1988–
APRIL 14, 1988

On February 8, 1988, Gorbachev offered to withdraw Soviet troops from Afghanistan during a ten-month period to begin on May 15 if a Geneva agreement was signed by March 15.[1] He also agreed in principle to front-loading the withdrawal. Previously, withdrawal had routinely been linked to Afghan national reconciliation, but in this announcement the issues were explicitly uncoupled. Pakistan and the United States were faced with a dilemma. They had called for the withdrawal of Soviet forces repeatedly and now the Soviets were prepared to withdraw. However, Pakistan wanted, and the United States supported, an interim government, a proposal with which the Soviets refused to go along.

What became the final round of negotiations at Geneva began on March 2, but Gorbachev's March 15 deadline came and went. The sticking point was symmetry. The Soviets wanted to supply the Najibullah government, and demanded that the United States and Pakistan cease supplying opposition groups. The United States Senate resolved on March 1 that the

> U.S. government should not "cease, suspend, diminish, or otherwise restrict assistance to the Afghan Resistance" until it was "absolutely clear" that the Soviets had terminated their military occupation and that the mujahideen were "well enough equipped" to maintain their integrity during the transition period.[2]

Shevardnadze met with American Secretary of State George Schultz in Washington from March 21–23 where symmetry was discussed but not resolved. Riaz M. Khan, who was involved in the entire United Nations negotiating process, wrote that "the last week of March marked a low point in hopes for the success of the Geneva round."[3] This issue was finally resolved with what seems a sleight of hand. Two private communications between the United States and the Soviet Union were exchanged. The American communication said that the United States would reserve the right to provide military assistance to factions in Afghanistan. The Soviet response is said to have implicitly acquiesced.[4] Riaz has written that "to reconcile these communications and statements with the text of the Geneva Accords could be an international law expert's nightmare."[5] The text of the Accords, for example, banned "support for political or other groups acting on the territory of one of the contracting parties against the government of another contracting party."[6] In any case, some sort of understanding was established in this area as well as in others and Diego Cordovez, the United Nations representative, scheduled the signing for April 14.

Gorbachev had made progress in his battle with the military, KGB, and other interests that opposed withdrawal from Afghanistan. He was close to an agreement in negotiations conducted through the United Nations and had announced a date for withdrawal. However, opposition to withdrawal was still relatively strong.[7] Gorbachev had to continue to strengthen support for withdrawal, and television could be used to increase support among the masses, and among some in the elite, countering those who opposed pulling out.

As in the American case, Soviet withdrawal from Afghanistan was pursued regardless of the fact that their ally's ability to defend itself against aggression had not been adequately strengthened. In a comment that is striking for its similarity to American comments on withdrawing from Vietnam, Yuli Vorontsov, former first deputy foreign minister, said that the leadership wanted Afghan President Najibullah to survive, "at least for a decent interval."[8] The February 1988 directive on the framing of withdrawal noted this was particularly important for third parties:

> We must also keep in mind the fears expressed in one form or another in certain circles among friends and national liberation organizations, which wonder if the Soviet Union, by removing its troops from Afghanistan, is retreating from principled internationalist positions or is showing "excessive pliancy."[9]

But what about Soviet-American relations? What is particularly interesting is that the Soviets tried in a number of ways to convince the United States that withdrawal from Afghanistan was precisely what it was portrayed to be. Gorbachev is quoted as saying that "it would have been a very great stimulus if the United States had recognized that we were serious and had shown a desire to help us get out through the U.N. process."[10] This comment does not support the argument that Gorbachev was excessively concerned with appearing to lack resolve. Breslauer argues that "[w]hat Gorbachev sought to justify was a policy that decisively subordinated—even abandoned—the anti-imperialist struggle to the higher imperatives of great power collaboration."[11] If the United States would continue to acknowledge Soviet great power status, concessions in Afghanistan were acceptable. Even at the last minute, when the United States refused an agreement that would restrict American aid to the mujahedeen, the Soviets agreed to the final Geneva Accords. The separate letters acknowledging that the United States would not be prevented from sending aid were kept secret from the Soviet public and the rest of the world with American assent.[12] Overall then, there is little evidence that the Soviets were as concerned about their reputation with the United States as deterrence theory suggests.[13] They seem to have been more concerned with what third parties and domestic audiences believed about the Soviet ability to project power.

Explaining Withdrawal during the Negotiation Period

Soviet troops are leaving Afghanistan with the consent of the Afghan government, having completely fulfilled their international duty.

Koenker and Bachman, *Revelations*[14]

Gorbachev's official announcement on February 8, 1988 was the lead story on Soviet news that evening, taking up nearly twenty minutes of the forty-seven minute newscast.[15] The twenty minutes were divided between two stories, both presented by the reader with no accompanying graphics or film. The first story contained the reading of Gorbachev's official pronouncement on Afghanistan and the second covered Najibullah's announcement on Afghan television. Gorbachev's statements legitimized the announcement of withdrawal on February 8th by focusing on Afghan success in national reconciliation and the strong role of the Soviet Union in pursuing international negotiations. For example, he said that "the national reconciliation policy provided a political foundation for everyone who wants peace in Afghanistan."[16] And his statement that national reconciliation did "not manifest weakness, but strength of spirit, wisdom, the dignity of free, honest and responsible political leaders"[17] addressed those who feared that withdrawal would make the Soviet Union appear weak.

After Gorbachev's speech, national reconciliation remained central to the framing of withdrawal, and specific directives were set out for media coverage of this issue in the February 13, 1988 resolution of the Secretariat of the Central Committee "On propaganda support of the political settlement concerning Afghanistan."[18] First, the document said that the Soviet mass media should:

> Resolutely advance the idea that a political settlement in Afghanistan that excludes a military solution of the problem and a policy of national reconciliation are concrete paths to a peaceful solution of the Afghan problem, based on new political thinking, and are an example of realistic possibilities in the task of resolving the most complex regional situations and conflicts.[19]

Second, television had to report that a settlement could and should be reached because the Afghan government could control the situation without Soviet military involvement. So, even though Gorbachev decoupled national reconciliation and Soviet withdrawal, and the Soviets knew that the Afghan government was weak, the directive said that they should be linked in the media's explanation of withdrawal: "The mutually beneficial influence and interrelationships of a policy of national reconciliation and its practical realization with improvement in the general situation in international relations must be shown."[20]

In addition, the document clearly addressed how to counter Western reports that the Soviets had lost the war in Afghanistan and was weak:

> To counterbalance this, it should be explained that Soviet troops are leaving Afghanistan with the consent of the Afghan government, having completely fulfilled their international duty, that the USSR will withdraw its troops in light of reliable preconditions for a future settlement in the country in the interest of the broad masses of the Afghan people, the establishment of peace, and an end to bloodshed on Afghan land. It should be recalled that, arriving in Afghanistan, Soviet troops defended the freedom and independence of this country and foiled the attempts of imperialism to tie it to its path of development by military means. It was our military assistance that enabled the creation of objective conditions for the realization of a policy of national reconciliation, the discovery of a path to a peaceful settlement.[21]

Soviet television, then, was instructed to show the withdrawal not as a defeat, but as evidence of the successful protection of Afghanistan and Gorbachev's policy of new thinking. Soviet prestige was tied to avoiding its depiction as excessively pliant, again tying into the notion of power in the international system. The audiences here are allies, domestic elite, and the general public. The Central Committee resolution ordered television to "illuminate" the policy of national reconciliation:

> In illuminating the policy of national reconciliation of Afghanistan it is necessary to show objectively its successes and difficulties, not to embellish the state of affairs, and not to simplify the complexity of the path of the Afghan people towards this goal, which requires sincere, committed movement by diverse political forces and currents towards each other.[22]

To understand more concretely how television legitimized withdrawal, every *Vremya* broadcast was analyzed and coded for the final negotiation period, February 8–April 14, 1988. Within this period 57 days were coded and 5.4 percent of all news time during this period was spent on stories about Afghanistan. This is up from both the war waging baseline (0.7 percent) and the reassessment period sample (2.2 percent). Almost one-third of the *Vremya* stories about Afghanistan during this period dealt with the Afghan domestic situation, including stories that acknowledged past mistakes by the Afghan government.[23] This is important because previous television coverage of the war blamed it entirely on outside interference, particularly by the United States and Pakistan. One story, broadcast on February 15, 1988, assessed Soviet aid in Afghanistan, and focused on the building of a bread factory—certainly not a new type of story. What was different was that correspondent Alexander Tikhomirov noted that in the past many Afghan people had not supported the government due to leadership mistakes, especially in rural areas. Now, Tikhomirov reported that "more and more people find themselves siding with the government against the rebels." In another story broadcast on March 11, 1988, Tikhomirov discussed the many different sides involved in the situation in Afghanistan, including the various opposition groups, and reported that "many mistakes have been made by the current [Afghan] government" including bureaucratism and the mishandling of relations with the rural population.

Although the Afghan government was presented as having made mistakes, *Vremya* stories also clearly showed the Afghan leadership pursuing a successful program of national reconciliation. For example, the coverage of Afghan domestic politics included a story about the April 5th elections in which Mikhail Leshchinskii reported from the voting center with shots of men waiting in line to vote.[24] He stated that on this day no one was working, but people were out on the streets early—"on the democratic path." The election was for the national parliament, "the highest organ of government power in the country," that would determine the new Afghan constitution. Leshchinskii explained that the elections would go on for ten days so that people from all parts of the country could participate. There were a variety of parties, including the Democratic, Islamic and Peasants parties and he described the voting process: "The election process may be interesting to you. One at a time a person enters the hall and votes by placing a ballot in the box with the picture of the deputy of his choice. Many are illiterate but all know the faces of the candidates."[25] The polls were open for ten days so voters from all parts of the country could participate.

One strategy for legitimizing withdrawal was to use television to link the policy to historical precedence. Many of the stories that discussed historical precedents for withdrawal were done by Leshchinskii and one in particular was ordered in the propaganda resolution: "It would be appropriate to make propaganda use of the anniversary of the signing of the February 1921 Treaty of Friendship between the Soviet state and Afghanistan to promote our policy on the Afghan problem."[26] On February 28, Leshchinskii reported on the 1921 agreements on Soviet-Afghan friendship under Lenin, saying that the Soviet attempt to resolve conflict in Afghanistan went back to Leninist tradition and to this first agreement. There were shots of the documents and the museum where they were kept. Interestingly, Leshchinskii also showed another document, signed by opponents to the 1921 agreement. Leshchinskii remarked that "the relatives of those people [who signed the opposition document] are now part of the opposition: History repeats itself, no it continues." He paraphrased Lenin: "the Afghan people have one way and we have another, but we must respect Afghan independence." Leshchinskii concluded by saying that the Soviet Union happily wanted its neighbor to be independent and peaceful.[27] There is a certain tension between this strategy of attempting to legitimize withdrawal through historical precedent and the presentation of the policy as a new step forward, a new way of thinking.

From February 8 through April 14, 1988 the Soviet decision to withdraw from Afghanistan was presented on television in an international context. Negotiations were depicted as moving forward, in particular, due to a revitalized United Nations. Television stories presented withdrawal as evidence of a new international environment and the Soviet Union was leading the way toward peace. More than 80 percent of all news stories during this period were about negotiations and depicted the Soviet Union as an actor, driving the process in Geneva. Thus the Soviet Union was shown as a great power playing its proper role on the international stage. Due to this focus on the UN talks, the United Nations, the United States, and Pakistan were linked to Afghan stories in much of the coverage. The United Nations played a part in 45 percent of all Afghan stories during this time period.

News stories during this negotiation period depicted Gorbachev and the Soviet Union as pursuing peaceful proposals. New initiatives brought forward by the Soviets were possible due to New Thinking in the Soviet Union. In a February 10, 1988 editorial on *Vremya*, *Izvestia's* Stanislav Kondrashev said that Gorbachev's initiative "clearly demonstrates to all our new thinking, especially to the West but not only to the West."[28] This was repeated in stories about relations with countries other than Afghanistan as well. For example, another February 10th story about Shevardnadze's meeting with the Nicaraguan ambassador reported that Gorbachev's announcement on Afghanistan had been discussed as a new political line to eliminate regional conflict in the future.[29] In addition, there were a number of stories that covered foreign reaction to the Soviet initiative. In all of these stories the foreigners interviewed expressed support for Gorbachev's announcement and the Soviet desire for peace. These stories addressed the Soviet concern about maintaining credibility with allies and third parties.

Television presented a story of politicians negotiating an end to the conflict in Afghanistan. Ordinary people make up the second largest group of newsmakers in these stories, and they are generally supportive of Gorbachev and his decision to withdraw forces from Afghanistan. Other groups of people are poorly represented in news stories about Afghanistan during this time. Military newsmakers, for example, made up only 2.9 percent of the total newsmakers. The implied message was that the military had been and remained subservient to the political system and the goals of the leadership. Intellectuals and professionals comprised even less of the total newsmakers.

While many stories focused on the Geneva negotiations during this period, *Vremya* stories often cited the American supply of money and weapons to the opposition as hindering the chance for peace. In a February 18, 1988 editorial the situation was presented as: Moscow and Kabul were doing everything so that an agreement could finally be completed; meanwhile the United States was supplying money to the opposition.[30] The editorial said that both the United States and the Soviet Union had to compromise—"peace can only come with compromise."

EXPLAINING WITHDRAWAL APRIL 1988– FEBRUARY 15, 1989

Concern about withdrawal continued even after the Geneva Accords were signed and the Soviet Union began its withdrawal. A Politburo protocol from January 24, 1989—just a month before the completion of the pull out—stated that "the Afghan comrades are seriously worried as to how the situation will turn out."[31] As late as the first days of February 1989 "a decision was being made . . . as to whether to withdraw all the troops or not."[32] Yakovlev said:

> [T]here was indeed some tough talking, disagreement. Each side tried—how shall I put it—to force the other to accept responsibility. If you make this decision you must accept responsibility for the consequences. So this shining, gleaming ping-pong ball of responsibility flew back and forth. Where would the buck stop?[33]

The military predicted the Afghan government would collapse as soon as the Soviet troops were withdrawn. Gorbachev made the final decision and Yakovlev described the situation:

> Mikhail Sergeyevich [Gorbachev], of course, had had the final say. Enough hesitation, he said, the troops must be withdrawn. That's all there is to it. They must be withdrawn.[34]

Between April 1988 and February 1989, the process of withdrawal and the ability of the Afghan government to deal with the opposition on its own were the major themes on Soviet television. It is clear from interviews with Soviet officials that these themes were meant to legitimize withdrawal. Soviet officials did not want to dwell on the problems of soldiers returning home or on the inability of Soviet forces to achieve a victory in Afghanistan. The television sample analyzed for withdrawal included all broadcasts in 1988 and a sample week from January and February 1989.

After the accords were signed, and until the final withdrawal, television emphasized the completion of each phase of the withdrawal. For example, on August 15, 1988 *Vremya* covered the completion of the first phase with a story on the press conference of General B. V. Gromov, the commander of the limited contingent. Gromov discussed the withdrawal of Soviet troops, saying that 50,000 soldiers had already "crossed the border between war and peace and have returned home."[35] He continued by saying that the troops in Afghanistan had completed their mission—they had stabilized the political situation in Afghanistan and the country was still whole. Gromov, thus, legitimized the decision to withdraw by saying that Soviet political goals that were pursued with military means had been accomplished.

The framing of withdrawal can also be seen in the depiction of the Afghan domestic scene and national reconciliation. On May 25, 1988, for example, Leshchinskii did a story on troops moving from Jalalabad, through Kabul and on to Termez in the Soviet Union. There were shots of the trucks and tanks, and Leschchinskii reported that the convoy stopped to receive their last mail in Afghanistan. The camera panned over Afghan and Soviet soldiers standing side by side as Leshchinskii reported that the road was extremely important for trade, but also extremely dangerous. Interviewing an Afghan captain, Leshchinskii asked him if he was ready to take over the defense of this dangerous and important road. The 28-year-old captain replied that the Afghan military understood the danger, but "our soldiers have good weapons and plans." He said that "after the Soviet soldiers leave, we ourselves will defend the people and the land."[36] Among Soviet leaders, however, there were serious reservations about whether or not the Afghan government would survive for any length of time.

In stories about Afghan national reconciliation, *Vremya* focused on the return of refugees and negotiations with the opposition. In a May 26 story on national reconciliation, Petrova reported that people were returning to Afghanistan and the process was difficult.[37] In one interview a man said that he had heard that life was much better in

Afghanistan and had decided to return. His family would return soon as well. It was hard to return to Afghanistan, however, Petrova reported. There was a lack of housing, for example, and in part, because of this many had joined the army. The Minister of Repatriation was interviewed and said that the process had to be regularized, and commented that he needed a staff of 30 to 40 people, and he planned to use television, radio, and newspapers to tell people what to do.

One interesting view of Afghan national reconciliation came in *Vremya* stories about the role of Islam in Afghanistan. In October 1988 the Muslim Peace Conference was held in Afghanistan and *Vremya* stories about it were broadcast on October 22 and 23. In introducing the first story the TV news reader said that the situation was strained in Afghanistan and the peace conference would address the conflict. The role of Muslims in the Afghan government was reported to be extremely strong: "Today the strength of the government comes in no small part from the support of religious leaders and groups." Najibullah was shown addressing the conference, saying that Afghanistan was on the road to peace through the power of negotiation within Afghanistan and with other countries of the world. On the second day of the conference Leshchinskii interviewed a sheikh who said that the conference showed that Muslims all over the world were interested in peace. A mufti added: "This is a great push/impulse toward the solving of regional issues and promoting peace." The stories showed the importance of Islam yet there was an attempt to co-opt it for the legitimation of Soviet policy.

In addition to an emphasis on Afghan reconciliation, the Soviet leadership emphasized that the Soviet Union would continue to support Afghanistan with medical, material and technical aid, if not military personnel. These stories stressed that the Soviet Union was not abandoning its ally. On May 24, 1988, for example, Petrova reported on the opening of an institute where Afghan officials, with the help of Soviet doctors, were fitting prostheses on those who had lost arms and legs in the war. Petrova commented that "today in Afghanistan, it is not only necessary to rebuild buildings."[38] A doctor said that thousands required this care, and added that physicians who worked at the institute would take additional training in the Soviet Union. In another story with film about Soviet assistance for the Afghan health program, Petrova interviewed Minister of Health Nadzhm who had recently returned to his country from abroad. Nadzhm said that the country desperately needed Soviet help to implement a functioning national health service. Soviet doctors had been going into the streets and out to the countryside distributing medicine, particularly vaccines shipped from the Soviet Union because there were none in Afghanistan, according to Dr. Nadzhm.

The continued friendship of the Soviet Union and Afghanistan was also emphasized in stories about the joint Soviet-Afghan space flight in August–September 1988. Presented as the continuation of the cooperative relationship between the two countries, stories covered the space flight, including one in which the cosmonauts called for all parties to the Geneva Accords to follow the agreement. Direct reference was made to Pakistan and the United States.[39] The return of the cosmonauts was also heavily covered, including their decoration by the Presidium of the Supreme Soviet.[40]

While television stressed Soviet aid, friendship, and the success of national reconciliation, there was also coverage of the ongoing fighting in Afghanistan. For example, on September 9, 1988 *Vremya* reported that 16 people had died after a Stinger rocket supplied by the United States struck an Afghan plane. Among the dead were two Afghan generals and an Afghan colonel. Another story on October 19, 1988 reported that Kabul had been under attack for six hours and nine people had died.[41] On October 20th Leshchinskii showed the devastation of the attack on Kabul that had been described the day before on *Vremya*, and viewers saw him standing on a road near cars and trucks that had been blown up or hit. He said that the hostile forces were organized and were trying to cause panic among the people. One man said he was offered a lot of money to fight against state power, and a village elder added his voice, saying that political methods had to succeed if peace was to be achieved. The story showed these Afghan men calling for political dialogue, precisely what the Soviets wanted, and it is interesting to note that the terminology changed according to directives from above:

> Given that we completely subscribe to the policy of national reconciliation and are actively supporting the proposal of President Najibullah for the creation of a coalition government with the participation of all political groupings who are prepared for it, we also need to shift to a new terminology in our propaganda. It is hardly appropriate to speak of reconciliation with "counterrevolution," or participation in a government coalition with "bandits" or "dushman" [which in translation mean "enemies"]. These terms may be used: "opposition," "opposition forces," "Islamic parties"; expressions such as "armed opposition," or "military forces of the opposition" may be used in reference to their armed forces.[42]

The themes, characterizations, and language for the story of withdrawal were clearly set out in the directive from above, shaping the context for the public at large.

In February 1989, *Vremya* covered the last days of withdrawal, showing returning soldiers, many of whom look very serious and distant. This was a different depiction from the limited withdrawal of troops in 1986 when television covered great celebrations. On the final day of the withdrawal, *Vremya* gave extensive coverage to the end of the Soviet military presence in Afghanistan. Soviet soldiers were praised for doing their internationalist duty, and Gromov was the last to cross the bridge between Afghanistan and the Soviet Union—the bridge "between peace and war, life and death,"— before an emotional meeting with his son.

Afgantsy

It is clear that Gorbachev wanted to use television to legitimize withdrawal from Afghanistan, and it was logical to expect the central government would also use it as a way of covering the return of Soviet soldiers from Afghanistan. The treatment of veterans can directly affect relationships among the military, political officials, and society at large. In the case of Soviet soldiers returning from Afghanistan, the inability of the leadership to deal with the problems of veterans could have led to resentment. As a result, a final group of *Vremya* stories during withdrawal addressed the problems of the Soviet veterans of Afghanistan—the *Afgantsy*. Few in number, and often emphasizing the resolution of problems, the stories nonetheless touched on the reality of war and its effect on individual soldiers. In one January 29, 1989 example, a correspondent reported that the wounds of *Afgantsy* were both physical and mental. The camera panned over a modern building, swimming pool, and beautiful grounds, and showed a group of *Afgantsy* sitting in a clean, new hospital, listening to music, with blank stares, expressionless. There was a feeling in the hospital, said the correspondent, that "these people know more than us" about the horrors of war.[43] A few *Afgantsy* were interviewed, and they talked about the problems they were having and said that their main desire was to be able to deal with their families better. In this story the scars of war were quite clear. In spite of the new hospital and rehabilitation programs, the road to recovery would be difficult.

In another example, on September 6, 1988 Nikulin reported with film on the treatment of injured young *Afgantsy*. Soldiers sitting in the hospital watched cosmonauts on a donated television. One unidentified veteran said that the donated televisions were important because they were expressions of moral support, showing that the soldiers had not been forgotten. The story took a turn at the end, however, as the correspondent commented that the gift was only six television sets. These men, he reported, had done their internationalist duty and now the country must do its duty. Moreover, televisions weren't the issue. Transportation and jobs were what was needed. The story was clearly designed to show *Afgantsy* receiving help, but the correspondent shifted the focus by minimizing the donation and calling for more concrete help from the government.

The leadership took more of a lead in issues relating to *Afgantsy* after these stories were broadcast. In a TASS report (not a correspondent story) aired on February 3, 1989, *Vremya* reported that *Afgantsy* faced severe problems that needed to be rectified. This TASS report, specifically put out by the central leadership, attempted to press for better treatment of *Afgantsy* and sought to blame republican (i.e., regional) officials for the problems. Focusing on the Belorussian Republic, the report said that *Afgantsy* "had to fight for perestroika" because Party and government officials "had forgotten the needs of those who served in Afghanistan, including the hurt, the blind, and families of the dead." In an action labeled as heartless, more than 1000 Belorussian apartments that had been designated for Afghanistan veterans were "wrongly assigned" to many well-known people in the republic.

Although the analysis here focuses on *Vremya*, Soviet citizens learned about the soldiers' experience through other programs as well. Compelling for its black and white footage, *Return (Vozvrashchenie)*, was broadcast on October 10, 1988. The lack of color highlighted the somber, and indeed, tragic tone of the film. *Return* focused on the psychological anguish, stress, and pain of the *Afgantsy* and highlighted the problems of the veterans caused by a war in which "no one made the decision to participate." Shunned when he returned to the Soviet Union, one man said, "When I returned home I realized that no one needs us. No one cares about us. Everyone is afraid of us. They treat us like monsters." The final comment from another soldier finished with a sad question for all Soviet people: "I won't be able to live in peace. Whatever happens in this country is my business. They teach the wrong things. We're taught to kill and repress, but they don't teach us how to change things peacefully. What do I do with these memories?"

TELEVISION

Believe your own eyes—this is the secret behind the success of any broadcast which transports us great distances and makes us witnesses to events.

Kravchenko, "Television Head Outlines Program Plans"[44]

It is clear that during withdrawal the Soviet leadership and television professionals continued to stress the importance of certain techniques for effective television. Leonid Kravchenko, then first deputy chair of *Gostelradio*, understood the importance of correspondent reports from the field and more visually striking news reporting.[45] In an interview with Kravchenko in 1988 he emphasized again and again the need for timely information (*operativnost*) in the Soviet Union and quoted *Pravda* as saying that "the most important factor in the effectiveness of information is timeliness."[46]

The leadership believed television to be more effective when there was direct visual information given and when the information did not come from TASS. Kravchenko, emphasized the importance of direct visual information:

> Television possesses splendid technical merits. With its help it is possible to be at one and the same minute both in space and on another continent—present at an event the moment it happens. This "effect of being there" and being up-to-the-minute has a colossal impact. Therefore we are thinking of making more frequent use of direct open transmissions and further expanding "live" broadcasting. Satellite broadcasting systems now embrace the whole world. Yet direct air means a problem of trust. Believe your own eyes—this is the secret behind the success of any broadcast which transports us great distances and makes us witnesses to events.[47]

Kravchenko also spoke about the importance of the readers and correspondents:

> Of course, we are not yet managing to do everything the way we would like to, but we now understand the need to make better use of television's amazing potential. For example, it possesses absolute pitch with regard to the truth. Television does not have the right to sing out of tune, and its voice must be confiding, for it comes into our home, our apartment, our family. Announcers, moderators, and commentators are becoming our good acquaintances. How do they look and behave, how do they speak, are they intelligent? Do they find the requisite confiding key? All this is very important, and so responsible! To whom in television do we entrust the right to be in the shot and be our intermediary? Then you see how much still has to be done in order not to disappoint television viewers.[48]

The formatting of the stories during this period of withdrawal was very similar to both the reassessment and final negotiation periods. Readers presenting the news made up 44 percent of the stories and correspondent reports made up 49 percent. Non-TASS reports made up 90 percent of the coverage.

Leshchinskii continued to dominate the filmed news stories, although the percentage of correspondent stories by him dropped significantly. Thirty-six percent of all correspondent stories were done by Leshchinskii during this period while his wife, Petrova, accounted for 6 percent. This was a decrease from the reassessment period when Leshchinskii alone accounted for 67 percent of the Afghan stories. During this withdrawal period other correspondents were introduced, including Tikhomirov who reported 12 percent of the stories. This can be accounted for, at least in part, because there were many reports from locales other than Afghanistan, including Geneva and the United States.

Another explanation for this involves problems *Gostelradio* officials were reportedly having with Leshchinskii. It was rumored that he had a hard time with the change in policy, that is, the decision to withdraw forces from Afghanistan.[49] He acknowledged that he was very close to the military officers who served in the field. Sharing the same experience in Afghanistan, he said he had more in common with these military men than with his superiors at *Gostelradio*.[50] Certainly, his reports had to be approved by the leadership; however, there have been suggestions that he was overly patriotic and that he neglected to do stories on the problems of soldiers and their return to Soviet society. Leshchinskii, for his part, claimed that he supported withdrawal from the beginning of his time in Afghanistan.[51]

Afghan national reconciliation supplied a <u>valid</u> rationale for withdrawal without an acknowledgement of Soviet defeat. In the Soviet case, it seems more important that the political elite, and particularly the military, had a story they could live with. Withdrawal was presented as legitimate because the Soviets had achieved their intended goals. In an extensive *Vremya* news story on July 1, 1988, for example, General Gromov insisted that the Soviet military had done its job:

> Now they say and write a lot about our defeat in the West. About the fact that we allegedly lost the war in Afghanistan. Juggling with historical facts, turning the truth upside down, our enemies and malignants of all kinds do not want, or to be exact, are not willing to understand that we came to Afghanistan with a mission of a best will, we came to defend the people, their children and women, peaceful kishlaks and cities, finally national independence and sovereignty of this country. And we have accomplished this task. (applause) And we have accomplished this task, at an expensive price, but we have accomplished it with <u>honor</u>.
>
> . . .
>
> We believe that care about defense of our country, about the readiness to rise to its defense when it is necessary, is urgent as before.

> The position of some people, who try to assert that the military threat for our country is an archaic concept, cannot be understood. Unfortunately, it is far from being so. And the reality does not confirm this.[52]

So, here, as in the American case, honor was invoked, a superpower did not fail, and military strength was celebrated. Interestingly, the leadership believed that the story of Afghan national reconciliation was important to the general public, in part, due to the fear of a "Vietnam" reaction in which the public would lose confidence in the state's ability to project power.[53]

But, what happened after withdrawal? If the Soviet leadership did not present the repercussions of withdrawal as a central issue during withdrawal itself, did they deal with the issue after withdrawal was complete? The answer is no—the Soviet leadership did not, to any great degree, address this central issue. The leadership continued to feel that dwelling on Afghanistan would not advance any policy goals. Yakovlev said that the leadership did not explicitly think about the American experience in Vietnam. However, he also said that while it was permissable to criticize the government for using military force, he did not approve of criticism of the soldiers.[54]

ONE YEAR AFTERMATH MARCH 1989– MARCH 1990

The last Soviet troops left Afghanistan on February 15, 1989. After the Soviet withdrawal, the war in Afghanistan intensified. The Soviets continued to aid the Afghan government, and the United States and Pakistan continued to aid the opposition. There were estimates that, at least in 1989, the Soviets were spending $250 million a month trying to forestall the Afghan government's collapse.[55] Still, the Soviets called for the United States and Pakistan to adhere to the Geneva Accords that restricted foreign interference. The Soviet political goal was to support the stability of the Afghan government without military intervention. It is important to note that after the Soviet withdrawal from Afghanistan, and as proponents of New Thinking gained strength, the framing of the Soviet Union as "normal" and "democratic" was extended to include a thorough-going critique of Soviet policies generally. In fact, during this period a number of high-level Soviet governmental officials explicitly called the invasion of Afghanistan a mistake, including Shevardnadze and Vorontsov.[56] The December 1989 report of the USSR Supreme Soviet Committee on International Affairs flatly reported that "the decision to send Soviet troops into

Afghanistan merits moral and political condemnation," and clearly blamed the Soviet political system for presenting a fait accompli to the party and the people: "New thinking intends excluding the possibility of any repetition of anything like the 1979 action."[57] Yet, the document also pointed out that despite armed opposition, the Afghan government had not fallen. The Soviet Union, the report asserted, had defended the Afghan government and should and would continue to do so.

TELEVISION

As with Vietnamization, national reconciliation supplied a rationale for withdrawal without having to acknowledge defeat; and, as in the American case, the scenario gave Soviet political elites and the public a story they could live with. Withdrawal was presented as legitimate because the Soviets had achieved their intended goals. As far as television was concerned there was no leadership strategy to heal the wounds of the Afghanistan experience. Domestic politics took precedence. A sample of eight weeks of *Vremya* coverage during this year showed that 1.4 percent of the total *Vremya* coverage in this sample dealt with Afghanistan or the return of soldiers who had fought there. This is more than during war waging (0.7%), but less than during negotiations (2.2%) and withdrawal (5.4%).

Television did report on events in Afghanistan and it routinely covered instability in Afghanistan and continued aggression by the opposition. Reporting from Afghanistan in March 1989, Alexander Shkirando used the word "unstable" to describe Afghanistan. Shkirando interviewed the chairman of the National People's Alliance of Pushtunistan who said he thought that fighting would end when Soviet troops left, but "the war has not only not ended—on the contrary it has become even larger in scale."[58] The correspondent then talked about the shelling of Jalalabad over shots of burned out buildings and damage to houses: "As has happened many times before, mosques and other sacred places of Islam are suffering at the hands of the so-called fighters for the faith." This theme about the destruction caused by so-called religious fighters appeared in other stories during this time. In a July 11, 1989 story, Shkirando reported that Kabul had been under attack from extremists despite the fact that "peace" had been declared. An inhabitant said that children were playing when the bombs hit and some were killed: "Those that did this aren't true Muslims." Another story reported that the opposition continued attacks on Kabul in spite of an Islamic holiday.[59]

As in earlier periods, Soviet television attempted to tie Soviet behavior to some historical precedent. For example, on May 26, 1989 Shkirando reported on the 70th anniversary of Soviet-Afghan diplomatic relations established by Lenin when the Afghans were fighting British colonialism. Shkirando interviewed an old man who remembered meeting Lenin in Moscow and said that without Soviet help then, there would be no independent Afghanistan. Clearly this story was designed to legitimize the Soviet involvement in Afghanistan, supporting the proposition that without Soviet intervention in the 1980s, Afghanistan would have collapsed under the weight of rival groups fighting amongst themselves. In fact, the Afghan Ambassador to the Soviet Union made this point the next day,[60] when he equated Lenin's help against the British, with Soviet aid to resist the imperialism of the United States and Pakistan.

Most stories in the aftermath of war were about opposition attacks and called on Pakistan and the United States to stop supporting the opposition. In most cases, these stories referred to the Afghan government's calls for a peaceful resolution of the conflict. For example, in March 1989, *Vremya* reported that the Afghan government had called for people to do all they could to stop the war and bring peace and security to Afghanistan. Pakistan and the United States were specifically mentioned.[61] Other stories focused on Afghan calls to the United Nations, or to Javier Perez de Cuellar, the secretary-general, to tell Pakistan and the United States to abide by the treaty. Most of these stories were very short and were simply read. In fact, 75 percent of the newsmakers in these stories were politicians.

While Soviet television supported the Geneva Accords and called on the United States and Pakistan to do the same, it was not used to address problems of *Afgantsy* returning to the USSR. There was only one story in this eight-week sample about returning soldiers, but the powerful emotional nature of the coverage created perhaps a greater impact than most stories about Afghanistan. The story covered a disabled veterans meeting in Moscow in July 1989. Men had been blinded and had lost arms and legs in Afghanistan, but the story emphasized that all had jobs and an inner strength that helped them to keep an optimistic outlook. There was a contradiction, however, as one mother was interviewed, crying and saying through her tears that the hardest part is that her son needed help with everything.

Another issue covered in only one story in the sample was prisoners of war. Television did cover Gorbachev's meeting with *Nadezhda* (Hope), a national committee dedicated to the freeing of Soviet prisoners of war in Afghanistan. Gorbachev was shown speaking to the representatives of this group in a large conference room, and representatives were reported as heading to Afghanistan where they would contact the Pakistani opposition. Gorbachev promised on camera that the Soviet government would use every channel—through Pakistan, Afghanistan, the Arab countries, the United States, and the UN to facilitate the release of POWs. "We must not forget all that happened in Afghanistan—that is clear to everyone."[62] But even though Gorbachev said that Afghanistan should not be forgotten, as in the American case, domestic political circumstances would steer attention away from the war and its aftermath.

Turning once again to questions about communication strategies, domestic politics, international identity and reputation, and television technique and access; one can see the interplay of the various factors. During withdrawal, Gorbachev continued to legitimize his policy by emphasizing Afghan reconciliation (the cognitive component of policy legitimacy). In addition, both great power identity and the New Thinking of the Soviet Union on international relations gave overlapping normative reasons to support withdrawal. Political officials claimed Soviet success in Afghanistan and focused on a new era of "normal" behavior within a cooperative and negotiated international environment. Gorbachev continued to use television to secure popular support against entrenched bureaucratic interests, and the more effective techniques associated with glasnost continued. After withdrawal, domestic conditions demanded more and more time as changes began to spin far beyond what Gorbachev wanted.

CHAPTER 6

Conclusions and
a Post–Cold War Assessment

War demands sacrifice; families send loved ones to fight and die for the objectives established by political leaders; nations commit resources and treasures. The common assumption is that leaders must legitimize war waging through timely and truthful statements about how success will be defined and achieved, and also through credible explanations of why the war is worth the costs. Above all, it is about convincing citizens that the appalling price of war is justified. The case studies of Vietnam and Afghanistan suggest that leaders' communication strategies are also shaped by state identity, domestic political factors, access to media, and leadership skill in using media. And in reckoning with these factors, legitimizing war can become entangled in messy, unattractive, and politically charged decisions. This chapter summarizes the findings of the Vietnam and Afghanistan cases, and then briefly addresses how, in the post–Cold War world, leaders' communication strategies have not significantly changed.

Without legitimation, significant elite and/or public opposition can hamper and even undermine a leader's ability to wage war effectively. Yet, in both war waging cases—the United States in Vietnam and the USSR in Afghanistan—leaders legitimized the war effort in peculiar and ultimately problematic ways. Why? The answer lies, in part, in the fact that identity constrained policies and explanations and made candor unattractive. Vietnam and Afghanistan were limited wars in which a nuclear superpower faced a much smaller, nonnuclear third-world country. And in both cases, the conflict between a policy of limited war and perceptions about superpower identity deeply affected the leadership's television strategy. Being a superpower meant winning wars, not accepting compromised peace. After World War II, these two powers had emerged with starkly different ideologies as competitors for prominence in the world, protecting their own allies, and challenging their rivals. Yet, in both countries there was a consensus among political elites and many in the public about the proper role of a great power. In the American case, Lyndon Johnson's general explanations fit within the accepted Cold War consensus and formed the normative component of policy legitimacy. However, when it came to the escalation in Vietnam, Johnson employed a media strategy of minimum candor and sought to limit debate and criticism. One reason for this was that a limited war did not fit neatly within the prevailing understanding of the role of a superpower. Critics on the right suggested that if the United States was to be involved in a war, the leadership should use all resources to pursue victory. Instead, Johnson chose a muted and incremental escalation that played to the middle. As David Green succinctly notes:

> Precisely because the war evolved as a "middle of the road" or "moderate" approach to fighting "communism," it drew broad support from self-styled liberals and conservatives alike. And because it developed slowly and gradually, each "escalation" was accompanied by the most careful ideological justification. As a result, by the time the war had reached its truly massive proportions, its supporters were ideologically trapped, unable to see their way out or appreciate the vehemence of domestic antiwar protests.[1]

Soviet leaders initially refused to allow television to show or discuss direct Soviet military combat in Afghanistan largely because it did not resemble the Great Patriotic War (World War II) in which the Soviet Union had been directly threatened. The Soviet Union did not use all of its resources to fight to a victory in Afghanistan and the population at home was not touched by direct attacks on the motherland. The media coverage the leadership did allow showed Soviet military personnel helping the Afghan people with economic and other aid.

In addition to the issue of identity there were domestic complexities, especially in the American case. Johnson wanted the Congress and the country to focus on his domestic policies and Great Society programs rather than the war in Vietnam. Too much attention to the war and to military spending might weaken his ability to get his domestic programs passed and implemented. In addition, wars cost money and Johnson wanted to spend money on his domestic programs. In the Soviet case, the political leadership thought it did not need policy legitimacy to fight the war. The political elite did not question approved policy, and citizens who spoke out against the war were silenced.

Soviet and American leaders' decisions had serious repercussions for policy legitimacy. In the United States the result was a credibility gap. Because Johnson was not candid about how or why he escalated the war, many Americans believed he consistently and deliberately misled them about Vietnam. When he was forthcoming—about Tet, for example— few Americans believed him. In the Soviet case, hundreds of thousands of citizens came to know that Soviet soldiers were fighting and dying in Afghanistan, not because the leadership told them via the official news on Soviet television, but because more and more families and friends were touched by a war that their own leaders would not acknowledge. The credibility of the Soviet leadership was undermined because it did not discuss the war in Afghanistan. Of course, a media strategy that limits information about war will not always lead to credibility problems. It is possible for leaders to keep information from the public, but only if the war is short in duration. The Falklands, Panama, Grenada and the 1991 Persian Gulf War come to mind. But this strategy becomes problematic if the war drags on, casualties increase, and opposition mounts.

The differences in the television strategies of these leaders during reassessment were directly related to who drove the policy reevaluation. In the American case it was not the president who moved reassessment. In January 1968 Johnson was touting progress in Vietnam. After Tet, however, events moved rapidly and when Johnson made his decision in March to de-escalate and not seek reelection, he announced this promptly to the American people. There was no preparation and little concrete planning on how withdrawal could be achieved. This caused major problems for Richard Nixon who had to withdraw while still seeking a negotiated settlement.

In the Soviet case, Gorbachev and his closest advisors pushed for reassessment of the war effort as he entered office in March 1985, changing mass media coverage during his first summer as leader. This reassessment period was relatively long, lasting two and a half years. Beginning with his decision to change the coverage of Afghanistan in June 1985, Gorbachev sought to show how withdrawal could successfully be achieved through Afghan national reconciliation, and why it was desirable because of New Thinking. While domestic considerations curtailed Johnson's candor, Gorbachev used expanded coverage of the Afghan War to counter those opposed to his policies more generally. This decision was facilitated by the centralization of the Soviet media, especially television. Furthermore, Gorbachev's understanding of the role of media was different from his predecessors' and led to more interesting and effective news stories. So, Soviet television helped prepare the public for the withdrawal.

In the American case, Nixon took office in January 1969 "promising that he would end the war, and though he also promised 'peace with honor,' he never publicly talked about military victory."[2] Still, it took Nixon four years to reach an agreement with North Vietnam. In the Soviet case, after Gorbachev's announcement that troops would withdraw in February 1988, an agreement was quickly reached and withdrawal was completed within a year. These differences deeply affected some aspects of the leaders' television strategies. Yet, in spite of the differences, in both the American and Soviet cases, leaders attempted to use television to legitimize withdrawal from war by using similar themes that fit with the context of great power identity.

These decisions to withdraw did not coincide with the achievement of political objectives, but with the leaders' determination that the costs of staying were too high. In the United States withdrawal was influenced by divisions within the Congressional elite and by vocal domestic opposition. Nixon and Kissinger clearly pursued withdrawal in accordance with domestic imperatives. In the Soviet Union, withdrawal was shaped by Gorbachev's New Thinking as he sought to fundamentally change both domestic and international relations. In neither case did the leaders say that the state had failed to accomplish its goals. In neither case did the leaders say that the costs were simply too high and in neither case did the leaders question the use of military power. Instead, American and Soviet leaders stressed the cognitive component of legitimacy or how withdrawal could be accomplished, and the normative component of how they had honorably lived up to their great power commitments.

There are many similarities in the themes used to legitimize withdrawal. Both Nixon and Gorbachev stressed the importance of negotiations, and also insisted that their ally could handle the situation. In the American case, Nixon and Kissinger repeatedly emphasized the importance of negotiations, even as the discussions dragged on and on. In the Soviet case, Gorbachev and Soviet television stressed the importance of the United Nations as an important international organization that could facilitate a peaceful resolution to the war in Afghanistan. Here the end of the war fit Gorbachev's New Thinking which stressed political settlement of the conflict and the emergence of the Soviet Union as a normal country in the international system. In the American case, Vietnamization became the term used to describe the South's ability to take over the war effort. In the Soviet case, national reconciliation described the ability of the Afghan government to control the situation within its country. Both Nixon and Gorbachev rejected the war-waging policy of the past without questioning the fundamental assumptions of their country's policies and certainly without recognizing failure. Finally, particularly striking during withdrawal were the leaders' attempts to elicit help from their great power adversaries to end the conflict. This was true in spite of the fact that leaders used reputation as a reason for fighting to begin with. Both American and Soviet leaders sought a decent interval before their Vietnamese and Afghan allies fell so that they could blame failure on them.

In the Soviet case, troops were not withdrawn in any significant way until after the signing of the Geneva Accords between Pakistan and Afghanistan.[3] In the American case, Nixon had tremendous difficulty because he was withdrawing forces even as he negotiated for a settlement. In addition, at various points he expanded the war by invading Cambodia and escalating the air war. Nixon and Kissinger said that these actions would culminate with negotiated settlement, but many saw them as contradicting the policy of withdrawal, something that contributed to Nixon's problems in legitimizing withdrawal. These cases show that consistency was crucial. If media strategy does not consistently support withdrawal, the population at large may question whether the leader does indeed favor it. This is especially true if credibility is at issue to begin with.

The final withdrawal of troops would seem to signal the end of war, but events are rarely so straightforward. First, in both cases fighting continued and the results affected how each country understood what it had or had not accomplished. Second, like it or not, societies must deal with the consequences of an unwinnable war. Finally, veterans must be reintegrated into society. In both the American and Soviet cases, other issues clearly took prominence over the return of veterans and their place in society. In the American case, Watergate consumed more and more of President Nixon's time and energy. In the Soviet Union, the immense internal turmoil that finally led to the demise of the country was central. In light of these significant domestic political concerns, there was little time to address the plight of veterans and the repercussions for society, even if any leader might have wanted to address these issues. But why would they? The contradictions of withdrawing forces from a failed war were never confronted to begin with, and it was unthinkable to do so once withdrawal had been completed.

These two cases raise interesting questions about reputation, identity, and framing in international relations. First, in each case leaders framed withdrawal as cognitively and normatively desirable. Not only could withdrawal be successfully accomplished by strengthening an ally, this fit within the broader context of great power identity. Second, legitimacy was particularly important for domestic audiences and third parties in both the Soviet and American cases. This suggests a more complicated explanation of domestic costs than one that asserts the type of political system as explanatory. Third, there was a more nuanced and sophisticated framing of withdrawal for the rival superpower than for public audiences. The United States and the Soviet Union communicated about withdrawal extensively and secretly, hoping to have the other facilitate a decent interval strategy, something not predicted by deterrence theory. A loss of reputation or credibility may, in fact, have little effect on adversaries, but Nixon and Gorbachev understood that credibility could deeply affect allies' perceptions, and elite and public opinion. Fourth, in both cases domestic audiences were able and willing to accept and live with a story that portrayed a great power as having withdrawn "honorably" despite fully expecting their erstwhile allies to be crushed within a short period of time.

In the American case, it was much more difficult for the leadership to control the content of war coverage. Because media are separate from government, leaders had to develop strategies to influence coverage that took into account the structure of news organizations and the norms of professional journalists. Both Johnson and Nixon were often irritated by their seeming inability to more fully control their messages on television. Johnson's response was reticence; Nixon strove to shape coverage much more deliberately and in ways that contradicted democratic impulses. In the Soviet case, television was centrally controlled during the entire period under study, and leaders dictated policies about news on Afghanistan that suited specific political and cultural needs.

Even in the American case, however, leaders had a great capacity to get their message on television. First, leaders had special information about the war including access to the latest reports from the field. Consequently, the president made war news. He had ultimate responsibility for maintenance of the country's resources and interests. Because of this high level of information and responsibility, the leader could report to the public on how the war was progressing. In addition, leaders could share information or withhold information. Secrecy within a context of national security plays an important role during war. After all, war demands the sacrifice of human beings and material resources. Leaders are obligated to protect these to the greatest extent possible. Plans about maneuvers, equipment, and personnel should not be in the hands of the enemy. Knowledge of these plans could very well help the enemy preempt or attack. Therefore, during war, the importance of secrecy and the primacy of national security considerations are increased. This is so even in "open" societies that stress the right of the media and public to information.[4]

An important difference between the American and Soviet cases was that in the American case, other elite groups could affect media messages. Hallin's research shows shifts in elite opinion were reflected by American media. In the Soviet case it was much easier for Gorbachev and his closes advisors to control coverage. Note that this does not necessarily mean that a leader's media strategy will be more effective. When media are centrally controlled, their credibility is usually lowered because the public knows that they are getting the leaders' view. Thus a leader may have trouble legitimizing a policy if he does not control coverage, and a leader may have trouble legitimizing a policy because he does control coverage.

Many have argued that American television's coverage of Vietnam caused public support of the war to falter. After all, television brought the gore and violence of the Vietnam conflict into American living rooms night after night, juxtaposing plans for economic development of the Mekong Delta against pictures of defoliated jungles, and contrasting optimistic statements of progress with casualty rates superimposed on maps showing Viet Cong advances.[5] The argument that this led to criticism of the war effort and the eventual withdrawal of American troops from Vietnam is simplistic at best. The dynamic is clearly more complicated and, in addition to media images, involves issues of national identity, the nature of the opposition, the behavior of the leader, demonstrable progress (or lack thereof), and the number of casualties. However, whether or not television's visual nature affected support for the war, leaders since the Vietnam War have behaved as if it had. This consideration has shaped leadership television strategy in the Falklands,[6] Grenada, Panama, and the two Persian Gulf Wars.[7] Even the Soviets themselves argued that they had avoided the mistakes of America's Vietnam, saying in a Statement of the Soviet Military Command in Afghanistan on the Withdrawal of Soviet Troops on February 14, 1989:

> Withdrawal of Soviet forces, precisely withdrawal, not flight, as was the case with the American troops in Vietnam, is carried out according to the plan, in strict accordance with the Geneva Agreements on Afghanistan, and according to the will of the Afghan and Soviet people, with the support from the world community.[8]

GREAT POWERS AFTER THE COLD WAR

The case studies of Vietnam and Afghanistan beg questions about post–Cold War international relations. Do leaders attempt to legitimize policies in cognitive and normative dimensions in the same way? In light of a new international system that is not built around an adversarial bipolar world, does great power identity matter as much? Have leaders learned anything from previous leaders' credibility problems? This brief afterword summarizes leadership communication strategies about Russian military actions in Chechnya and American military actions in Iraq. These cases cannot be described as categorical failures because conflicts in both areas are ongoing;[9] however, in both cases political goals have not been secured through military action, at least not yet. Chechnya and Iraq suggest that great power identity continues to matter for Russian and especially American leaders. Some lessons from the past have been learned including the need to pay careful attention to what makes communication effective. As Vietnam and Afghanistan made clear, however, promoting a coherent and believable message and maintaining credibility can become more elusive over time, especially when political leaders are less than forthright.

RUSSIA AND CHECHNYA

In December 1991 the Soviet Union ceased to exist and fifteen sovereign states (former republics) took its place. Economic and political reconstruction was complex and difficult, but perhaps most importantly for the world, it was also relatively peaceful. Chechnya, however, was a notable exception. Chechen separatists demanded an independent state and the Russian Federation resisted. In November 1994 the Russian military offensive that became known as the First Chechen War began. Despite President Boris Yeltsin's prediction that the war would end quickly, the Russian military did not gain control of Chechnya, and a peace agreement wasn't signed until August 31, 1996. In the following few years, various factions, including Islamic fundamentalist groups, fought for influence and power, and continued to demand independence from Russia. Levels of violence increased and in October 1999 the Russian military invaded again, and began the Second Chechen War. The Russians were more successful in pushing rebels into hiding than during the first war, but intermittent violence continues as this is written in early 2006, and many see no end in sight.

Leadership communication strategies during the First Chechen War were reminiscent of those used during Afghanistan in some important ways. Yeltsin and his government attempted to limit information about the conflict, claiming that the military was engaged only in "pinpoint" bombing and emphasizing the cruelty of Chechen rebels. Moreover, the government's argument was that rebels were destabilizing a part of the Russian Federation. Government pronouncements stressed battlefield successes even as the troops became bogged down. One strategy that certainly failed was the Russian leadership's attempt to curtail coverage by denying journalists access to Russian soldiers. In part this failed because Russian journalists turned instead to Chechen fighters for news and information about the war. In addition, Russian politicians and the military viewed journalists as enemies, hardly helping to facilitate favorable coverage.

While government strategies resembled past practices, Russian television's coverage of the war presented a sharp contrast with previous media models. After the fall of the Soviet Union in 1991, some of Russian television was commercialized and became less prone to government control. In 1994, NTV, the largest private television station in Russia, covered the First Chechen War extensively. Indeed, on the first day of the war, NTV had four crews on the ground in Chechnya.[10] NTV's coverage of the war went beyond the limited governmental statements, as reporters covered battlefield atrocities, death, and destruction, and proved that "pinpoint" bombing claims were false.[11] NTV's president, Igor Malashenko, recognizing the new prerogatives of the media "reminded the government that Chechnya was not Afghanistan".[12]

Russian political leaders miscalculated the time it would take to stabilize the situation in Chechnya, and public opinion was consistently hostile to the war effort with between 58 and 63 percent of poll respondents opposed to the war.[13] One reason was that television showed the inconsistencies in Russian reports about the war, and showed the destruction and bloodshed.[14] Government credibility was questioned as television exposed divisions in elite and public opinion. In a public opinion survey taken in January 1995, when respondents were asked, "What do you think? How should a real patriot of Russia regard the operation in Chechnya?" 52 percent said a real patriot should speak out against the operation. Nineteen percent said a real patriot should support the operation.[15]

Finally, Russian identity was in a state of flux in the early 1990s. The political leadership was concerned about Russian international prestige and influence as support for negotiations shifted to support for the use of force.[16] But there was also a faction within the political elite and a large percentage of the general public that emphasized that Russia was now a "normal" country in Europe, and emphasized negotiations. For example, in 1996 only 29 percent of polled respondents said that Russia should have a great and powerful army by any means possible.[17] Some of the strongest criticism of intervention in Chechnya came from within the Russian military, and especially from veterans of the Afghan conflict.[18]

The Second War would be another story. Russian leaders, including Vladimir Putin, whom Yeltsin appointed as president in December 1999 and who was elected in March 2000, were critical of NTV's coverage of the First Chechen War. This led, in part, to a reassertion of governmental control over the media. Thomas argues that changes occurred because the Russians had analyzed "their public relations disaster of the first war," studied NATO's press handling in Kosovo, and appointed experienced people to supervise press operations.[19] More important was the government's challenge to television ownership and threats to journalists if they did not report the government's story.[20] The leadership's television strategy was to control information, press their description of their opponents as terrorists, and emphasize military success. Rebel bombings (in Moscow, for example) and hostage-taking supported government assertions about terrorism. The government claimed that security would be restored and law and order reasserted.

Access to the battlefield was extremely restricted and journalists had to obtain special credentials and stay in certain regions. In a move that clearly revealed the government's impatience with NTV, the military refused to take NTV journalists to the front but did allow access to correspondents from other media outlets. "Censorship is now the rule of the game in Chechnya," said Oleg Panfilov, head of the Center for Journalism in Extreme Situations. "The republic is an isolated territory. We do not get any information from there. Comparing our press now to what it was during the first war would be like comparing the European press to the North Korean press."[21] Acting according to directives that are certainly reminiscent of Soviet ways, government spokesmen had specific rules on how to present the war, including calling the opposition "terrorists" and citing the bravery of the great Russian army and its soldiers.

By 1999 there was a change in the mood of the Russian people about Chechnya and Russian identity as well. In January 2000, a Russia-wide poll showed that 67 percent of respondents approved of military actions by Russian forces in Chechnya.[22] Between 1996 and 2000, those who supported having a great and powerful army by any means increased from 29 percent to 49 percent.[23] In addition, the percentage of respondents who felt that there was an enemy "out there" rose from 44 percent in August 1997 to 73 percent in April 1999.[24] In 2000 especially, Putin's communication strategy emphasized the great power status of the Russian Federation.[25] This corresponds with a shift in the general public.[26] Anna Politkovskaya, a journalist who covered the war extensively, wrote "Chechnya provides the yeast for the growth of the great-power mentality, the basis of Putin's state morality."[27] The indecisive outcome in Chechnya in 1996, combined with nearly a decade of economic and political upheaval, increased the public's desire for stability and order.

Still more recently the Russian public has become disillusioned with, if not vocally opposed to, the operations in Chechnya. For example, after a year and a half of fighting, in June 2001, 46 percent (down from 67 percent) of respondents in a Russia-wide poll disapproved of Russian military actions in Chechnya, while 42 percent approved.[28] Meanwhile the Russian media depicted "Chechnya as 'returning to normal,' and the ongoing military campaign as having no alternative."[29] The leadership emphasized normalization and muted public discussion of Chechnya,[30] even as violence continued. According to governmental guidelines, media should avoid mentioning Chechnya and "setbacks should continue to be referred to as events 'in the context of international terrorism.' "[31]

In the Russian case of Chechnya, leaders, the political elite, and the public seem to have settled with an uncomfortable, and perhaps unstable, agreement about a story they can live with. The lesson leaders took from the First Chechen War was that a freer press was dangerous, and they moved to constrain journalists and control information more concretely in the second war. The public, meanwhile, has shown considerable support for what they perceive to be the security and order associated with strong leadership. A call for renewed Russian power can be appealing under such circumstances. Still, beneath the surface (and sometimes above) are serious questions of credibility.

THE UNITED STATES AND IRAQ

The First Iraq War (the Gulf War) began in January 1991 when the United States led a coalition force of 34 countries to remove Iraq's army from occupied Kuwait. The coalition force first launched an air war and then quickly moved ground troops through Kuwait and into Iraq. President George Bush declared Kuwait liberated on February 27. Later, Bush and former National Security Advisor Brent Scowcroft explained why they had not moved to overthrow Saddam Hussein: it would have severely divided the coalition and the political and human costs would have been too high.[32] More than a decade later, in March 2003, the United States military forces returned to Iraq under the direction of President George W. Bush when the United States led a "coalition of the willing" after the United Nations refused to support a military intervention in Iraq.[33] Bush subsequently declared major combat completed (or "mission accomplished") on May 1, 2003. Violence continued, however, with a growing armed insurgency against American occupation and reconstruction of Iraq. The limited objectives of the First Iraq War had been replaced by the much broader objective of democratizing Iraq. In June 2004 the United States announced the transfer of sovereignty to Iraq, but approximately 150,000 American troops were on the ground in Iraq in early 2006.

In the First Iraq War on January 16, 1991, George H. W. Bush stressed the Iraqi violation of United Nations resolutions and said that through this war a new world order would be established:

> This is an historic moment. We have in this past year made great progress in ending the long era of conflict and cold war. We have before us the opportunity to forge for ourselves and for future generations a new world order—a world where the rule of law, not the law of the jungle, governs the conduct of nations. When we are successful—and we will be—we have a real chance at this new world order, an order in which a credible United Nations can use its peacekeeping role to fulfill the promise and vision of the U.N.'s founders.[34]

Bush's communication strategy emphasized the interdependent nature of the international system, and the ability of states to cooperate against overt aggression. Domestically, the American public and political elites supported the coalition actions in Iraq.[35] On January 12, 1991, Congress authorized the use of the military to force Iraq out of Kuwait. In this case, the war had limited and clearly defined objectives, and coalition ground troops were withdrawn when these were accomplished.

The military and political leaders took some lessons from the American experience with media during Vietnam. First, the Pentagon's media rules in the First Iraq War were highly restrictive. Press pools were established, for example, and reporters were not allowed wide access. In addition, the military supplied a significant amount of the information that went to the press hoping to curtail independent reporting. Compelling video footage of missiles hitting their targets supplied a hi-tech, and some would say video-game aura, to the combat coverage that was immensely popular with audiences. One significant difference with Vietnam was the growing level of technological sophistication in the media and the emergence of various other information outlets, including the internet. Satellite technology, for example, allowed televised pictures of air strikes in Baghdad. Even though some journalists balked at the new Pentagon press rules, the conflict's short time frame did not allow for a prolonged discussion about the war or its coverage. Troops came home and the media turned to other stories. Even the continuing air strikes were not covered extensively.

The Second Iraq War began with air strikes on March 20, 2003. In the beginning of the military effort, Bush's communication strategy consistently tied the war to the presence of weapons of mass destruction and a worldwide fight against terrorism. Despite the end of major combat activities, after May 1, 2003, violence continued and American ground forces met determined resistance and suffered escalating numbers of U.S. casualties over time.[36] Bush emphasized success, even as violence continued. Steps that highlighted democratic processes received considerable attention including the June 2004 handing over of "sovereignty" to the Coalition Provisional Authority, the 2005 drafting of a constitution, and the holding of elections. The ability of the Iraqis to defend themselves militarily was a major focus, even as reports surfaced that the Iraqis were not prepared. In the normative context, Bush emphasized the threat from terrorism and he often linked 9-11, al Qaeda, and Iraq: "The terrorists who attacked us— and the terrorists we face—murder in the name of a totalitarian ideology that hates freedom, rejects tolerance, and despises all dissent."[37] The Cold War rhetoric also became more explicit over time. In October 2005 Bush noted that "[t]he murderous ideology of the Islamic radicals is the great challenge of our new century. Yet, in many ways, this fight resembles the struggle against communism in the last century."[38] He then compared Islamic radicals to communism, always beginning his comments with "Like the ideology of communism." This comparison, however, seems to lack resonance with the American people.

While Bush sought to reassure the American people about the war in Iraq, another important element of the government's communication strategy was the embedding of journalists with military units in Iraq.[39] The Pentagon's new plan set out the rationale for embedding as follows:

Ultimate strategic success in bringing peace and security to this region will come in our long-term commitment to supporting our democratic ideals. We need to tell the factual story—good or bad—before others seed the media with disinformation and distortions, as they most certainly will continue to do. Our people in the field need to tell our story.[40]

Approximately 600 reporters (mostly American and British) covered the war from positions with the troops.[41] Many journalists appreciated the access afforded through embedding, especially those from smaller media outlets that might not have had access otherwise.[42] Some did suggest that their stories were shaped by the camaraderie they developed with soldiers in the field. Overall, the use of embedded journalists focused coverage on the everyday experiences of soldiers. Critics of embedding argued that journalists lost objectivity and could not focus on the forest for the trees.

The American public and political elites again supported intervention in Iraq. In October 2002, the House of Representatives and the Senate had approved resolutions that gave the president authority to use means that he deemed to be appropriate. Pew Center polls showed that around 70 percent of those polled supported the military intervention.[43] This support continued into 2005 when public support eroded and Congressional critics grew more outspoken. The success promised by the administration was contradicted by continued violence. In addition, a growing opposition movement in the United States took to the internet and the streets. Three years after the declaration of "mission accomplished," there is growing concern about American involvement in Iraq. The Pew Research Center reported that in their April 7 through 16, 2006 poll that the nation was divided on whether or not the right decision was made to use military force in Iraq (47 percent supportive, 46 percent opposed, 7 percent unsure); and whether or not to keep troops in Iraq or bring them home (48 percent keep and 48 percent bring home).[44] Specifically related to how Americans viewed the Bush administration's communication on Iraq, a CBS poll conducted in the first week of April 2006 showed that 63 percent of Americans polled reported that they thought the Bush administration had not clearly explained U.S. goals in Iraq; and 63 percent said President Bush was making things in Iraq sound better than they really were.[45]

Questions about the veracity of the governmental rationale for the war, including issues associated with intelligence reports about weapons of mass destruction, and the rising casualty rates among American forces began to undermine the leaders' legitimation strategy. The administration's credibility is also undermined at home by its use of certain forms of public diplomacy abroad. Unlike the Vietnam case, media have become globalized and even more pervasive as the internet, and cable and satellite television facilitate the transmission of views from around the world. Credibility becomes even more important when there are so many points of access and so many mode of reception.

Still, a heavy-handed approach has often been the strategy of the Bush administration during the Second Iraq War. In 2002 the Office of Strategic Influence, designed to develop and plant true (and false) stories in the foreign media, was closed after public criticism;[46] but the military later acknowledged in late 2005 that it was covertly paying to run news stories in the Iraqi Press.[47] Secretary of Defense Donald Rumsfeld defended the program, not recognizing that it undermines credibility both at home and abroad, saying:

> The U.S. military command, working closely with the Iraqi government and the U.S. embassy, has sought nontraditional means to provide accurate information to the Iraqi people in the face of an aggressive campaign of disinformation. Yet this has been portrayed as inappropriate; for example, the allegations of someone in the military hiring a contractor, and the contractor allegedly paying someone to print a story—a true story—but paying to print a story. For example, the resulting explosion of critical press stories then cause everything, all activity, all initiative, to stop, just frozen. Even worse, it leads to a chilling effect for those who are asked to serve in the military public affairs field.[48]

In at least some quarters of the Bush administration they have forgotten nothing, but have learned nothing.

In the Iraq wars, American leaders sought to legitimize policies in both cognitive and normative dimensions. Both Bushes emphasized successful operations and the responsibility of the United States, as the lone superpower, to act. The Second Iraq war is marked by a focus on the ability of Iraqis to handle the situation both militarily and politically, reminiscent of Vietnamization. American leaders seek to control images, and restrict information, but doing so has prompted serious questions of credibility as the public now questions the leader's explanations for the war.

Finally, one may ask why any of this is important after the end of the Cold War? The answer is that the communist versus capitalist framing of the international system that characterized the Cold War was layered on top of already existing great power identities of the United States and the Soviet Union. The end of the Cold War did not mean the end of great power identities. English notes this when discussing the "underlying continuity between liberal-Westernizing and statist-great power thought."[49] Gorbachev, for example, recognized that Soviet hard-liners believed in a great power Russia, and said that he "tried to show that only incorrigible 'hawks' could see anathema in a policy that did away with the hyper-militarization of the country, turned the world back from the nuclear precipice and created the basis for our integration into the economic and political structures of the world."[50] In a post–Cold War world, both American and Russian leaders continued to behave according to previously held beliefs about great powers and international relations.

As Jepperson, Wendt, and Katzenstein argue, "constancy in underlying identity helps to explain underlying regularities in national security interests and policy."[51] This raises interesting questions about the repercussions of maintaining and bolstering a great power identity. Today one need only look to security statements to see the continuity of a worldview based on super- or great power considerations.[52] The 2002 American National Security Strategy sets out this view:

> It is time to reaffirm the essential role of American military strength. We must build and maintain our defenses beyond challenge. Our military's highest priority is to defend the United States. To do so effectively, our military must:
>
> - assure our allies and friends;
> - dissuade future military competition;
> - deter threats against US interests, allies, and friends; and
> - decisively defeat any adversary if deterrence fails.
>
> . . .
>
> Through our willingness to use force in our own defense and in defense of others, the United States demonstrates its resolve to maintain a balance of power that favors freedom.[53]

The American wars in Afghanistan and Iraq show clearly how beliefs about American power have played out in a post–Cold War world. Russia, for its part, is concerned about maintaining its great power status. The 2000 Russian National Security Concept says:

> Russia's national interests in the international sphere lie in upholding its sovereignty and strengthening its position as a great power and as one of the influential centers of a multipolar world.[54]

Questions for the future include the degree to which these powers' identities will shape intervention and how leaders explain going in and getting out. If things go badly, one should expect apologies or a recognition of failure only if the peoples' understanding of a great power's role changes. This is true because domestic political concerns are central to world leaders' behavior. This change in how great powers are expected to behave can come from leaders, the elite, or the public at large. But unless and until the leaders of great powers recognize and acknowledge that they, too, can fail, the patterns of denial will simply continue.

Appendix

Coding Subject for Soviet Television

Political

1. Soviet-Afghan political/diplomatic meetings
2. UN-Geneva talks
3. Soviet-Pakistani political/diplomatic meetings
4. Afghan-Opposition contacts/meetings
5. United States-Soviet political/diplomatic contacts/meetings
6. Soviet-Indian political/diplomatic contacts/meetings
7. Soviet-Iranian political/diplomatic contacts/meetings
8. Soviet-Chinese political/diplomatic contacts/meetings
9. United States-Iranian political/diplomatic contacts/meetings
10. United States-Pakistani political/diplomatic contacts/meetings

War

1. Actions of bandits/counterrevolutionaries/dushmani/opposition
2. United States interference in the war
3. Pakistani interference in the war
4. Interference (general/unnamed) in war
5. Casualties
6. Bandit attacks
7. Military action (general)
8. Afghani defense
9. Drugs and war
10. Chemical weapons
11. Weapons
12. Amnesty
13. Withdrawal
14. Refugees
15. Cease-fire
16. Spies

(Note: there would not be double coding within this section, i.e., if chemical weapons were coded for, weapons would not be coded. The rule was to code for the most specific category available.)

Afghanistan—Domestic Issues/Stories

1. Legal issues
2. Domestic politics
3. Economics
4. Party politics
5. Medical issues
6. Education
7. Holidays
8. National reconciliation
9. Religion
10. Elections
11. Life/lifestyle stories
12. Interim government
13. International aid—nonmilitary
14. Afghan foreign policy—not related to the war

The Soviet-Afghan Experience

1. Soviet soldiers' bravery
2. Afghanis thanking Soviets
3. Soviet soldiers returning home
4. Awards
5. New Thinking, specifically mentioned with regard to the Afghan War
6. Soviet tradition—for example, World War II
7. Soviet antiwar sentiment
8. Soviet reaction to returning vets
9. Problems of returning vets
10. POWs

Soviet-Afghan Cooperation

1. Soviet help for Afghanistan (specifically mentioned in those terms)
2. Soviet-Afghan Cooperation (general)
3. Space

NOTES

CHAPTER 1 POLITICAL COMMUNICATION AND POLICY LEGITIMACY: EXPLAINING FAILURE

1. Douglas A. Borer, *Superpowers Defeated: Vietnam and Afghanistan Compared* (London: Frank Cass, 1999).
2. Fred S. Siebert, Theodore Peterson and William Schramm, *Four Theories of the Press* (Urbana, IL: University of Illinois Press, 1956); J. Herbert Altschull, *Agents of Power* (New York: Longman, 1984); Doris Graber, "The Media and Democracy: Beyond Myths and Stereotypes," *Annual Review of Political Science*, vol. 6, 2003, 141.
3. Reuveny and Aseem argue that "the official media also began showing signs of independence in its war reporting" in 1981 (705). The examples they give are from newspapers (not television) and provide "hints" of Soviet involvement. These examples do not appear to me to be "signs of independence," but even if they are, they prove the rule, that the political leadership had a substantial degree of control over media messages. In fact, the "flood of reports and letters to newspapers against the Afghanistan war" (706) came after the directive commanding a change in coverage and follows the pattern of media campaigns of the past in many ways. Rafael Reuveny and Aseem Prakash, "The Afghanistan War and the Breakdown of the Soviet Union," *Review of International Studies*, vol. 25, no. 4, 1999, 693–708.
4. Richard Nixon, *Public Papers of the Presidents of the United* States (Washington, DC: Office of the Federal Register, National Archives and Records Service, 1970), 409.
5. Anatoly Chernyaev, *My Six Years with Gorbachev* (University Park: The Pennsylvania State University Press, 2000), 106.
6. Small and Singer coded the winners by following "the consensus among the acknowledged specialists in deciding which side 'won' each war." Melvin Small and J. David Singer, *Resort to Arms: International and Civil Wars, 1816–1980* (Beverly Hills, CA: Sage Publications, 1982), 182.
7. For each case the *New York Times*, the Foreign Broadcast Information Service, and the secondary literature were consulted for official leadership statements on the military outcome of the conflict.
8. "Yahya Khan Addresses Nation on Continuation of War," *Foreign Broadcast Information Service*, December 16, 1971, Q1.

9. Steven V. Roberts, "Caramalis on TV," *New York Times*, August 16, 1974, 61.
10. "Education Minister Makes Statement to Muscat Radio," *Foreign Broadcast Information Service*, March 14, 1978, B4.
11. "Shastri Welcomes Peace, Denounces Pakistan," *Foreign Broadcast Information Service*, September 24, 1965, 1.
12. "Transcript of the President's Address Announcing Agreement to End the War," *New York Times*, January 25, 1973, 19.
13. "Text of Gorbachev Statement Setting Forth Soviet Position on Afghan War," *New York Times*, February 9, 1988, A14.
14. Mary Stuckey, *The President as Interpreter-In-Chief* (Chatham, NJ: Chatham House Publishers, 1991); Jeffrey Tulis, *The Rhetorical Presidency* (Princeton: Princeton University Press, 1987); Robert E. Denton, Jr. and Dan F. Hahn. *Presidential Communication* (New York: Praeger, 1986).
15. Alexander George, "Domestic Constraints on Regime Change in US Foreign Policy: The Need for Policy Legitimacy," in G. J. Ikenberry, ed., *American Foreign Policy: Theoretical Essays* (Glenview: IL: Scott, Foresman & Co., 1989), 583–608.
16. For a good discussion of the conceptual issues involved in political legitimacy see Lisa Weeden, *Ambiguities of Domination* (Chicago: University of Chicago Press, 1998), 5–12.
17. George, *Domestic Constraints*, 584.
18. Ibid., 585.
19. Tulis, *Rhetorical Presidency*, 4.
20. Stuckey, *President as Interpreter-In-Chief*.
21. B. Thomas Trout, "Rhetoric Revisited: Political Legitimation and the Cold War," *International Studies Quarterly*, vol. 19, no. 3, September 1975, 256.
22. George, *Domestic Constraints*, 235.
23. Ibid.
24. Michael Billig, "Political Rhetoric," in David O. Sears, Leonie Huddy, and Robert Jervis, eds., *Oxford Handbook of Political Psychology* (Oxford: Oxford University Press, 2003), 233.
25. Frank Schimmelfennig, *The EU, NATO and the Integration of Europe: Rules and Rhetoric* (Cambridge: Cambridge University Press, 2003).
26. John Hutcheson, David Domke, Andre Billeaudeaux, and Philip Garland, "U.S. National Identity, Political Elites, and a Patriotic Press Following September 11," *Political Communication*, vol. 21, no. 1, January 2004, 28.
27. Jack Snyder, *Myths of Empire* (Ithaca, NY: Cornell University Press, 1991), 17.
28. Ibid., 2.
29. Thomas Remington, *The Truth of Authority: Ideology and Communication in the Soviet Union* (Pittsburgh: University of Pittsburgh Press, 1988).

30. Stephen M. Meyer, "The Sources and Prospects of Gorbachev's New Political Thinking on Security," *International Security*, vol. 13, no. 2, Fall 1988, 130, fn. 13.

31. Mikhail Gorbachev, *Perestroika* (New York: Harper & Row, 1987); Stephen F. Cohen, and Katrina Vanden Heuvel, *Voices of Glasnost: Interviews with Gorbachev's Reformers* (New York: W. W. Norton & Co., 1989).

32. Ellen Mickiewicz, *Split Signals* (New York: Oxford University Press, 1988). Samizdat, or underground publications, did serve this purpose, but reached so many fewer people than mass media in the Soviet Union.

33. Mary Buckley, *Redefining Russian Society and Polity* (Boulder: Westview Press, 1993).

34. Ellen Mickiewicz, *Changing Channels: Television and the Struggle for Power in Russia* (New York: Oxford University Press, 2000a), 31.

35. Mikhail Gorbachev, *Memoirs* (New York: Doubleday, 1995), 203.

36. Thomas Schelling, *Arms and Influence* (New Haven: Yale University Press, 1966); Alexander George and Richard Smoke, *Deterrence in American Foreign Policy: Theory and Practice* (New York: Columbia University Press, 1974); Glenn Snyder and Paul Diesing, *Conflict Among Nations* (Princeton: Princeton University Press, 1977); Richard Ned Lebow, "Is Crisis Management Always Possible?" *Political Science Quarterly*, vol. 102, no. 2, 1987, 181–192; Paul Huth and Bruce Russett, "What Makes Deterrence Work? Cases from 1900–1980," *World Politics*, vol. 36, no. 4, July 1984, 496–526; Paul Huth, "Extended Deterrence and the Outbreak of War," *The American Political Science Review*, vol. 82, no. 2, June 1988, 423–443.

37. George and Smoke, *Deterrence in American Foreign Policy*, 11.

38. Robert Jervis, "Introduction: Approach and Assumptions," in Robert Jervis, Richard Ned Lebow, and Janice Gross Stein, eds., *Psychology and Deterrence* (Baltimore: The Johns Hopkins University Press, 1985), 9.

39. Jonathan Mercer, *Reputation and International Politics* (Ithaca, NY: Cornell University Press, 1996), 10. See also Daryl Press, *Calculating Credibility* (Ithaca, NY: Cornell University Press, 2005).

40. Ted Hopf, *Peripheral Visions: Deterrence Theory and American Foreign Policy in the Third World, 1965–1990* (Ann Arbor: University of Michigan Press, 1994).

41. The cases here were chosen in part because they involved a substantial number of American and Soviet troops, continued over a significant period of time, and involved a large number of American and Soviet casualties and wounded. Withdrawal from this type of war would seem to be the most likely to affect reputation.

42. Robert Jervis, *The Logic of Images in International Relations* (New York: Columbia University Press, 1989), 156.

43. Patrick M. Morgan, "Saving Face for the Sake of Deterrence," in Robert Jervis, Richard Ned Lebow, and Janice Gross Stein, eds., *Psychology & Deterrence* (Baltimore: The Johns Hopkins University Press, 1985), 151.

44. James D. Fearon, "Signaling Foreign Policy Interests: Tying Hands Versus Sinking Costs," *Journal of Conflict Resolution*, vol. 41, no. 1, February 1997, 68–90; Alexandra Guisinger and Alastair Smith, "Honest Threats: The Interaction of Reputation and Political Institutions in International Crises," *Journal of Conflict Resolution*, vol. 46, no. 2, April 2002, 175–200; Lisa Martin, "Credibility, Costs, and Institutions: Cooperation on Economic Sanctions," *World Politics*, vol. 45, no. 3, April 1993, 406–432.

45. Ted Hopf, *Social Construction of International Politics: Identities and Foreign Policies, Moscow, 1955 & 1999* (Ithaca, NY: Cornell University Press, 2002); Jeffrey Checkel, "Social Constructivisms in Global and European Politics: A Review Essay," *Review of International Studies*, vol. 30, no. 2, April 2004, 229–244; Jeffrey Checkel, *Ideas and International Political Change: Soviet/Russian Behavior and the End of the Cold War* (New Haven: Yale University Press, 1997); Yosef Lapid and Friedrich Kratochwil, *The Return of Culture and Identity in IR Theory* (Boulder: Lynne Reinner, 1996); Alexander Wendt, *Social Theory of International Politics* (Cambridge, UK: Cambridge University Press, 1999); Vendulka Kubalkova, ed., *Foreign Policy in a Constructed World* (Armonk, NY: ME Sharpe, 2001); Peter J. Katzenstein, ed., *The Culture of National Security: Norms and Identity in World Politics* (New York: Columbia University Press, 1996).

46. Marc Lynch, *State Interests and Public Spheres* (New York: Columbia University Press, 1999), 22.

47. Alexander Wendt, "Identity and Structural Change in International Politics," in Lapid and Kratochwil, eds., *The Return of Culture and Identity in IR Theory*, 57.

48. Lynch, *State Interests and Public Spheres*; Thomas Risse, "Let's Argue: Communicative Action in World Politics," *International Organization*, vol. 54, no. 1, Winter 2000, 1–39; Thomas Risse-Kaplan, "Ideas Do Not Float Freely: Transnational Coalitions, Domestic Structure, and the End of the Cold War," *International Organization*, vol. 48, no. 2, Spring 1994, 185–214; Thomas Risse-Kaplan, "Constructivism and International Institutions: Toward Conversations Across Paradigms," in Ira Katznelson and Helen Milner, eds., *Political Science: State of the Discipline* (New York: W. W. Norton & Co., 2002), 597–623; Schimmelfennig, *EU, NATO and the Integration of Europe*; Harald Muller, "Arguing, Bargaining and All That: Communicative Action, Rationalist Theory, and the Logic of Appropriateness in International Relations," *European Journal of International Relations*, vol. 10, no. 3, September 2004, 395–435; Darren Hawkins, "Explaining

Costly International Institutions: Persuasion and Enforceable Human Rights Norms," *International Studies Quarterly*, vol. 48, no. 4, December 2004, 779–804.

49. Lynch, *State Interests and Public Spheres*, 44.
50. Checkel, "Social Constructivisms in Global and European Politics," 234.
51. Lynch, *State Interests and Public Spheres*, 18.
52. Denton and Hahn, 276.
53. Stephen Ansolabehere, Roy Behr, and Shanto Iyengar, *The Media Game: American Politics in the Television Age* (New York: Macmillan, 1993), 103. See also, Benjamin Page, *Who Deliberates? Mass Media in Modern Democracy* (Chicago: University of Chicago Press, 1996); Doris Graber, *Media Power in Politics* (Washington, DC: CQ Press, 2000).
54. Mickiewicz, *Changing Channels*.
55. Ellen Mickiewicz, "Institutional Incapacity, the Attentive Public, and Media Pluralism in Russia," in Richard Gunther and Anthony Mughan, eds., *Democracy and the Media: A Comparative Perspective* (Cambridge: Cambridge University Press, 2000b), 95.
56. Mickiewicz, *Changing Channels*, 52.
57. Mickiewicz, *Split Signals*.
58. Ibid., 32.
59. Roper Organization, *An Extended View of Public Attitudes Toward Television and Other Mass Media* (New York: Television Information Office, 1971).
60. Fred S. Siebert, Theodore Peterson, and William Schramm, *Four Theories of the Press* (Urbana, IL: University of Illinois Press, 1956); J. Herbert Altschull, *Agents of Power* (New York: Longman, 1984).
61. Barbara Pfetsch, "Government News Management," in Doris Graber, Denis McQuail, and Pippa Norris, eds., *The Politics of News The News of Politics* (Washington, DC: Congressional Quarterly Press, 1998), 70–93; Ansolabehere, Behr and Iyengar, *The Media Game*, 1993.
62. Michael Baruch Grossman and Matha Joynt Kumar, *Portraying the President: The White House and the News Media* (Baltimore: The Johns Hopkins University Press, 1981), 29.
63. Grossman and Kumar, *Portraying the President*, 28.
64. Shanto Iyengar and Donald R. Kinder, *News that Matters* (Chicago: University of Chicago, 1987), 124. See also Roy L. Behr and Shanto Iyengar, "Television News, Real-World Cues, and Changes in the Public Agenda," *Public Opinion Quarterly*, vol. 49, no. 1, Spring 1985, 38–57.
65. Richard E. Neustadt, *Presidential Power* (New York: John Wiley and Sons, 1980), 236.
66. David L. Paletz and Robert M. Entman, *Media, Power, Politics* (New York: The Free Press, 1981), 56.
67. Michael Baruch Grossman and Frances E. Rourke, "The Media and the Presidency: An Exchange Analysis," *Political Science Quarterly*, vol. 91, no. 3, Fall 1976, 456–457.

68. Edward Jay Epstein, *News from Nowhere* (New York: Random House, 1973), xviii.
69. For information and literature on more recent organizational issues see Jan E. Leighley, *Mass Media and Politics: A Social Science Perspective* (Boston: Houghton Mifflin Co., 2004), especially chapter 4, "Newsgathering, Business, Profession, and Organization."
70. Epstein, *News from Nowhere*, 261.
71. Grossman and Kumar, *Portraying the President*, 253.
72. Gaye Tuchman, "Objectivity as Strategic Ritual: An Examination of Newsmen's Notions of Objectivity," *American Journal of Sociology*, vol. 77, no. 4, January 1972, 660–679.
73. Epstein, *News from Nowhere*, 1973; Leighley, *Mass Media and Politics*, 2004.
74. I purposely avoid the term persuade here, as it is conceptually very fuzzy. Persuasion is sometimes defined to mean that "A gets B to do or believe or accept or reject something which he would not otherwise do or believe or accept or reject, by exhibiting reasons or by exhibiting consequences of alternatives confronting B." Peter Burnell and Andrew Reeve, "Persuasion as a Political Concept," *British Journal of Political Science*, vol. 14, no. 4, October 1984, 394–395. Others use the term quite loosely to mean convince or change the beliefs of others. The point here is not that the audience is convinced to believe due to reasoned argument, but that the views held by elite and public allow the leader to rule without significant challenge or constraints.
75. Ellen Mickiewicz, *Media and the Russian Public* (New York: Praeger, 1981).
76. Joseph J. Mathews, *Reporting the Wars* (Minneapolis: University of Minneapolis Press, 1957).
77. Ibid., 175.
78. Ibid.
79. Denton and Hahn, *Presidential Communication*, 275.
80. Mickiewicz, *Split Signals*, 57.
81. Karen S. Johnson-Cartee, *News Narratives and News Framing: Constructing Political Reality* (Lanhan, MD: Rowman & Littlefield, 2005), 129.
82. Lynch, *State Interests and Public Spheres*, 262.
83. Erving Goffman, *Frame Analysis: An Essay on the Organization of Experience* (Cambridge: Harvard University Press, 1974); Todd Gitlin, *The Whole World is Watching: Mass Media in the Making and Unmaking of the New Left* (Berkeley: University of California Press, 1980); Doug McAdam, John D. McCarthy, and Mayer N. Zald, eds., *Comparative Perspectives on Social Movements: Political Opportunities, Mobilizing Structures, and Cultural Framing* (New York: Cambridge University Press, 1996).
84. Stephen D. Reese, Oscar H. Gandy, Jr., August E. Grant, eds., *Framing Public Life: Perspectives on Media and Our Understanding*

of the Social World (Mahwah, NJ: Lawrence Erlbaum Associates, 2001); Gadi Wolfsfeld, *Media and Political Conflict: News from the Middle East* (Cambridge: Cambridge University Press, 1997); Robert Entman, R. *Projections of Power: Framing News, Public Opinion, and US Foreign Policy* (Chicago: University of Chicago Press, 2004); Dietram A. Scheufele, "Framing as a Theory of Media Effects," *Journal of Communication*, vol. 49, no. 1, Winter 1999, 103–122.

85. Amos Tversky and Daniel Kahneman, "Rational Choice and the Framing of Decisions," in Robin M. Hogarth and Melvin W. Reder, eds., *Rational Choice: The Contrast Between Economics and Psychology* (Chicago: University of Chicago Press, 1987); James N. Druckman, "Political Preference Formation: Competition, Deliberation, and the (Ir)relevance of Framing Effects," *American Political Science Review*, vol. 98, no. 4, November 2004, 671–686; George A. Quattrone and Amos Tversky, "Contrasting Rational and Psychological Analyses of Political Choice," *American Political Science Review*, vol. 82, no. 3, September, 1988, 719–736.

86. McAdam, McCarthy, and Zald, *Comparative Perspectives on Social Movements*, 6.

87. Entman, *Projections of Power*, 5.

88. Wolfsfeld, *Media and Political Conflict*, 35.

89. James W. Tankard, Jr., "The Empirical Approach to the Study of Media Framing," in Reese, Gandy, and Grant, *Framing Public Life*, 98.

90. Entman, *Projections of Power*, 4.

91. Robin Brown, "Getting to War: Communications and Mobilization in the 2002–2003 Iraq Crisis," in Philip Seib, ed., *Media and Conflict in the Twentieth Century* (New York: Palgrave, 2005).

92. Zhongdang Pan and Gerald Kosicki, "Framing as a Strategic Action in Public Deliberation," in Reese, Gandy, and Grant, *Framing Public Life*, 59.

93. David A. Snow, E. Burke Rochford, Steven K. Worden, and Robert D. Benford, "Frame Alignment Processes: Micromobilization and Movement Participation," *American Sociological Review*, vol. 51, no. 4, August 1986, 464–481.

94. Gaye Tuchman, *Making News: A Study in the Construction of Reality* (New York: Free Press, 1978), 209.

95. Robert H. Miller, "Vietnam: Folly, Quagmire, or Inevitiability?" *Studies in Conflict and Terrorism*, vol. 5, no. 2, April 1992, 114–115.

96. Soviet television coverage was obtained for this period from the International Media and Communications Program at Emory University.

97. Alexander George, "Case Studies and Theory Development." Draft Paper prepared for the Second Annual Symposium on Information Processing in Organizations, Carnegie-Mellon University, October 15–16, 1982. See also Alexander George and Andrew Bennett,

Case Studies and Theory Development in the Social Sciences (Cambridge: MIT Press, 2005).

98. Richard Nixon, *RN: The Memoirs of Richard Nixon* (New York: Grosset & Dunlap, 1978); Henry Kissinger, *Ending the Vietnam War* (New York: Simon & Schuster, 2003) and Henry Kissinger, *White House Years* (Boston: Little, Brown and Co., 1979); Herbert Klein, *Making it Perfectly Clear* (Garden City, NY: Doubleday, 1980); Raymond Price, *With Nixon* (New York: Viking Press, 1977); H. R. Haldeman, *The Haldeman Diaries: Inside the Nixon White House* (New York: G. P. Putnam's Sons, 1994).

99. This period included 19 full weeks of coverage: 4 weeks in 1985, 7 weeks in 1986, 7 in 1987 and 1 in 1988.

Chapter 2   War Waging and Reassessment: Vietnam

1. The Vietnam War has been extensively studied by scholars. The major works used in this chapter include: Daniel Hallin, *The Uncensored War: The Media and Vietnam* (Berkeley: University of California Press, 1986); Kathleen Turner, *Lyndon Johnson's Dual War* (Chicago: University of Chicago, 1985); Stanley Karnow, *Vietnam: A History* (New York: The Viking Press, 1983); Herbert Schandler, *The Unmaking of a President* (Princeton: Princeton University Press, 1977); Leslie Gelb and Richard Betts, *The Irony of Vietnam: The System Worked* (Washington, DC: The Brookings Institution, 1979); Brian VanDeMark, *Into the Quagmire* (New York: Oxford University Press, 1991); Melvin Small, *Johnson, Nixon, and the Doves* (New Brunswick: Rutgers University Press, 1988); David Halberstam, *The Powers That Be* (New York: Bantam Doubleday Dell Publishing Group, 1979); Lyndon Baines Johnson, *The Vantage Point* (New York: Holt, Rinehart and Winston, 1971); Robert Dalek, *Flawed Giant: Lyndon Johnson and his Times, 1961–1973* (New York: Oxford University Press, 1998). In addition, primary sources from *Vietnam, The Media, and Public Support for the War: Selections from the Holdings of the Lyndon B. Johnson Library* (Frederick, MD: University Publications of America, 1986), microfilm, 11 reels.

2. Small, *Johnson, Nixon, and the Doves*, 24–60.

3. Jane E. Holl, "From the Streets of Washington to the Roofs of Saigon: Domestic Politics and the Termination of the Vietnam War," PhD Dissertation, Stanford University, 1989, 101.

4. David M. Barrett, ed., *Lyndon B. Johnson's Vietnam Papers: A Documentary Collection*, (College Station, TX.: Texas A&M University Press, 1997), 108.

5. Michael Beschloss, *Reaching for Glory: Lyndon Johnson's Secret White House Tapes, 1964–1965* (New York: Simon & Schuster, 2001), 181–182; Conversation with Everett Dirksen, Wednesday, February 17, 1965, 6:20 p.m.

6. Beschloss, *Reaching for Glory*, 166. LBJ to Robert McNamara, February 26, 1965.
7. Beschloss, *Reaching for Glory*, 211. Conversation with Richard Russell, March 6, 1965, 12:05 p.m.
8. Ibid., 213. Conversation with Richard Russell, March 6, 1965, 12:05 p.m.
9. Dalek, *Flawed Giant*, 257.
10. Karnow, *Vietnam*, 420.
11. Turner, *Lyndon Johnson's Dual War*, 145–146.
12. Beschloss, *Reaching for Glory*, 378, LBJ to Robert McNamara, July 2, 1965.
13. Doris Kearns Goodwin, *Lyndon Johnson and the American Dream* (New York: Harper & Row, 1976), 253.
14. Quoted in Kearns, *Lyndon Johnson and the American Dream*, 253.
15. U.S. President. "Annual Message to the Congress on the State of the Union," *Public Papers of the Presidents of the United States Lyndon B. Johnson* (Washington, DC: Office of the Federal Register,1965), vol.1, January 4, 3.
16. Karnow, *Vietnam*, 414.
17. Hallin, *Uncensored War*, 92.
18. "Annual Message to the Congress on the State of the Union," *Public Papers of the President Lyndon B. Johnson, 1965*, vol. 1, January 4, 3.
19. *Public Papers of the President Lyndon B. Johnson, 1965*, vol. 1, 134, 153, 205.
20. Beschloss, *Reaching for Glory*, 192–193, Tapes, February 25, 1965, 10:25 a.m.
21. Beschloss, *Reaching for Glory*, 195.
22. *Public Papers of the Presidents, 1965*, vol. 1, 300–301.
23. Small, *Johnson, Nixon, and the Doves*, 33, 249.
24. Harry G. Summers, Jr., *On Strategy: A Critical Analysis of the Vietnam War* (Novato, CA: Presidio Press, 1982), 25.
25. *Public Papers of the Presidents, 1965*, vol. 1, 395.
26. Hallin, *Uncensored War*, 93.
27. *Public Papers of the Presidents, 1965*, vol. 1, 395–396.
28. *The Johnson Presidential Press Conferences*, vol. 1 (New York: Earl M. Coleman Enterprises, Inc., 1978).
29. *The Johnson Presidential Press Conferences*, vol. 1, 300.
30. Ibid., 301.
31. Ibid., 334 and 339.
32. Ibid., 339.
33. Hallin, *Uncensored War*, 101.
34. Turner, *Lyndon Johnson's Dual War*, 150.
35. Ibid., 145–146.
36. "Fact Sheet: The US Commitment to Freedom," *Vietnam, The Media, and Public Support for the War*, Reel 11.
37. *The Lyndon Johnson Presidential Press Conferences*, vol. 1, 349.

38. Hallin, *Uncensored War*, 61.
39. Kearns, *Lyndon Johnson and the American Dream*, 255.
40. *The Gallup Poll: Public Opinion 1935–1971*, vol. 3, (New York: Random House, 1972), 1925.
41. *The Gallup Poll*, 1967.
42. Turner, *Lyndon Johnson's Dual War*, 3.
43. Ibid., 147.
44. Hallin, *Uncensored War*, 29, 30.
45. Beschloss, *Reaching for Glory*, 309.
46. Ibid.
47. Ibid., 350, LBJ conversation with Robert McNamara, June 10, 1865, 6:40 p.m.
48. Turner, *Lyndon Johnson's Dual War*, 74; Dalek, *Flawed Giant*, 253.
49. Quoted in Kearns, *Lyndon Johnson and the American Dream*, 252.
50. Turner, *Lyndon Johnson's Dual War*, 115.
51. Beschloss, *Reaching for Glory*, 272. conversation with Arthur "Tex" Goldschmidt, director, Technical Assistance, Special Fund Operations, UN, April 8, 1965, 10:27 a.m.
52. Beschloss, *Reaching for Glory*, 186.
53. *Public Papers of the Presidents, 1965*, vol. 2, 923.
54. Turner, *Lyndon Johnson's Dual War*, 101.
55. Hallin, *Uncensored War*, 105.
56. Emmette S. Redford and Richard T. McCulley, *White House Operations: The Johnson Presidency* (Austin: University of Texas Press, 1986).
57. Turner, *Lyndon Johnson's Dual War*, 100–104.
58. Ibid., 103.
59. Small, *Johnson, Nixon, and the Doves*, 32.
60. Turner, *Lyndon Johnson's Dual War*, 113.
61. Ibid., 101.
62. Ibid.
63. Hallin, *Uncensored War*, 61.
64. Beschloss, *Reaching for Glory*, 216, Conversation with Robert McNamara, March 6, 1965, 2:32 p.m.
65. Turner, *Lyndon Johnson's Dual War*, 13.
66. Ibid., 102.
67. Quoted in Redford and McCulley, *White House Operations*, 169.
68. Turner, *Lyndon Johnson's Dual War*, 80.
69. Ibid., 106.
70. "Memorandum for the Record, August 3 (1965) Dinner Meeting on the Information Problem," *Vietnam, The Media, and Public Support for the War*, Reel 6. Emphasis in the original.
71. Ibid.
72. Ibid.
73. "Memorandum for Mr. Cater from Gordon Chase, August 23, 1965," *Vietnam, The Media, and Public Support for the War*, Reel 6.

74. "Memorandum for the Record. Public Affairs Policy Committee for Vietnam, August 23, 1965," *Vietnam, The Media, and Public Support for the War*, Reel 6.

75. "Memorandum for the Record. Public Affairs Policy Committee for Vietnam, November 9, 1965," *Vietnam, The Media, and Public Support for the War*, Reel 6.

76. "Memorandum for the Record. Public Affairs Policy Committee for Vietnam, November 29, 1965," *Vietnam, The Media, and Public Support for the War*, Reel 6.

77. Hallin, *Uncensored War*, 114–158.

78. Ibid., 142–147.

79. Ibid., 158.

80. *Public Papers of Lyndon B. Johnson, 1968–69*, vol. 1, 469–476.

81. Ibid., 2.

82. Ibid., 25.

83. Ibid.

84. Ibid.

85. Ibid., 469–476.

86. Small, *Johnson, Nixon, and the Doves*, 136–137.

87. Peter Braestrup, *Big Story: How the American Press and Television Reported and Interpreted the Crises of Tet in Vietnam and Washington* (Boulder: Westview, 1977); Small, *Johnson, Nixon, and the Doves*, 133; Turner, *Lyndon Johnson's Dual War*, 217–222.

88. Dalek, *Flawed Giant*, 526. Although Dalek argues that the polls were not decisive in LBJ's decision not to run.

89. Dalek, *Flawed Giant*, 528.

90. This group included Dean Acheson, General Omar Bradley, George Ball, Mac Bundy, Arthur Dean, Douglas Dillon, Abe Fortas, Averell Harriman, Henry Cabot Lodge, Robert Murphy, and Max Taylor.

91. Bundy, quoted in Small, *Johnson, Nixon, and the Doves*, 146.

92. Schandler, *Unmaking of a President*, 301.

93. Halberstam, *Powers That Be*, 711.

94. Turner, *Lyndon Johnson's Dual War*, 220.

95. Ibid., 221.

96. Ibid., 222; Holl, 157.

97. *Public Papers of the Presidents, 1968*, vol. 1, 155.

98. Small, *Johnson, Nixon, and the Doves*, 139.

99. Halberstam, *Powers That Be*, 711.

100. Turner, *Lyndon Johnson's Dual War*, 223.

101. Johnson, *Vantage Point*, 421.

102. *Public Papers of the Presidents, 1965*, vol. 1, 287.

103. Ibid., 414.

104. Ibid., 424.

105. Ibid., 469.

106. Ibid., 170.

107. Ibid.

108. *Public Papers of the Presidents, 1965*, vol. 1, 170.
109. Gallup, July 1967. Question: "In view of developments since we entered the fighting in Vietnam, do you think the U.S. made a mistake sending troops to fight in Vietnam?"
110. Quoted in Goodwin, *Lyndon Johnson and the American Dream*, 343.
111. Hallin, *Uncensored War*, 162.
112. Walter Cronkite's "*We are mired in Stalemate*" Broadcast, February 27, 1968, http://faculty.smu.edu/dsimon/Change%20—Cronkite.html Accessed October 23, 2005.
113. Johnson, *Vantage Point*, 380.
114. Small, Johnson, Nixon, and the Doves; Karnow, Vietnam.

CHAPTER 3 WITHDRAWAL AND
AFTERMATH: VIETNAM

1. Richard Nixon, *The Memoirs of Richard Nixon* (New York: Grosset & Dunlap, 1978), 392.
2. U.S. President, *Public Papers of the Presidents of the United States Richard Nixon* (Washington, DC: Office of the Federal Register, 1969), 718.
3. Ibid.
4. Stanley Karnow, *Vietnam: A History* (New York: The Viking Press, 1983), 697–699.
5. Jane E. Holl, "From the Streets of Washington to the Roofs of Saigon: Domestic Politics and the Termination of the Vietnam War," PhD Dissertation, Stanford University, 1989, 248; Henry Kissinger, *A History of America's Involvement In and Extrication From the Vietnam War* (New York: Simon & Schuster, 2003).
6. Henry Kissinger, *White House Years* (Boston: Little, Brown and Co., 1979), 271; see also Kissinger, *A History of America's Involvement*.
7. Kissinger, *White House Years*, 271.
8. Holl, "From the Streets of Washington," 232, fn. 47.
9. Ibid., 248.
10. Nixon, *Memoirs of Richard Nixon*, 413, cited in Holl, "From the Streets of Washington," 224, fn.39.
11. Memo, Herb Klein to the President, October 17, 1969, including Fact Sheet, folder "Action Memos," Box 5, Herbert G. Klein Files, White House Special Files (WHSF), Nixon Presidential Materials Staff.
12. "Presidential Objectives," October–December 1969, folder "HRH Public Relations," Box 141, H. R. Haldeman Files, WHSF, Nixon Presidential Materials Staff.
13. Herbert Klein, *Making It Perfectly Clear* (Garden City, NY: Doubleday, 1980), 311.
14. Harry G. Summers, Jr., *On Strategy: A Critical Analysis of the Vietnam War* (Novato, CA: Presidio Press, 1982), 105.
15. Summers, *On Strategy*, 177.

16. Fact Sheet comparing Vietnam conditions on January 20 and October 1969, folder "Action Memos," Box 5, Herbert G. Klein Files, White House Special Files (WHSF), Nixon Presidential Materials Staff, 2.
17. Jeffrey Kimball, *The Vietnam War Files: Uncovering the Secret History of Nixon-Era Strategy* (Lawrence: University Press of Kansas, 2004), 42–44; Daniel Hallin, *The Uncensored War: The Media and Vietnam* (Berkeley: University of California Press, 1986).
18. *Public Papers of the Presidents of the United States, Richard Nixon*, 908.
19. Richard Nixon, *No More Vietnams* (New York: Arbor House, 1985), 114.
20. *Public Papers of the Presidents of the United, States Richard Nixon*, 1969, 425.
21. Ibid., 906.
22. Ibid., 373.
23. Ibid., 407.
24. William E. Porter. *Assault on the Media: The Nixon Years* (Ann Arbor: University of Michigan Press, 1976), 61.
25. *Public Papers of the Presidents of the United States Richard Nixon*, 1970, 407.
26. Nixon, *Memoirs of Richard Nixon*, 452.
27. *Public Papers of the Presidents of the United States Richard Nixon*, 1970, 409.
28. Klein, *Making It Perfectly Clear*, 339.
29. Ibid., 340. Underlining in the original.
30. Ibid., 260.
31. *Public Papers of the Presidents of the United States Richard Nixon*, 1970, 480.
32. Ibid.,1971, 524.
33. Karnow, *Vietnam*, 645.
34. Kissinger, *White House Years*, 286.
35. Kimball, *Vietnam War Files*, 45.
36. Kissinger, *White House Years*, 286.
37. *Public Papers of the Presidents of the United States Richard Nixon*, 1970, 909.
38. Nixon, *Memoirs of Richard Nixon*, 410.
39. Ibid., 413.
40. The Gallup Poll: Public Opinion 1972–1977, vol. 1 (Wilmington, Delaware: Scholarly Resources, Inc., 1978), 2222.
41. *Public Papers of the Presidents of the United States Richard Nixon*, 1968, 914.
42. Holl, "From the Streets of Washington," 256.
43. Kissinger, *History of America's Involvement*.
44. Holl, "From the Streets of Washington," 268.
45. Nixon, *Memoirs of Richard Nixon*, 717.
46. Kissinger, *History of America's Involvement*, 409.

47. Nixon, *Memoirs of Richard Nixon*, 726.
48. Ibid., 734.
49. Ibid.
50. Kissinger, *History of America's Involvement*, 418.
51. Nixon, *Memoirs of Richard Nixon*, 741.
52. Klein, *Making It Perfectly Clear*, 389.
53. Ibid., 389.
54. Ibid.
55. Kimball, *Vietnam War Files*, 289.
56. "Transcript of the President's Address Announcing Agreement to End the War," *New York Times*, January 25, 1973, 19.
57. Kimball, *Vietnam War Files*, 289.
58. Ibid., 290.
59. Ibid.
60. The Gallup Poll, 93–93.
61. Ibid.
62. Kimball, *Vietnam War Files*, 139.
63. Anatoliy Dobrynin, *In Confidence: Moscow's Ambassador to America's Six Cold War Presidents, 1962–1986* (New York: Times Books, 1995), 200.
64. Kimball, *Vietnam War Files*, 139.
65. Ibid., 143.
66. Ibid., 145.
67. Patrick M. Morgan, "Saving Face for the Sake of Deterrence," in Robert Jervis, Richard Ned Lebow, and Janice Gross Stein, eds., *Psychology & Deterrence* (Baltimore: The Johns Hopkins University Press, 1985), 150.
68. Kimball, *Vietnam War Files*, 45.
69. *Public Papers of the Presidents of the United States, Richard Nixon, 1970*, 479.
70. Kimball, *Vietnam War Files*, 138–139, 186–193.
71. Kissinger, *History of America's Involvement*, 56.
72. Nixon, *Memoirs of Richard Nixon*, 354.
73. Klein, *Making It Perfectly Clear*, 285.
74. Richard Nixon, *Six Crises* (Garden City, NY: Doubleday, 1962), 423.
75. Klein, *Making It Perfectly Clear*, 76.
76. Memo, Haldeman to Chapin, Klein and Ziegler, March 20, 1969, Folder "Haldeman, 1 of 3," Box 1, Klein Files, WHSF, Nixon Presidential Materials Staff.
77. Nixon, *Memoirs of Richard Nixon*, 354.
78. Klein, *Making It Perfectly Clear*, 241.
79. Ibid., 61.
80. James Keogh, *President Nixon and the Press* (New York: Funk & Wagnalls, 1972), 39.
81. Nixon, *Memoirs of Richard Nixon*, 350.
82. News summary, September 1969, Folder "September 1969," Box 30, Presidential Office Files, WHSF, Nixon Presidential Materials Staff, Nixon's underlining. Emphasis in the original.

83. Ibid.
84. John Ehrlichman. *Witness to Power* (New York: Simon & Schuster, 1982), 273.
85. Porter, *Assault on the Media*, 26.
86. Ibid., 27.
87. Klein, *Making It Perfectly Clear*, 69.
88. Ibid., 105.
89. "Will the Press Be Out to 'Get' Nixon?" *US News & World Report*, December 2, 1968, 2; see also Joseph C. Spear, *Presidents and the Press: the Nixon Legacy* (Cambridge: MIT Press, 1984), 65.
90. Klein, *Making It Perfectly Clear*, 69.
91. Ibid., 285.
92. Memo, Haldeman to Buchanan, Price, Safire, Keogh, Moore, Ziegler, Klein, Colson, Chapin, Finch, Rumsfeld, June 22, 1970, Folder "Press and Media, #1, Part 2," Box 141, Haldeman Files, WHSF, Nixon Presidential Materials Staff.
93. Ibid.
94. Memo, Gregg Petersmeyer to Haldeman, July 28, 1970, Folder "Press and Media, #2, Part 1," Box 141, Haldeman Files, WHSF, Nixon Presidential Materials Staff.
95. Memo, Colson to Haldeman, June 24, 1970, Folder "Press and Media, #1, Part 2," Box 141, Haldeman Files, WHSF, Nixon Presidential Materials Staff.
96. Quoted in Porter, *Assault on the Media*, 35.
97. Of course, all presidents must rely on staff for reports and briefings. The news summaries produced by Buchanan and staff were, however, highly critical of television and its coverage of Richard Nixon and his policies. Klein, in fact, did not quite see it that way. Nixon was getting a highly skewed view of television coverage.
98. Memo, Haldeman to Klein, March 27, 1969, folder "Haldeman," 3 of 3, Box 1, Klein Files, WHSF, Nixon Presidential Materials Staff.
99. News Summary, July 1969, Folder "July 1969," Box 30, Presidential Office Files, WHSF, Nixon Presidential Materials Staff.
100. News Summary, September 1969, Folder "September 1969," Box 30, Presidential Office Files, WHSF, Nixon Presidential Materials Staff.
101. Saturday Night Television Coverage of the President, September 1969, Folder "September 1969," Box 30, Presidential Office Files, WHSF, Nixon Presidential Materials Staff.
102. News Summary, October 1969, Folder "October 1969," Box 31, Presidential Office Files, WHSF, Nixon Presidential Materials Staff.
103. Television Report, October 7, 1969, Folder "October 1969," Box 31, Presidential Office Files, WHSF, Nixon Presidential Materials Staff.
104. Press Commentators' Attitudes Toward the Nixon Administration and Memo, Haldeman to Klein, June 3, 1969, Folder "Haldeman," 1 of 3, Box 1, WHSF, Nixon Presidential Materials Staff.

105. Memo, Herbert Klein to the President, December 5, 1969, Folder "Press and Media, #2," Part 2, Box 141, WHSF, Haldeman, #141, Nixon Presidential Materials Staff.
106. News summary, December 1970, Folder "December 1970," Box 32, Presidential Office Files, WHSF, Nixon Presidential Materials Staff.
107. Ibid.
108. News summary, December 27, 1970. Folder "December 1970," Box 32, Presidential Office Files, WHSF, Nixon Presidential Materials Staff. The White House and PBS is a subject of much study; however, this book does not examine that particular facet of White House communication policy. See Porter, *Assault on the Media*, 145–154. The September 23, 1971 news summary contained the following passage:

    Robert MacNeil and Sander Vanocur will anchor a weekly political program on Public Broadcasting in '72. It will "try to reverse the usual focus of political reporting from the politician down to the people." Said Vanocur: "we have taken an institutional view of politics in the past . . . in a sense will be doing psychological reporting." (We can hardly wait.) . . . Sen. Ervin's Constitutional Rights sub-comm. will begin next week exploring the growing deterioration in relations between the press and the government.

    Nixon's marginalia reads, "This is the last straw. Cut all funds for Public Broadcasting immediately." (Just work it out so that the House appropriations committee gets the word.)

    News summary, September 23, 1971, Folder "September 1971," Box 33. Presidential Office Files, WHSF, Nixon Presidential Materials Staff.
109. Memo, Buchanan to the President (per Haldeman), September 28, 1969, Folder "September 1969," Box 30, Presidential Office Files, WHSF, Nixon Presidential Materials Staff. Emphasis in the original.
110. Quoted in Porter, *Assault on the Media*, 44.
111. Nixon, *Memoirs of Richard Nixon*, 411.
112. Ibid., 411.
113. Porter, *Assault on the Media* 46.
114. "Transcript of Address by Agnew Criticizing Television on Its Coverage of the News," *New York Times*, November 13, 1969.
115. Memo, Colson to Haldeman, February 5, 1970, Folder "Douglas Commission," Box 133, Charles W. Colson Files, WHSF, Nixon Presidential Materials Staff.
116. New summary, February 15, 1970, Folder "February 1970," Box 31, POF, WHSF, Nixon Presidential Materials Staff. Emphasis in the original.
117. Ibid.
118. Memo, Allin to Haleman and Magruder, July 7, 1970, Folder "Haldeman II," 2 of 5, Box 1, Klein Files, WHSF, Nixon Presidential Materials Staff.

119. Memo, Patrick Buchanan to the President (per HRH), June 23, 1970, folder Haldeman II, 1 of 5, Box #1, Klein Files, WHSF, Nixon Presidential Materials Staff. Emphasis in the original.

120. Memo, Haldeman to Klein, July 20, 1970, Folder "White House Action Memos," Box 6, Klein files, WHSF, Nixon Presidential Materials Staff.

121. Klein, *Making it Perfectly Clear*, 284–285.

122. Memo, Colson to Haldeman, September 25, 1970, Folder "Press and Media, #1, Part 1" Box 141, Haldeman Files, WHSF, Nixon Presidential Materials Staff.

123. Ibid.

124. Ibid.

125. See, for example, Spear, *Presidents and the Press*, 158–161.

126. Memo, Haldeman to Colson, September 21, 1970, Folder "Press and Media, #1, Part 1," Box 141, Haldeman Files, WHSF, Nixon Presidential Materials Staff.

127. Memo, Colson to Haldeman, September 25, 1970, Folder "Press and Media, #1, Part 1," Box 141, Haldeman Files, WHSF, Nixon Presidential Materials Staff.

128. News summary, September 1970, Folder "September 1970," Box 32, Presidential Office Files, WHSF, Nixon Presidential Materials Staff.

129. Nixon, *Memoirs of Richard Nixon*, 496.

130. Memo, Scali to Colson, April 14, 1871, Folder "Action Memos, 5 of 7," Box 1, Scali Files, WHSF, Nixon Presidential Materials Staff.

131. Ibid.

132. *Public Papers of the Presidents of the United States, Richard Nixon*, 1974, 210.

133. Ibid., 325.

134. Nixon, *Memoirs of Richard Nixon*, 514–515.

CHAPTER 4   WAR WAGING AND
REASSESSMENT: AFGHANISTAN

1. Mikhail Gorbachev, *Memoirs* (New York: Doubleday, 1995), 171.

2. "CC CPSU Politburo Session March 17–18, 1979," The September 11th Sourcebooks, Volume II: Afghanistan: Lessons from the Last War, in Svetlana Savranskaya, ed., *The Soviet Experience in Afghanistan: Russian Documents and Memoirs*, October 9, 2001, located in National Security Archive documents, http:// www.gwu.edu/~nsarchiv/ NSAEBB/NSAEBB57/r1.pdf Accessed October 14, 2005.

3. Igor Belyaev and Anatoly Gromyko, "Tak my voshli v Afhanistan," *Literaturnaya Gazeta*, 38, September 20,1989, 14; Sarah Mendelson, *Changing Course: Ideas, Politics, and the Soviet Withdrawal from Afghanistan* (Princeton: Princeton University Press, 1998); Michael McGwire, *Perestroika and Soviet National*

Security (Washington, DC: The Brookings Institution, 1991). The broader literature on the war in Afghanistan includes Diego Cordovez and Selig S. Harrison, *Out of Afghanistan: The Inside Story of the Soviet Withdrawal* (New York: Oxford University Press, 1995); Mark Galeotti, *Afghanistan: The Soviet Union's Last War* (London: Frank Cass, 1994); Fred Halliday, "Soviet Foreign Policymaking and the Afghanistan War: From 'Second Mongolia' to 'Bleeding Wound,' " *Review of International Studies*, vol. 25, no. 4, October 1999, 675–691; Rafael Reuveny and Aseem Prakash, "The Afghanistan War and the Breakdown of the Soviet Union," *Review of International Studies*, vol. 25, no. 4, October 1999, 693–708; Riaz M. Khan, *Untying the Afghan Knot: Negotiating Soviet Withdrawal* (Durham: Duke University Press, 1991); Amin Saikal and William Maley, eds., *The Soviet Withdrawal from Afghanistan* (Cambridge: Cambridge University Press, 1989); Carolyn McGiffert Ekedahl and Melvin A. Goodman, *The Wars of Eduard Shevardnadze* (University Park: The Pennsylvania State University Press, 1997); Lester W. Grau and Michael A. Gress, *The Soviet–Afghan War: How a Superpower Fought and Lost* (Lawrence: University Press of Kansas, 2002). Soviet/Russian sources include Aleksandr Antonovich Liakhovskii, *Plamia Afgana* (Moskva: Vagrios, 1999); Aleksandr Antonovich Liakhovskii, *Tragedia I Doblest Afgana* (Moskva: GPI Iskona, 1995); Gennadii Korzh, *Afganskoe dos'e: istoriia voiny SSSR v Afganistane* (Khar'kov: Folio, 2003); Anatoly S. Chernyaev, *My Six Years with Gorbachev* (University Park: The Pennsylvania State University Press, 2000); Georgi Arbatov, *The System: An Insider's Life in Soviet Politics* (New York: Random House, 1992); Georgii Khosroevich Shakhnazarov, *Tsena Svobody: Reformatisiya Gorbacheva Glazami evo pomoshchnika* (Moskva: Rossika Zevs, 1993); B. V. Gromov, *Ogranchennyi Kontingent* (Moskva: Izd-kaia gruppa "Progress,"1994). Archival data are included in Diane Koenker and Ronald D. Bachman, eds., *Revelations from the Russian Archives: Documents in English Translation* (Washington, DC: Library of Congress, 1997); *The Soviet Union and Afghanistan, 1978–1989: From the Russian and East German Archives.* http://www.wilsoncenter.org/index. cfm?topic_id = 1409&fuseaction = library.document&id = 39, *Afghanistan: Lessons from the Last War.* http://www.gwu.edu/~ nsarchiv/NSAEBB/NSAEBB57/soviet.html; and "New Evidence on the Soviet Intervention in Afghanistan," *The Cold War International History Project.* http://www.wilsoncenter.org/ index.cfm?topic_id = 1409&fuseaction = library.Collection&class = New%20Evidence%20on%20the%20Soviet%20Intervention%20in% 20 Afghanistan. A work that compares the Soviet and American military efforts is Douglas A. Borer, *Superpowers Defeated: Vietnam and Afghanistan Compared* (London: Frank Cass, 1999).

4. Korzh, *Afganskoe dos'e*, 448–453.
5. "Transcript of CPSU CC Politburo Discussions on Afghanistan, 17–19 March 1979." *The Soviet Union and Afghanistan, 1978–1989: From the Russian and East German Archives.* http://www.wilsoncenter. org/index.cfm?topic_id=1409&fuseaction=library.document&id= 39 Accessed October 26, 2005.
6. Ibid.
7. Ibid.
8. Ibid.
9. Halliday, "Soviet Foreign Policymaking and the Afghanistan War," 679.
10. The September 11th Sourcebooks, Volume II: Afghanistan: Lessons from the Last War. Svetlana Savranskaya, ed., *The Soviet Experience in Afghanistan: Russian Documents and Memoirs*, October 9, 2001. National Security Archive documents, http://www.gwu.edu/~ nsarchiv/ NSAEBB/NSAEBB57/r1.pdf Accessed October 14, 2005.
11. Ibid.
12. Koenker and Bachman, *Revelations from the Russian Archives*, 758.
13. Liakhovskii, *Tragedia I Doblest Afgana*, 177.
14. Ibid.
15. McGwire, *Perestroika and Soviet National Security*, 225.
16. Mark Urban, *War in Afghanistan* (London: Macmillan Press, 1988), 159–160.
17. Lewarne, Stephen, "Soviet Press and Afghanistan," *International Perspectives*, vol. 17, July—August 1985, 17–20.
18. Frederick Barghoorn and Thomas Remington, *Politics USSR* (Boston: Little, Brown & Co., 1986), 181.
19. Ellen Mickiewicz, *Split Signals* (New York: Oxford University Press, 1988), 5.
20. "O Nashik shagakh v cvyazi s razvitiem obstanovki vokrug Afganistana," in Liakhovskii, *Tragedia I Doblest Afgana*, 141.
21. "O Propagandistskom obespechenii nashei aktsii v otnoshenii Afganistana," in Liakhovskii, *Tragedia I Doblest Afgana*, 141–142.
22. Alexander Yakovlev, Mikhail Leshchinskii, interviews by author, Moscow, May 1992. Liakhovskii, *Tragedia I Doblest Afgana*, 141. Also, Moscow Central Television First Program, "Political Investigation—Behind the Scenes of War," December 27, 1991 as cited in Foreign Broadcast Information Service—Soviet Union, (FBIS-SOV), December 31, 1991, 3–5. Nicholas S. Daniloff, "Afghan War Finally Hits Soviets' Home Front," *US News and World Report*, December 16, 1985, 41–42.
    Reuveny and Prakash, ("The Afghanistan War and the Breakdown of the Soviet Union," 705) argue that "the official media also began showing signs of independence in its war reporting" in 1981. The examples they give are from newspapers (not television) and provided "hints" of Soviet involvement. These examples do not appear to me to

be "signs of independence." In fact, the "flood of reports and letters to newspapers against the Afghanistan War" (706) came after the directive commanding a change in coverage (in June 1985) and follows the pattern of Soviet media campaigns of the past.

23. Liakhovskii, *Tragedia I Doblest Afgana*, 198.
24. Liakhovskii was a personal aide to the Head of the USSR Defense Ministry Operations Group in Afghanistan, Army General Valentina Varennikov, who served as Afghan President Najibullah's military advisor.
25. "Rabochaya Zapis Zasedaniya Politburo CC CPSS 30 July 1981," in Liakhovskii, *Tragedia I Doblest Afgana*, 199.
26. Because the Soviet leadership controlled the content of television coverage, we can learn a significant amount about leadership communication goals and strategies by studying this coverage. Unfortunately archives of Soviet television dating back to December 1979 do not exist. Fortunately, the archive of the International Media and Communications Program at Emory University does contain Soviet television broadcasts dating back to 1984. Hence the three month sample of the nightly news program *Vremya* was taken—October through December 1984—as a baseline against which to compare coverage under Gorbachev. During this period Konstantin Chernenko was the General Secretary of the Communist Party of the Soviet Union and Soviet troops were waging war in Afghanistan.
27. Thomas Remington, "Policy Innovation and Soviet Media Campaigns," *Journal of Politics*, vol. 45, no. 1, February 1983, 220–227.
28. Mickiewicz, *Split Signals*, 225.
29. The shortest *Vremya* broadcast was 30 minutes long. The longest was 1 hour and 15 minutes long. The political agenda drove the length of the broadcast, not any need to keep the broadcast within a scheduled timeframe. This highlights the leadership's control over the messages broadcast on Soviet television.
30. *Vremya*, December 28, 1984.
31. *Vremya*, October 9, 1984.
32. Joseph L. Nogee and Robert H. Donaldson, *Soviet Foreign Policy since World War II* (New York: Macmillan, 1992), 321.
33. Ibid., 388.
34. The Soviets were concerned with American media depictions of their activity in Afghanistan, particularly those transmitted via Voice of America. In February 1980 a Central Committee degree said, "In its broadcasts *to the Soviet Union*, American propaganda has attempted to prove that the Soviet Union miscalculated the consequences of its actions in Afghanistan. . . ." The Soviet mass media have responded to this situation in their counterpropaganda efforts and are energetically exposing the aggressive policies of the United States." Koenker and Bachman, *Revelations from the Russian Archives*, 763. In 1982 orders

were given to have *Pravda* and *Isvestia* run articles about American interference in the internal affairs of Afghanistan. Liakhovskii, *Tragedia I Doblest Afgana*, 263.

35. Mikhail Leshchinskii, interview by author, Moscow, May 1992. This issue is, and will continue to be, murky as the years have gone by and individuals have had to adjust to a new political reality. See also, Halliday, "Soviet Foreign Policymaking and the Afghanistan War," 677, fn. 7.
36. Seth Mydans, "Afghan War: The Russian Public is Still a Believer," *New York Times*, December 3, 1984, A2.
37. Ellen Mickiewicz, *Media and the Russian Public* (New York: Praeger, 1981).
38. "Meeting of CC CPSU Politburo" November 13, 1986. *Afghanistan: Lessons from the Last War*, National Security Archives. http://www.gwu.edu/~nsarchiv/NSAEBB/NSAEBB57/r18.pdf Accessed October 26, 2005.
39. Mendelson, *Changing Course*, 24.
40. Yakovlev, Leshchinskii, interviews by author, May 1992.
41. See scenarios listed in "On the Measures Pertaining to the Impending Withdrawal of Soviet Forces from Afghanistan." *The Soviet Union and Afghanistan, 1978– from the Russian and East German Archives.* National Security Archives, 91–95 of 97.
42. Mendelson, *Changing Course*, 35.
43. Ibid., 30.
44. "Meeting of CC CPSU Politburo 13 November 1986," *Afghanistan: Lessons from the Last War*, National Security Archives http://www.gwu.edu/~nsarchiv/NSAEBB/NSAEBB57/r18.pdf Accessed October 25, 2005.
45. Richard Herrmann, "The Soviet Decision to Withdraw from Afghanistan: Changing Strategic and Regional Images," in Robert Jervis and Jack Snyder, eds., *Dominoes and Bandwagons: Strategic Beliefs and Great Power Competition in the Eurasian Rimland* (New York: Oxford University Press, 1991), 235.
46. "Meeting of CC CPSU Politburo 13 November 1986," *Afghanistan: Lessons from the Last War*, located in National Security Archives http:// www.gwu.edu/~nsarchiv/NSAEBB/NSAEBB57/r18.pdf Accessed October 25, 2005.
47. Ibid., 87 of 97.
48. Ibid., 88–89 of 97.
49. Ibid., 90 of 97.
50. Herrmann, "Soviet Decision to Withdraw from Afghanistan," 235.
51. Sarah Mendelson, "Internal Battles and External Wars: Politics, Learning, and the Soviet Withdrawal from Afghanistan," *World Politics*, vol. 45, no. 3, 1993, 327–360; Cordovez and Harrison, *Out of Afghanistan*, 249; Korzh, *Afganskoe dos'e*, 554.
52. *New York Times*, July 22, 1987, 1.

53. Laura Roselle, "The Role of Political Communication in the Diffusion of Ideas: Soviet Television and New Thinking in International Security, 1985–1991." Paper prepared for the American Political Science Association Annual Meeting, Boston, 2002. For more on New Thinking see, Robert English, *Russia and the Idea of the West: Gorbachev, Intellectuals, and the End of the Cold War* (New York: Columbia University Press, 2000); Andrew Bennett, *Condemned to Repetition? The Rise, Fall, and Reprise of Soviet-Russian Military Interventionism, 1973–1996* (Cambridge, MA: MIT Press, 1999); Ted Hopf, *Peripheral Visions: Deterrence Theory and American Foreign Policy In the Third World, 1965–1990* (Ann Arbor: University of Michigan Press, 1994); Seweryn Bialer, "New Thinking and Soviet Foreign Policy," *Survival*, July/August 1988, 291–310; Matthew Evangelista, "The New Soviet Approach to Security," *World Politics Journal*. vol. 3, 1986, 561–599; Robert Legvold. "The Revolution in Soviet Foreign Policy," *Foreign Affairs*, vol. 68, no. 1, 1989, 82–98; Stephen Meyer, "Sources and Prospects of Gorbachev's New Political Thinking in Security," *International Security*. vol. 13, no. 2, Fall 1988, 124–163; F. Stephen Larrabee, "Gorbachev and the Soviet Military," *Foreign Affairs*, vol. 66, no. 5, 1988, 1002–1026; David Holloway, "State, Society, and the Military Under Gorbachev," *International Security*, vol. 14, no. 3, Winter 1989/1990, 5–24; Mikhail Gorbachev, *Perestroika* (New York: Harper & Row, 1987); Robert G. Herman, "Identity, Norms, and National Security: The Soviet Foreign Policy Revolution and the End of the Cold War," in Peter J. Katzenstein, ed., *The Culture of National Security: Norms and Identity in World Politics* (New York: Columbia University Press, 1996).
54. Stephen White and Stephen Revell, "Revolution and Integration in Soviet International Diplomacy, 1917–1991," *Review of International Studies*, vol. 25, 1999, 641–654.
55. See Mendelson, "Internal Battles and External Wars."
56. Gorbachev, *Memoirs*, 402.
57. "Anatoly Chernaev's Notes from the Politburo Session, February 23 and 26, 1987," Translated by Svetlana Savranskaya. *Afghanistan: Lessons from the Last War*, National Security Archives. http://www.gwu.edu/~nsarchiv/NSAEBB/NSAEBB57/soviet.html#docs Accessed October 25, 2005.
58. Liakhovskii, *Tragedia I Doblest Afgana*, 296–298.
59. Ibid., 298.
60. Ibid., 297.
61. Leshchinskii, interview with author, Moscow, May 1992.
62. Ibid.
63. Ibid.
64. Ibid.
65. It is difficult to determine who exactly was in this group (Halliday, "Soviet Foreign Policymaking and the Afghanistan War"; Aleksander Yakovlev, Interview, Moscow, 1992; Mendelson, "Internal Battles and

External Wars,"; *Changing Courses;* G. Myre, "Gorbachev Says Painful Lessons of Afghanistan Haven't Been Learned," *Associated Press,* February 19, 1999, Lexis-Nexis, Accessed September 14, 2004), but members of the military and KGB are often mentioned.
66. Foreign Broadcast Information Service, December 31, 1991, 4.
67. Ibid., 4.
68. Yakovlev, interview with author, Moscow, May 1992.
69. Leshchinskii, interview with author, Moscow, May 1992.
70. Georgii Khosroevich Shakhnazarov, Tsena Svobody: Reformatsiia Gorbacheva glazami ego pomoshchnika (Moskva: Rossika, 1993), 87.
71. Gorbachev, *Memoirs,* 203.
72. Leshchinskii, interview with author, May 1992.
73. Ibid. Some would say that he grew too close to the military. Leonid Kravchenko, Eduard Sagalaev, interviews with author, May 1992.
74. Dusko Doder and Louise Branson, *Gorbachev: Heretic in the Kremlin* (New York: Viking, 1990), 228.
75. *Vremya,* December 11, 1985.
76. Ibid.
77. *Vremya,* March 20, 1985.
78. *Vremya,* September 9, 1985.
79. *Vremya,* September 12, 1985.
80. *Vremya,* July 11, 1986.
81. Leshchinskii, interview with author, Moscow, 1992.
82. Ibid.
83. *Vremya,* October 19, 1986.
84. *Vremya,* March 18, 1987.
85. "Gorbachev Exhorts Media on Restructuring," *The Current Digest of Soviet Press,* XXXIX, no. 28, 1987, 7.
86. Mickiewicz, *Split Signals.*
87. Mickiewicz notes that Aksyonov "understood very little of the revolution that glasnost was unleashing." Ellen Mickiewicz, *Changing Channels: Television and the Struggle for Power in Russia* (Durham: Duke University Press, 1999).
88. E. I. Popa, *TV: Informatsiya v structure respublikanskovo yeshchaniy* (Kishinev: Shtiintsa, 1989), 12.
89. Mickiewicz, *Split Signals,* 179–203.
90. Ibid., 52–56.
91. Ibid., 56–57.
92. "Gorbachev Exhorts Media," 7.

Chapter 5   Withdrawal and Aftermath: Afghanistan

1. Kornienko says that Gorbachev put in the date of withdrawal without getting approval from the rest of the leadership. In Sergei Fedorovich Akhromeyev and G. M. Kornienko, *Glazami Marshala I Diplomata* (Moscow: Mezhdunarodiye Otnosheniye, 1992). Also cited in Fred

Halliday, "Soviet Foreign Policymaking and the Afghanistan War: From 'Second Mongolia' to 'Bleeding Wound,'" *Review of International Studies*, vol. 25, no. 4, October 1999, 686.

2. Riaz M. Khan, 1991, *Untying the Afghan Knot: Negotiating Soviet Withdrawal* (Durham, NC: Duke University Press, 1991), 270.
3. Ibid., 273.
4. Ibid., 276.
5. Ibid., 274.
6. Ibid., 275.
7. Aleksander Yakovlev, Leonid Kravchenko, Mikhail Leshchinskii, interviews by the author, Moscow, May 1992.
8. Diego Cordovez and Selig S. Harrison, *Out of Afghanistan: The Inside Story of the Soviet Withdrawal* (New York: Oxford University press, 1995), 254.
9. Diane Koenker and Ronald D. Bachman, eds., *Revelations from the Russian Archives: Documents in English Translation* (Washington, DC: Library of Congress, 1997), 765–766.
10. Cordovez and Harrison, *Out of Afghanistan*, 245.
11. George Breslauer, "How Do You Sell a Concessionary Foreign Policy?" *Post-Soviet Affairs*, vol. 10, no. 3, 1994, 281.
12. Cordovez and Harrison, *Out of Afghanistan*, 266.
13. Sarah Mendelson, "Internal Battles and External Wars: Politics, Learning, and the Soviet Withdrawal from Afghanistan," *World Politics*, vol. 45, no. 3, 1993, 354.
14. February 13, 1988 resolution of the Secretariat of the Central Committee "On propaganda support of the political settlement concerning Afghanistan," in Koenker and Backman, *Revelations from the Russian Archives*, 765.
15. The news could vary in length if Soviet leaders determined that specific speeches or announcements would be read.
16. *Vremya*, February 8,1988.
17. Ibid.
18. Koenker and Bachman, *Revelations from the Russian Archives*, 765–766.
19. Ibid.
20. Ibid.
21. Ibid.
22. Ibid.
23. All *Vremya* stories during this time period were reviewed.
24. *Vremya*, April 5, 1988.
25. *Vremya*, April 15, 1988.
26. Koenker and Bachman, *Revelations from the Russian Archives*, 766.
27. *Vremya*, February 28, 1988.
28. *Vremya*, February 10, 1988.
29. Ibid.
30. *Vremya*, February 18, 1988.

31. "Minutes of the Session of CC CPSU Politburo, January 23, 1989." The September 11th Sourcebooks, Volume II: Afghanistan: Lessons from the Last War, in Svetlanka Savranskaya, ed., located in the National Security Archive, http://www.gwu.edu/~nsarchiv/NSAEBB/NSAEBB57/r22.pdf Accessed October 5, 2001.
32. "Yakovlev's Role in Afghanistan Discussed," Foreign Broadcast Information Service (FBIS-SOV), December 31, 1991, 5.
33. Ibid.
34. Ibid.
35. *Vremya*, August 15, 1988.
36. *Vremya*, May 25, 1988.
37. *Vremya*, May 26, 1988
38. *Vremya*, May 24, 1988.
39. *Vremya*, September 4, 1988.
40. *Vremya*, September 7, 1988.
41. *Vremya*, October 19, 1988.
42. Koenker and Bachman, *Reflections from the Russian Archives*, 766.
43. *Vremya*, January 20, 1989.
44. "Television Head Outlines Program Plans," FBIS-SOV, February 12, 1988, 65.
45. Kravchenko, interview by author, Moscow, December 1988. It is interesting that Kravchenko went on to become Chair of the State Committee for Television and Radio in November 1990 when he was highly criticized for his tight control over Soviet television. He declared when he took the job, "I have come to execute the will of the President" (*New York Times*, February 8, 1991, A6). Yet, even he supported more correspondent reports and visually interesting television. This is because he understood that these were more effective.
46. Kravchenko, interview by author, Moscow, December 1988.
47. "Television Head Outlines Program Plans," 65.
48. "Television Head Outlines Program Plans," FBIS, February 12, 1988, 64–65. Kravchenko left *Gostelradio* in early 1988 but the understanding of what constituted effective communication did not change. Kravchenko eventually became Chairman of *Gostelradio* in December 1990.
49. Yakovlev, Kravchenko, Eduard Sagalaev, interviews by author, Moscow, May 1992.
50. Leshchinskii, interview by author, Moscow, May 1992.
51. Ibid.
52. *Vremya*, July 1, 1988. Emphasis added.
53. Leshchinskii, interview by author, Moscow, May 1992.
54. Yakovlev, interview by author, Moscow, May 1992.
55. Khan, *Untying the Afghan Knot*, 295.
56. Ibid., 294 and 374, fn. 12.
57. "Report of A. S. Dzasokhov, Chairman of the USSR Supreme Soviet Committee on International Affairs, to the Second Congress of USSR

People's Deputies on the Political Assessment of the Decision to Send Soviet Troops into Afghanistan in December 1979," in Patrick J. Rollins, ed., *First Congress of People's Deputies of the USSR, 25 May—9 June 1989, The Stenographic Record*, vol. 1 (Gulf Breeze, FL: Academic International Press, 1993).

58. *Vremya*, March 27, 1989.
59. *Vremya*, July 14, 1989.
60. This was a common occurrence. On special national holidays or anniversaries of Soviet friendship, the ambassador from the other country would "speak" to the Soviet people on television.
61. *Vremya*, July 14, 1989.
62. Ibid.

Chapter 6   Conclusions and a Post–Cold War Assessment

1. David Green, *Shaping Political Consciousness: The Language of Politics in America from McKinley to Reagan* (Ithaca: Cornell University Press, 1987), 254–255.
2. Daniel Hallin. *The Uncensored War* (New York: Oxford University Press, 1986), 178.
3. Chapter 4 mentions that there was an earlier troop withdrawal in 1986, but this was used as more of a signal than the beginning of substantive withdrawal.
4. George does argue that the phrase "national interest" has become "part of the shopworn political rhetoric that every administration in recent times has employed in order to justify questionable or arbitrary policies and decisions." Alexander George, "Domestic Constraints on Regime Change in US Foreign Policy: The Need for Policy Legitimacy," in G. John Ikenberry, ed., *American Foreign Policy: Theoretical Essays* (Glenview, IL: Scott Foresman, 1989), 584.
5. Kathleen Turner, *Lyndon Johnson's Dual War* (Chicago: University of Chicago Press, 1985), 4.
6. Robert Harris, *Gotcha! The Media, Government and the Falklands Crisis* (London: Faber & Faber, 1983).
7. Howard Tumber and Jerry Palmer, *Media at War: The Iraq Crisis* (London: Sage, 2004).
8. "Excerpt from Statement of the Soviet Military Command in Afghanistan on the Withdrawal of Soviet Troops, February 14, 1989," Source: Alexander Lyakhovsky, *Tragedy and Valor of Afghan*, Iskon, Moscow 1995, Appendix 11, Translated by Svetlana Savranskaya, The September 11th Sourcebooks, Vol. II, Afghanistan: Lessons from the Last War, National Security Archive Briefing Book No. 57, John Prados and Svetlana Savranskaya, eds., October 9, 2001, http://www.gwu.edu/~nsarchiv/NSAEBB/NSAEBB57/r23.doc Accessed October 25, 2005.

9. A full analysis of leadership communication strategies for Chechnya and Iraq cannot be completed due to data considerations. Archival data and internal memoranda are not available. Much of the discussion here is necessarily drawn from media sources themselves. Conclusions should be seen as preliminary. Additionally, Chechnya and Iraq are very different cases. Chechnya is contained within the Russian Federation.

10. Francesca Mereu and Simon Saradzhyan, "Smokescreen Around Chechnya," *The Moscow Times* (independent), Moscow, Russia, March 18, 2005.

11. Ellen Mickiewicz, *Changing Channels: Television and the Struggle for Power in Russia* (Durham: Duke University Press, 1999); Olga V. Malinkina and Douglas M. McLeod, "The Russian Media Role in the Conflicts in Afghanistan and Chechnya: A Case Study of Media Coverage by *Izvestia*," in Eytan Gilboa, ed., *Media and Conflict: Framing Issues and Making Policy Shaping Opinions* (Ardsley, NY: Transnational Publishers, 2002), 213–238.

12. Mickiewicz, *Changing Channels*, 10.

13. Ibid., 256–257.

14. This does not mean that television *caused* the lack of support for the war. As Mickiewicz (*Changing Channels*, 258) writes, "the bloody events of the Chechen war had pushed their moods into greater disorientation."

15. Mickiewicz, *Changing Channels*, 255.

16. Andrew Bennett, *Condemned to Repetition? The Rise, Fall, and Reprise of Soviet-Russian Military Intervention, 1973–1996* (Cambridge, MA: MIT Press, 1999), 295–347.

17. A. Petrova, "A Great and Powerful Army—By Any Means Necessary," The Public Opinion Foundation Database, August 24, 2000. http://bd.english.fom.ru/report/cat/societas/rus_im/Great_Power/eof003401 Accessed October 17, 2005.

18. Bennett, *Condemned to Repetition?*, 339.

19. Timothy L. Thomas, "Manipulating the Mass Consciousness: Russian and Chechen 'Information War' Tactics in the 2nd Chechen-Russian Conflict," Foreign Military Studies Office Publications. http://fmso.leavenworth.army.mil/documents/chechiw.htm Accessed October 17, 2005.

20. Anna Politkovskaya, *A Dirty War: A Russian Reporter in Chechnya* (London: The Harvill Press, 2001).

21. Mereu and Saradzhyan, "Smokescreen Around Chechnya."

22. A. Petrova, "Attitudes Towards Military Actions in Chechnya are Changing," The Public Opinion Foundation, Russia-wide poll of urban and rural populations. January 15 and July 8, 2000; January 27 and June 9, 2001. 1500 respondents each. June 14, 2001, http://bd.english.fom.ru/report/cat/societas/Chechnya/truck_war/eof012102, accessed October 17, 2005.

23. "We Are Peace-Lovers and they Want a War . . ." The Public Opinion Foundation Database, September 2002. http://bd.english.fom.ru/report/cat/societas/rus_im/Great_Power/ed021832, 9 Accessed October 10, 2005.

24. A. Petrova, "A Great and Powerful Army—By Any Means Necessary," The Public Opinion Foundation Database, August 24, 2000. http://bd.english.fom.ru/report/cat/societas/rus_im/Great_Power/eof003401 Accessed October 17, 2005.

25. Putin's vision of "Russia as a normal great power" is discussed by Andrei P. Tsygankov, "Vladimir Putin's Vision of Russia as a Normal Great Power," *Post-Soviet Affairs*, vol. 21, no. 2, April–June 2005, 132–158.

26. The tie between strict controls over media and Russian opinions on the war in Chechnya are discussed in Theodore P. Gerber and Sarah E. Mendelson, "Russian Public Opinion on Human Rights and the War in Chechnya," *Post-Soviet Affairs*, vol. 18, no. 4, 298–299.

27. Anna Politkovskaya, "Remember Chechnya," *Washington Post*, November 14, 2001. http://www.cdi.org/russia/johnson/5545-6.cfm, Johnson's Russia List. Accessed October 10, 2005.

28. Ibid.

29. Fred Weir, "Quietly, Tide of Opinion Turns On Chechen war," *Christian Science Monitor*, November 17, 2004. http://www.csmonitor.com/2004/1117/p04s01-woeu.html. Accessed October 17, 2005.

30. Mark Kramer, "The Domestic Political Context of Russia's War in Chechnya." Paper presented at Conference on Post-Soviet In/Securities: Theory and Practice, October 7, 2005. The Mershon Center, The Ohio State University.http://www.mershon.ohio-state.edu/Events/05-06events/hopfconference/KramerPaper.pdf Accessed October 17, 2005.

31. See Friedemann Weckbach-Mara, " 'Terror und Gräueltaten auf beiden Seiten': Putin-Beraterin will sich für internationale Beobachter in Tschetschenien einsetzen," *Welt am Sonntag* (Hamburg), May 10, 2004, 1. Cited in Kramer, "Domestic Political Context," 5–6, fn. 11.

32. George H. W. Bush and Brent Scowcroft, *A World Transformed* (New York: Alfred A. Knopf, 1998).

33. After the 1991 war a no-strike zone was set up.

34. "George Bush: Address to the American People" in Brooke Barnett, 2005. *The Iraq Wars and the War on Terror & Index*. The Greenwood Library of American War Reporting, Vol. 8 (Westport, CT: Greenwood Press, 2005), 26.

35. Andrew Kohut and Robert C. Toth. "Arms and the People," *Foreign Affairs*, November/December, 1994. http://www.foreignaffairs.org/19941101faessay5150/andrew-kohut-robert-c-toth/arms-and-the-people.html accessed October 18, 2005; Robert Denton, Jr., ed., *The Media and the Persian Gulf War* (Westport, CT: Praeger, 1993); For a discussion of polling during the Persian Gulf War see John

Mueller, "The Polls—A Review American Public Opinion and the
Gulf War: Some Polling Issues" *Public Opinion Quarterly*, vol. 57, no. 1,
Spring 1993, 80–97; for another view see Kurt Taylor Gaubatz,
"Intervention and Intransitivity: Public Opinion, Social Choice, and
the Use of Military Force Abroad," *World Politics*, vol. 47, no. 4, July
1995, 534–554.

36. Casualties passed 1000 in September 2004 and on April 1, 2006
stood at 2325. http://web1.whs.osd.mil/mmid/casualty/oif-deaths-
total.pdf

37. "President Addresses Nation, Discusses Iraq, War on Terror," Fort
Bragg, North Carolina, June 28, 2005. http://www.whitehouse.gov/
news/releases/2005/06/20050628-7.html Accessed October 21,
2005.

38. "President Discusses War on Terror at National Endowment for
Democracy" Ronald Reagan Building and International Trade Center
Washington, DC, October 6, 2005. http://www.whitehouse.gov/
news/releases/2005/10/20051006-3.html Accessed October 21,
2005.

39. Bill Katovsky and Timothy Carlson, *Embedded: The Media At War in
Iraq* (Guilford, CT: Lyons Press, 2003).

40. "Military Embed Ground Rules," *MilitaryCity.com*, March 3, 2003.
http://www.militarycity.com/iraq/1631270.html Accessed October 21,
2005.

41. http://www.pbs.org/newshour/bb/media/jan-june03/
embeds_04-01.html

42. Katovsky and Carlson, *Embedded*, 2003.

43. http://www.pbs.org/newshour/bb/middle_east/jan-june03/
opinion_3-30.html Accessed October 21, 2005.

44. www.pollingreport.com/iraq.htm Accessed April 22, 2006.

45. Ibid.

46. www.fair.org/index.php?page=1859 Accessed April 22, 2006.

47. Mark Mazzetti and Borzou Daragahi, "U.S. Military Covertly Pays to
Run Stories in Iraqi Press," Los Angeles *Times*, November 30, 2005.
www.latimes.com/news/nationworld/world/la-fg-
infowar30nov80,0,4578768 Accessed April 22, 2006.

48. "New Realities in the Media Age: A Conversation with Donald
Rumsfeld," Council on Foreign Relations, February 17, 2006. http://
www.cfr.org/publication/9900/Accessed April 22, 2006.

49. Robert English, *Russia and the Idea of the West: Gorbachev,
Intellectuals, and the End of the Cold War* (New York: Columbia
University Press, 2000), 237.

50. Mikhail Gorbachev, *Memoirs* (NY: Doubleday, 1995) 336.

51. Ronald L. Jepperson, Alexander Wendt, and Peter J. Katzenstein,
"Norms, Identity, and Culture in National Security," in Peter J.
Katzenstein, ed., *The Culture of National Security: Norms and Identity
in World Politics* (New York: Columbia University Press, 1996), 61.

52. I am not arguing that these identities are static in nature, but that they may ebb and flow based on a number of factors.

53. *The National Security Strategy of the United States of America.* September 2002. http://www.whitehouse.gov/nsc/nss.html Accessed October 25, 2005.

54. "Russia's National Security Concept," January 2000. Arms Control Association online newsletter. Jan-Feb. 2000. http://www.armscontrol. org/act/2000_01-02/docjf00.asp Accessed October 25, 2005.

Sources Consulted and Selected Bibliography

Holdings of the Nixon Archive

White House Special Files (WHSF)

Patrick J. Buchanan	Special Assistant to the President
Dwight Chapin	President's Appointments Secretary
Charles W. Colson	Special Counsel to the President
John D. Ehrlichman	Counsel to the President, Assistant to the President for Domestic Affairs
H. R. Haldeman	Chief of Staff, Assistant to the President
Herbert G. Klein	Director of Communications for the Executive Branch

President's Office Files (containing Annotated News Summaries)

John A. Scali	Special Assistant to the President
Ronald L. Ziegler	Press Secretary

Holding of the International Media and Communications Program at Emory University *Vremya* coverage, Moscow, First Program, October 1984–March 1990.

Vietnam, The Media, and Public Support for the War: Selections from the Holdings of the Lyndon B. Johnson Library, (Frederick, MD: University Publications of America, 1986), microfilm, 11 reels.

Selected Bibliography

Books

Akhromeyev, Sergei Fedorovich and G. M. Kornienko. *Glazami Marshala I Diplomata*. Moscow: Mezhdunarodiye Otnosheniye, 1992.

Altschull, Herbert. *Agents of Power*. New York: Longman, 1984.

Ansolabehere, Stephen, Roy Behr, and Shanto Iyengar. *The Media Game: American Politics in the Television Age*. New York: Macmillan, 1993.

Arbatov, Georgi. *The System: An Insider's Life in Soviet Politics*. New York: Random House, 1992.

Barrett, David M., ed., *Lyndon B. Johnson's Vietnam Papers: A Documentary Collection*. College Station, TX: Texas A&M University Press, 1997.

Beschloss, Michael. *Reaching for Glory: Lyndon Johnson's Secret White House Tapes, 1964–1965.* New York: Simon & Schuster, 2001.

Borer, Douglas A. *Superpowers Defeated: Vietnam and Afghanistan Compared.* London: Frank Cass, 1999.

Braestrup, Peter. *Big Story: How the American Press and Television Reported and Interpreted the Crises of Tet in Vietnam and Washington.* Boulder: Westview, 1977.

Buckley, Mary. *Redefining Russian Society and Polity.* Boulder: Westview Press, 1993.

Bush, George H. W. and Brent Scowcroft. *A World Transformed.* New York: Alfred A. Knopf, 1998.

Checkel, Jeffrey. *Ideas and International Political Change: Soviet/Russian Behavior and the End of the Cold War.* New Haven: Yale University Press, 1997.

Chernyaev, Anatoly S. *My Six Years with Gorbachev.* University Park: The Pennsylvania State University Press, 2000.

Cohen, Stephen F. and Katrina Vanden Heuvel. *Voices of Glasnost: Interviews with Gorbachev's Reformers.* New York: W. W. Norton & Co., 1989.

Cordovez, Diego and Selig S. Harrison. *Out of Afghanistan: The Inside Story of the Soviet Withdrawal.* New York: Oxford University Press, 1995.

Dalek, Robert. *Flawed Giant: Lyndon Johnson and his Times, 1961–1973.* New York: Oxford University Press, 1998.

Denton, Jr., Robert, ed. *The Media and the Persian Gulf War.* Westport, CT: Praeger, 1993.

Denton, Robert E., Jr. and Dan F. Hahn. *Presidential Communication.* New York: Praeger, 1986.

Dobrynin, Anatoliy. *In Confidence: Moscow's Ambassador to America's Six Cold War Presidents, 1962–1986.* New York: Times Books, 1995.

Doder, Dusko and Louise Branson. *Gorbachev: Heretic in the Kremlin.* New York: Viking, 1990.

Ehrlichman, John. *Witness to Power.* New York: Simon & Schuster, 1982.

Ekedahl, Carolyn McGiffert and Melvin A. Goodman. *The Wars of Eduard Shevardnadze.* University Park: The Pennsylvania State University Press, 1997.

English, Robert. *Russia and the Idea of the West: Gorbachev, Intellectuals, and the End of the Cold War.* New York: Columbia University Press, 2000.

Entman, Robert. *Projections of Power: Framing News, Public Opinion, and US Foreign Policy.* Chicago: University of Chicago Press, 2004.

Epstein, Edward Jay. *News from Nowhere.* New York: Random House, 1973.

Galeotti, Mark. *Afghanistan: The Soviet Union's Last War.* London: Frank Cass, 1994.

Gelb, Leslie and Richard Betts. *The Irony of Vietnam: The System Worked.* Washington, DC: The Brookings Institution, 1979.

George, Alexander and Richard Smoke. *Deterrence in American Foreign Policy: Theory and Practice.* New York: Columbia University Press, 1974.

Gitlin, Todd. *The Whole World is Watching: Mass Media in the Making and Unmaking of the New Left.* Berkeley: University of California Press, 1980.

Goffman, Erving. *Frame Analysis: An Essay on the Organization of Experience.* Cambridge: Harvard University Press, 1974.

Goodwin, Doris Kearns. *Lyndon Johnson and the American Dream.* New York: Harper & Row, 1976.

Gorbachev, Mikhail. *Memoirs.* New York: Doubleday, 1995.

———. *Perestroika.* New York: Harper & Row, 1987.

Graber, Doris. *Media Power in Politics.* Washington, DC: CQ Press, 2000.

Grau, Lester W. and Michael A. Gress. *The Soviet-Afghan War: How a Superpower Fought and Lost.* Lawrence: University Press of Kansas, 2002.

Green, David. *Shaping Political Consciousness: The Language of Politics in America from McKinley to Reagan.* Ithaca: Cornell University Press, 1987.

Gromov, B. V. *Ogranichennyi Kontigent.* Moskva: Izd-kaia gruppa "Progress," 1994

Grossman, Michael Baruch and Matha Joynt Kumar. *Portraying the President: The White House and the News Media.* Baltimore: The Johns Hopkins University Press, 1981.

Halberstam, David. *The Powers That Be.* New York: Bantam Doubleday Dell Publishing Group, 1979.

Haldeman, H. R. *The Haldeman Diaries: Inside the Nixon White House.* New York: G. P. Putnam's Sons, 1994.

Hallin, Daniel. *The Uncensored War: The Media and Vietnam.* Berkeley: University of California Press, 1986.

Harris, Robert. *Gotcha! The Media, Government and the Falklands Crisis.* London: Faber & Faber 1983.

Hopf, Ted. *Social Construction of International Politics: Identities and Foreign Policies, Moscow, 1955 & 1999.* Ithaca: Cornell University Press, 2002.

———. *Peripheral Visions: Deterrence Theory and American Foreign Policy in the Third World, 1965–1990.* Ann Arbor: University of Michigan Press, 1994.

Iyengar, Shanto and Donald R. Kinder. *News that Matters.* Chicago: University of Chicago, 1987.

Jervis, Robert. *The Logic of Images in International Relations.* New York: Columbia University Press, 1989.

Johnson, Lyndon Baines. *The Vantage Point.* New York: Holt, Rinehart and Winston, 1971.

Johnson-Cartee, Karen S. *News Narratives and News Framing: Constructing Political Reality.* Lanhan, MD: Rowman & Littlefield, 2005.

Karnow, Stanley. *Vietnam: A History.* New York: The Viking Press, 1983.

Katovsky, Bill and Timothy Carlson. *Embedded: The Media at War in Iraq.* Guilford, CT: Lyons Press, 2003

Katzenstein, Peter J. ed., *The Culture of National Security: Norms and Identity in World Politics.* New York: Columbia University Press, 1996.

Keogh, James. *President Nixon and the Press.* New York: Funk & Wagnalls, 1972.

Khan, Riaz M. *Untying the Afghan Knot: Negotiating Soviet Withdrawal.* Durham: Duke University Press, 1991.

Kimball, Jeffrey. *The Vietnam War Files: Uncovering the Secret History of Nixon-Era Strategy.* Lawrence: University Press of Kansas, 2004.

Kissinger, Henry. *Ending the Vietnam War.* New York: Simon & Schuster, 2003.

———. *White House Years.* Boston: Little, Brown and Co., 1979.

Klein, Herbert. *Making it Perfectly Clear.* Garden City, NY: Doubleday, 1980.

Koenker, Diane and Ronald D. Bachman, eds. *Revelations from the Russian Archives: Documents in English Translation.* Washington, DC: Library of Congress, 1997.

Korzh, Gennadii. *Afganskoe dos'e: istoriia voiny SSSR v Afganistane.* Khar'kov: Folio, 2003.

Kubalkova, Vendulka, ed. *Foreign Policy in a Constructed World.* Armonk, NY: ME Sharpe, 2001.

Lapid, Yosef and Friedrich Kratochwil. *The Return of Culture and Identity in IR Theory.* Boulder: Lynne Reinner, 1996.

Leighley, Jan E. *Mass Media and Politics: A Social Science Perspective.* Boston: Houghton Mifflin Co., 2004.

Liakhovskii, Aleksandr Antonovich. *Plamia Afgana.* Moskva: Vagrios, 1999.

Lynch, Marc. *State Interests and Public Spheres.* New York: Columbia University Press, 1999.

Mathews, Joseph J. *Reporting the Wars.* Minneapolis: University of Minneapolis Press, 1957.

McAdam, Doug, John D. McCarthy, and Mayer N. Zald, eds. *Comparative Perspectives on Social Movements: Political Opportunities, Mobilizing Structures, and Cultural Framing.* New York: Cambridge University Press, 1996.

McGwire, Michael. *Perestroika and Soviet National Security.* Washington, DC: The Brookings Institution, 1991.

Mendelson, Sarah. *Changing Course: Ideas, Politics, and the Soviet Withdrawal from Afghanistan.* Princeton: Princeton University Press, 1998.

Mercer, Jonathan. *Reputation and International Politics.* Ithaca, NY: Cornell University Press, 1996.

Mickiewicz, Ellen. *Changing Channels: Television and the Struggle for Power in Russia.* New York: Oxford University Press, 2000a.

———. *Media and the Russian Public.* New York: Praeger, 1981.

———. *Split Signals.* New York: Oxford University Press, 1988.

Neustadt, Richard E. *Presidential Power.* New York: John Wiley and Sons, 1980.

Nixon, Richard. *No More Vietnams.* New York: Arbor House, 1985.

———. *RN: The Memoirs of Richard Nixon.* New York: Grosset & Dunlap, 1978.

———. *Six Crises.* Garden City, NY: Doubleday, 1962.

Nogee, Joseph L. and Robert H. Donaldson. *Soviet Foreign Policy since World War II.* New York: Macmillan, 1992.

Page, Benjamin. *Who Deliberates? Mass Media in Modern Democracy.* Chicago: University of Chicago Press, 1996.

Paletz, David L. and Robert M. Entman. *Media, Power, Politics.* New York: The Free Press, 1981.

Politkovskaya, Anna. *A Dirty War: A Russian Reporter in Chechnya.* London: The Harvill Press, 2001.

Porter, William E. *Assault on the Media: The Nixon Years.* Ann Arbor: University of Michigan Press, 1976.

Press, Daryl. *Calculating Credibility.* Ithaca, NY: Cornell University Press, 2005.

Price, Raymond. *With Nixon.* New York: Viking Press, 1977.

Redford, Emmette S. and Richard T. McCulley. *White House Operations: The Johnson Presidency.* Austin: University of Texas Press, 1986.

Reese, Stephen D., Oscar H. Gandy, Jr., and August E. Grant, eds. *Framing Public Life: Perspectives on Media and Our Understanding of the Social World.* Mahwah, NJ: Lawrence Erlbaum Associates, 2001.

Remington, Thomas. *The Truth of Authority: Ideology and Communication in the Soviet Union.* Pittsburgh: University of Pittsburgh Press, 1988.

Saikal, Amin and William Maley, eds. *The Soviet Withdrawal from Afghanistan.* Cambridge: Cambridge University Press, 1989.

Schandler, Herbert. *The Unmaking of a President.* Princeton: Princeton University Press, 1977.

Schelling, Thomas. *Arms and Influence.* New Haven: Yale University Press, 1966.

Schimmelfennig, Frank. *The EU, NATO and the Integration of Europe: Rules and Rhetoric.* Cambridge: Cambridge University Press, 2003.

Shakhnazarov, Georgii Khosroevich. *Tsena Svobody: Reformatisiya Gorbacheva Glazami evo pomoshchnika.* Moskva: Rossika Zevs, 1993.

Siebert, Fred S., Theodore Peterson, and William Schramm. *Four Theories of the Press.* Urbana, IL: University of Illinois Press, 1956.

Small, Melvin. *Johnson, Nixon, and the Doves.* New Brunswick: Rutgers University Press, 1988.

Snyder, Glenn and Paul Diesing. *Conflict Among Nations.* Princeton: Princeton University Press, 1977.

Snyder, Jack. *Myths of Empire.* Ithaca: Cornell University Press, 1991.

Spear, Joseph C. *Presidents and the Press: The Nixon Legacy.* Cambridge: MIT Press, 1984.

Stuckey, Mary. *The President as Interpreter-In-Chief.* Chatham, NJ: Chatham House Publishers, 1991.

Summers, Jr., Harry G. *On Strategy: A Critical Analysis of the Vietnam War.* Novato, CA: Presidio Press, 1982.

Tuchman, Gaye. *Making News: A Study in the Construction of Reality.* New York: Free Press, 1978.

Tulis, Jeffrey. *The Rhetorical Presidency.* Princeton: Princeton University Press, 1987.

Tumber, Howard and Jerry Palmer. *Media at War: The Iraq Crisis.* London: Sage, 2004.

Turner, Kathleen. *Lyndon Johnson's Dual War.* Chicago: University of Chicago, 1985.

Urban, Mark. *War in Afghanistan.* London: Macmillan Press, 1988.

VanDeMark, Brian. *Into the Quagmire.* New York: Oxford University Press, 1991.

Weeden, Lisa. *Ambiguities of Domination.* Chicago: University of Chicago Press, 1998.

Wendt, Alexander. *Social Theory of International Politics.* Cambridge, UK: Cambridge University Press, 1999.

Wolfsfeld, Gadi. *Media and Political Conflict: News from the Middle East.* Cambridge: Cambridge University Press, 1997.

Articles and Chapters

Behr, Roy L. and Shanto Iyengar. "Television News, Real-World Cues, and Changes in the Public Agenda," *Public Opinion Quarterly*, vol. 49, no. 1, Spring 1985, 38–57.

Bialer, Seweryn. "New Thinking and Soviet Foreign Policy," *Survival*, July—August 1988, 291–310.

Billig, Michael. "Political Rhetoric," in David O. Sears, Leonie Huddy, and Robert Jervis, eds., *Oxford Handbook of Political Psychology* (Oxford: Oxford University Press, 2003), 222–250.

Breslauer, George. "How Do You Sell a Concessionary Foreign Policy?" *Post-Soviet Affairs*, vol. 10, no. 3, 1994, 227–290.

Brown, Robin. "Getting to War: Communications and Mobilization in the 2002–2003 Iraq Crisis," in Philip Seib, ed., *Media and Conflict in the Twentieth Century* (New York: Palgrave, 2005).

Burnell, Peter and Andrew Reeve. "Persuasion as a Political Concept," *British Journal of Political Science*, vol. 14, no. 4, October 1984, 393–410.

Checkel, Jeffrey. "Social Constructivisms in Global and European Politics: A Review Essay," *Review of International Studies*, vol. 30, no. 2, April 2004, 229–244.

Druckman, James N. "Political Preference Formation: Competition, Deliberation, and the (Ir)relevance of Framing Effects," *American Political Science Review*, vol. 98, no. 4, November 2004, 671–686.

Fearon, James D. "Signaling Foreign Policy Interests: Tying Hands Versus Sinking Costs," *Journal of Conflict Resolution*, vol. 41, no. 1, February 1997, 68–90.

Gaubatz, Kurt Taylor. "Intervention and Intransitivity: Public Opinion, Social Choice, and the Use of Military Force Abroad," *World Politics*. vol. 47, no. 4, July 1995, 534–554.

George, Alexander. "Case Studies and Theory Development." Draft Paper prepared for the Second Annual Symposium on Information Processing in Organizations, Carnegie-Mellon University, October 15–16, 1982.

———. "Domestic Constraints on Regime Change in US Foreign Policy: The Need for Policy Legitimacy," in G. J. Ikenberry, ed., *American Foreign Policy: Theoretical Essays* (Glenview, IL: Scott, Foresman & Co., 1989), 583–608.

George, Alexander and Andrew Bennett. *Case Studies and Theory Development in the Social Sciences.* Cambridge: MIT Press, 2005.

Gerber, Theodore P. and Sarah E. Mendelson. "Russian Public Opinion on Human Rights and the War in Chechnya," *Post-Soviet Affairs*, vol. 18, no. 4, 271–306.

Graber, Doris. "The Media and Democracy: Beyond Myths and Stereotypes," *Annual Review of Political Science*, vol. 6, 2003, 139–160.

Grossman, Michael Baruch and Frances E. Rourke. "The Media and the Presidency: An Exchange Analysis," *Political Science Quarterly*, vol. 91, no. 3, Fall 1976, 456–457.

Guisinger, Alexandra and Alastair Smith, "Honest Threats: The Interaction of Reputation and Political Institutions in International Crises," *Journal of Conflict Resolution*, vol. 46, no. 2, April 2002, 175–200.

Halliday, Fred. "Soviet Foreign Policymaking and the Afghanistan War: From 'Second Mongolia' to 'Bleeding Wound,'" *Review of International Studies*, vol. 25, no. 4, October 1999, 675–691.

Hawkins, Darren. "Explaining Costly International Institutions: Persuasion and Enforceable Human Rights Norms," *International Studies Quarterly*, vol. 48, no. 4, December 2004, 779–804.

Herrmann, Richard. "The Soviet Decision to Withdraw from Afghanistan: Changing Strategic and Regional Images," in Robert Jervis and Jack Snyder, eds. *Dominoes and Bandwagons: Strategic Beliefs and Great Power Competition in the Eurasian Rimland* (New York: Oxford University Press, 1991), 220–249.

Holloway, David. "State, Society, and the Military under Gorbachev," *International Security*, vol. 14, no. 3, Winter 1989–1990, 5–24.

Hutcheson, John, David Domke, Andre Billeaudeaux, and Philip Garland. "U.S. National Identity, Political Elites, and a Patriotic Press Following September 11," *Political Communication*, vol. 21, no. 1, January 2004, 27–50.

Huth, Paul. "Extended Deterrence and the Outbreak of War," *The American Political Science Review*, vol. 82, no. 2, June 1988, 423–443.

Huth, Paul and Bruce Russett. "What Makes Deterrence Work? Cases from 1900–1980," *World Politics*, vol. 36, no. 4, July 1984, 496–526.

Jepperson, Ronald L., Alexander Wendt, and Peter J. Katzenstein. "Norms, Identity, and Culture in National Security," in Peter J. Katzenstein, ed., *The Culture of National Security: Norms and Identity in World Politics* (New York: Columbia University Press, 1996).

Jervis, Robert. "Introduction: Approach and Assumptions," in Robert Jervis, Richard Ned Lebow, and Janice Gross Stein, eds., *Psychology and Deterrence* (Baltimore: The Johns Hopkins University Press, 1985).

Larrabee, F. Stephen. "Gorbachev and the Soviet Military," *Foreign Affairs*, vol. 66, no. 5, 1988, 1002–1026.

Lebow, Richard Ned. "Is Crisis Management Always Possible?" *Political Science Quarterly*, vol. 102, no. 2, 1987, 181–192.

Legvold, Robert. "The Revolution in Soviet Foreign Policy," *Foreign Affairs*, vol. 68, no. 1, 1989, 82–98.

Lewarne, Stephen. "Soviet Press and Afghanistan," *International Perspectives*. vol. 17, July–August 1985, 17–20.

Malinkina, Olga V. and Douglas M. McLeod. "The Russian Media Role in the Conflicts in Afghanistan and Chechnya: A Case Study of Media Coverage by Izvestia" in Eytan Gilboa, ed., *Media and Conflict: Framing Issues and Making Policy Shaping Opinions* (Ardsley, NY: Transnational Publishers, 2002), 213–238.

Martin, Lisa. "Credibility, Costs, and Institutions: Cooperation on Economic Sanctions," *World Politics*, vol. 45, no. 3, 406–432.

Mendelson, Sarah. "Internal Battles and External Wars: Politics, Learning, and the Soviet Withdrawal from Afghanistan," *World Politics*, vol. 45, no. 3, 1993, 327–360.

Meyer, Stephen M. "The Sources and Prospects of Gorbachev's New Political Thinking on Security," *International Security*, vol. 13, no. 2, Fall 1988, 124–163.

Mickiewicz, Ellen. "Institutional Incapacity, the Attentive Public, and Media Pluralism in Russia," in Richard Gunther and Anthony Mughan, eds., *Democracy and the Media: A Comparative Perspective* (Cambridge: Cambridge University Press, 2000b), 85–121.

Miller, Robert H. "Vietnam: Folly, Quagmire, or Inevitability?" *Studies in Conflict and Terrorism*, vol. 5, no. 2, April 1992, 114–115.

Morgan, Patrick M. "Saving Face for the Sake of Deterrence," in Robert Jervis, Richard Ned Lebow, and Janice Gross Stein, eds., *Psychology & Deterrence* (Baltimore: The Johns Hopkins University Press, 1985), 125–152.

Mueller, John. "The Polls—A Review American Public Opinion and the Gulf War: Some Polling Issues" *Public Opinion Quarterly*, vol. 57, no. 1, Spring 1993, 80–97.

Muller, Harald. "Arguing, Bargaining and All That: Communicative Action, Rationalist Theory, and the Logic of Appropriateness in International Relations," *European Journal of International Relations*, vol. 10, no. 3, September 2004, 395–435.

Pan, Zhongdang and Gerald Kosicki. "Framing as a Strategic Action in Public Deliberation," in Stephen D. Reese, Oscar H. Gandy, Jr., and August E. Grant, eds., *Framing Public Life: Perspectives on Media and Our Understanding of the Social World* (Mahwah, NJ: Lawrence Erlbaum Associates, 2001).

Pfetsch, Barbara. "Government News Management," in Doris Graber, Denis McQuail, and Pippa Norris eds. *The Politics of News The News of Politics* (Washington, DC: Congressional Quarterly Press, 1998), 70–93.

Quattrone, George A. and Amos Tversky. "Contrasting Rational and Psychological Analyses of Political Choice," *American Political Science Review*, vol. 82, no. 3, September 1988, 719–736.

Remington, Thomas. "Policy Innovation and Soviet Media Campaigns," *Journal of Politics*, vol. 45, no. 1, February 1983, 220–227.

Reuveny, Rafael and Aseem Prakash. "The Afghanistan War and the Breakdown of the Soviet Union," *Review of International Studies*, vol. 25, no. 4, October 1999, 693–708.

Risse, Thomas. "Let's Argue: Communicative Action in World Politics," *International Organization*, vol. 54, no. 1, Winter 2000, 1–39.

Risse-Kaplan, Thomas. "Constructivism and International Institutions: Toward Conversations Across Paradigms," in Ira Katznelson and Helen Milner, eds., *Political Science: State of the Discipline* (New York: W. W. Norton & Co., 2002), 597–623.

———. "Ideas Do Not Float Freely: Transnational Coalitions, Domestic Structure, and the End of the Cold War," *International Organization*, vol. 48, no. 2, Spring 1994, 185–214.

Scheufele, Dietram A. "Framing as a Theory of Media Effects," *Journal of Communication*, vol. 49, no. 1, Winter 1999, 103–122.

Snow, David A., E. Burke Rochford, Steven K. Worden, and Robert D. Benford. "Frame Alignment Processes: Micromobilization and Movement Participation," *American Sociological Review*, vol. 51, no. 4, August 1986, 464–481.

Tankard, Jr. James W. "The Empirical Approach to the Study of Media Framing," in Stephen D. Reese, Oscar H. Gandy, Jr., and August E. Grant, eds., *Framing Public Life: Perspectives on Media and Our Understanding of the Social World* (Mahwah, NJ: Lawrence Erlbaum Associates, 2001), 95–106.

Thomas, Timothy L. "Manipulating the Mass Consciousness: Russian and Chechen 'Information War' Tactics in the 2nd Chechen-Russian Conflict," Foreign Military Studies Office Publication. http://fmso.leavenworth.army.mil/documents/chechiw.htm Accessed October 17, 2005.

Trout, B. Thomas. "Rhetoric Revisited: Political Legitimation and the Cold War," *International Studies Quarterly*, vol. 19, no. 3, September 1975, 251–284.

Tsygankov, Andrei P. "Vladimir Putin's Vision of Russia as a Normal Great Power," *Post-Soviet Affairs*, vol. 21, no. 2, April–June 2005, 132–158.

Tuchman, Gaye. "Objectivity as Strategic Ritual: An Examination of Newsmen's Notions of Objectivity," *American Journal of Sociology*, vol. 77, no. 4, January 1972, 660–679.

Tversky, Amos and Daniel Kahneman. "Rational Choice and the Framing of Decisions," in Robin M. Hogarth and Melvin W. Reder, *eds., Rational Choice: The Contrast between Economics and Psychology* (Chicago: University of Chicago Press, 1987).

Wendt, Alexander. "Identity and Structural Change in International Politics," in Yoself Lapid and Friedrich Kratochwil, eds., *The Return of Culture and Identity in IR Theory* (Boulder: Lynne Rienner, 1996), 47–64.

White, Stephen and Stephen Revell. "Revolution and Integration in Soviet International Diplomacy, 1917–1991," *Review of International Studies*, 25, 1999, 641–654.

INDEX

LAURA ROSELLE is Professor of Political Science
at Elon University. She has published works
on both Russian and American media and politics.